Fiction of
Chitra Banerjee Divakaruni

Fiction of Chitra Banerjee Divakaruni

Edited by

SUMAN BALA

Delta Book World

New Delhi

Published by
Delta Book World
New Delhi
in association with
Prestige Books International
New Delhi

ISBN: 978-81-926244-5-7

Printed in India

Contents

Introduction
The Fiction of Chitra Banerjee Divakaruni

SUMAN BALA
S.B.S. College, University of Delhi

Indian American writer Chitra Banerjee Divakaruni (born Chitralekha Banerjee, 1956) is an eminent author, poet, activist and teacher. She was born in Kolkata, graduated from the University of Calcutta in 1976 and received Masters and Ph.D. in English from the University of California. Her books have been translated into thirty languages. Her works have been made into films and plays. She has won several awards, including American Book Award and Light of India Prize. She teaches Creative Writing at the University of Houston. In 2015, she has been included by the *Economic Times* in the 'Twenty Most Influential Global Indian Women.'

Divakaruni's fiction is largely set in India and the United States. She lives in Houston with her husband Murthy, and two sons, Anand and Abhay, whose names she has freely used in her children's novels. In 1996, she published *Arranged Marriage*, a collection of short stories, which won the American Book Award along with the PEN Josephine Miles Award and the Bay Area Book Reviewers Award for Fiction. It was in 1997 that she wrote her first novel *The Mistress of Spices* which became immensely popular. It was made into a film by Gurinder Chadha starring Aishwarya Rai and Dylan McDermott. She published *Sister of My Heart* in 1998 and *The Vine of Desire* in 2002. Since then, she has published a number of novels and today she is regarded a leading writer of the Indian diaspora. Though hailing from Kolkata, Divakaruni has been living in the U.S. However, she has not forgotten her roots, "My Kolkata roots will always endure, I think," she says.

Recently, Chitra Divakaruni was in Delhi for the release of her novel *Oleander Girl* which is an interesting book. Basically, *Oleander Girl* is a coming-of-age story. It follows a mythic structure, that is, the hero's journey in search of parentage or self. A major theme in the book is the clash between old and new values. It is a superbly well-plotted and hard-hitting novel of family, marriage and class. She writes about India in a way that makes the rest of the world disappear around us.

The novel is the gripping story of a young woman who leaves India in pursuit of a shocking family secret and in the process learns far more about herself than she imagined. The protagonist of the book is an eighteen-year-old girl Karobi Roy who finds herself on a troubled search across post-9/11 U.S. after her grandfather's sudden death. She confronts the intrinsic truths about love, loss, grief, redemption and the choices we make. It turns out to be a family saga that reads like a detective novel. Divakaruni delivers an absorbing modern fairy tale about an orphan in search of the messy truths of family and love. The novel explores issues of class and politics in India and immigrant America, but the family issues at the heart of the novel give it a cross-cultural appeal.

Like Bharati Mukherjee and Jhumpa Lahiri, Divakaruni's fiction displays feminine sensibility in her fiction. Her writing shows deep insight into the female psyche and presents a full range of feminine experience. Speaking on writing women-centric books, Divakaruni says: "I understand them and respect the challenges they face and the dreams they dare to dream. I think it is important more now than ever, in view of the recent cases of violence against women, to portray them as courageous beings at the centre of a fictional universe."

Divakaruni's experience as a writer, teacher and person living in multicultural society has immensely influenced her writings. She has always been inspired by her mother and also by Mother Teresa with whom she closely worked: "In Kolkata, I volunteered with Mother Teresa in her orphanage, Shishu Bhavan. She was a small woman who embodied the joy that comes out of helping others. She taught me compassion. I hope some of that emerges through my books and my life."

Let us now look at two stories by Chitra Divakaruni where women leave their homes and plan to start life anew. Marital discord is indeed one of the major reasons of their taking such a step. In the story "The Disappearance," the wife disappears one fine morning all of a sudden. The husband is totally confused at this and announces a hefty reward of one hundred thousand dollars which indeed is beyond his means. He plans to have a second mortgage on the house if somebody turns up with his wife to claim the reward.

When the policeman comes for the investigation, he asks the husband if they had had a quarrel. The husband strongly denies this but as we go through the story presented from the husband's point of view, we feel that the wife had sufficient reasons to leave the house. Both the husband and the wife followed their own routines, though many a time the husband's wish was forced upon the woman. Sex, for example. This was one area where he was very firm. Though she always pleaded "Please, not tonight," and tried various methods to postpone it, he almost always had his way: "Surely, he couldn't be blamed for raising his voice or for grabbing her by the elbow and pulling her to the bed, like he did that last night. He was always careful not to hurt her. . . . And he always told himself he'd stop if she really begged him, if she cried." The night before she disappeared, he had raised his voice and grabbed her by the elbow and pulled her to the bed which is nothing less than marital rape.

The protagonist had adopted the same kind of attitude when he had gone for the selection of a bride. In a flashback, the husband gives us the whole incident of how his marriage was arranged. When his mother had started insisting on his marriage, he suggested that she may look for a quiet, pretty girl who may have done at least a year of college, someone he could introduce to his friends with pride. He had flown to Calcutta to view several suitable girls that his mother had shortlisted. Among the prospective brides was the girl he ultimately selected. She had sat there, head bowed, jasmine plaited into her hair, silk sari draped modestly over her shoulders. The cool, considering look in her eyes made him rush through the marriage and they were married within a week despite the protests by his mother.

Though the wife was taking full care of the family, the husband considers his mother a better housekeeper than his wife. After the wife disappears, the mother comes over within a week and takes charge of the house. She runs the house very well—the furniture is dusted daily, laundry is folded and put into drawers, all his favourite dishes are cooked. The little boy is also taken good care of—each afternoon, the grandmother goes with him for a walk in the park and brings him into her bed whenever he wakes up crying at night. His wife, on the other hand, had never done that because she wanted the boy to be independent. After the husband finds the jewellery missing, he removes everything from the house that could remind him of his wife. He even destroys all the photographs of his wife.

Within a year of the disappearance of the wife, the husband gets used to life without a wife; he stops thinking much about her. The boy also does not ask as often about his mother. The boy starts sleeping through the night again and puts on some weight because he likes the food prepared by his grandmother. Like his father, the boy starts calling his grandmother "Ma."

The husband removes the photographs of his wife from the picture frames and replaces them with pictures of himself with his son, the little boy on his grandma's lap, holding a red birthday balloon. He lets his mother remove his wife's clothes so that he has more space in the closet for his own clothes. They also have a prayer service done at the temple one year after the tragedy. The mother suggests that he should get married again. He decides to contact a lawyer to find out the legal procedure for marriage. He plans to ask his mother to find a simple girl from their ancestral village, someone whose family was not well off, who would appreciate the comforts he provided. This time he did not want a college-going girl. Nor were good looks very important. Completely constructed by patriarchy, the husband gives no importance to the feelings of his wife. He expects his wife to be fully satisfied if she is provided with food and basic comforts. He has no room for the finer feelings of his wife.

In traditional relationships, women are not expected to transgress beyond normative feminine behaviour. The husband cherishes the memories of his wife because it does not occur to him that she has deserted him. It is only when he finds that all her gold jewellery is missing from the old tea tin as well as the bank locker that it dawns on him that she has disappeared intentionally. It happens one night when his mother is cooking cauliflower curry, her specialty, and runs out of *hing*. She insists that hing is essential to the recipe. The husband remembers that sometimes his wife used to keep extra spices on the top shelf. So he climbs on a chair to look for it. There are no extra spices but he finds there something he had totally forgotten about—an old tea tin in which he had asked his wife to hide her jewellery. Nothing major was kept there. The expensive wedding items were all stored in a bank vault. The husband thought of taking all the jewellery to the bank in the morning but when he picked up the tin, it felt surprisingly light; and when he opened it, it was all empty. He stood there holding the tin, for a moment not breathing. Then he remembered that his wife was a careless woman and often left pieces of jewellery at odd places like the back of her make-up drawer or under a pile of books. He looked all around but found nothing anywhere. The next day, he took the afternoon off from work and went to the bank. In a small stuffy corner, he opened the safety deposit box kept in the bank locker and found that all her jewellery was gone. He finds it very hard to reconcile to the fact that his wife had gone away with somebody.

In the story "Affair," the protagonist Asha feels inspired by Meena's affair with her boss and her decision to divorce her husband Srikant. Abha also decides to become financially independent by taking up a job as a cook. The story starts with Abha's husband Ashok exploding the news on Abha: "You know, of course, that Meena is having an affair." The news so shocks Abha that the knife with which she is chopping vegetables slips and nicks her finger. Abha and Meena are best of friends and talk to each other on phone everyday, preferably before their husbands return from work. Abha is agitated over the fact that Meena has not taken her into confidence and has instead chosen her husband Ashok and confided in him. Ashok offers to reveal the name of the person if Abha asked him very nicely. However, Abha cannot bring herself to do it because that would mean accepting her defeat.

Meena's affair raises a number of questions in Abha's mind. She wonders why Meena is having an affair. Of course, she considers it very wrong: "Was she bored? Did she want to shake up Srikant? Make him sit up and stop taking her for granted? Or had she found someone she couldn't resist? And what kind of man would be worth giving up your principles for? What kind of man would be more important than being a good wife?" All her married life, Abha had tried to be the best wife to her husband. She has changed her life as per the wishes of her husband. However, she is neither as beautiful, nor as elegantly dressed as Meena.

Asian American writing is comparatively a new area of research. This area cropped up around the turn of the twentieth century, primarily with autobiographies. In the course of time, in the latter half of the twentieth century, fiction dominated the scene. It was in tune with the contemporary scene the world over. Fiction enjoyed immense popularity as it is said to be close to 'social reality.' This is true of India as well. It was in the early twentieth century that the writings of Bankimchandra, K.A. Abbas, Raja Rao, Mulk Raj Anand, R.K. Narayan gained popularity.

In the latter half of the twentieth century, there was a spate of migrations from India to the west, especially the U.K., Canada and U.S.A. The Indian diaspora was qualified and knowledgeable which took up well paid-up jobs and with the passage of time made inroads into the literary scene in the country of their adoption. In America, many women writers published their works and received worldwide recognition. Some of these are: Anita Desai, Kiran Desai, Bharati Mukherjee, Jhumpa Lahiri and Chitra Banerjee Divakaruni. These writers have produced a rich body of fictional work that has drawn a plethora of critical response and evaluation of their writings. A number of scholars and academics have done stupendous research on these women writers of the Indian diaspora.

I wish to draw attention to some books that have admirably evaluated the writings of the Indian diaspora. Keya Majumdar's book entitled *Diaspora Space: Emergence of Transnational Literature* is made up of discussions and introspection of scholarly trajectories of different theories regarding diaspora culture and history, power and memory, travelling across intellectual landscapes.

Yet another important publication is P. Shailaja and T. Vinoda's *Expatriate Indian Writing in English* (3 vols.). These are comprehensive volumes that discuss various issues pertaining to problems of identity in the diaspora writing. They deal with specific writers as also with theoretical issues related to this domain of writing. The first volume highlights women's concerns in the fiction of Bharati Mukherjee, Suniti Namjoshi, Sunetra Gupta,

Jhumpa Lahiri, Meena Alexander, Anita Rau Badami and also Chitra Divakaruni. The second volume discusses the dynamics of diaspora and deals with issues of nation, identity and belonging. It includes treatment of history by writers like Salman Rushdie, Amitav Ghosh, Anita Desai and Meera Syal. The third volume is more significant as it introduces various area of diasporic writing like Indo-American Writing, Indo-British Writing, Indo-African Writing. Further, it includes a comprehensive bibliography on various diaspora writers and various issues related to the migrant literature. In all, it is a highly useful anthology that introduces and critically examines diaspora writings by Indians, settled in U.S.A., Canada, U.K., Australia and West Indies. In her introductory chapter, T. Vinoda writes: "In the contemporary scene of letters, it is an undeniable fact that almost all the major writers in English write from diaspora spaces in the West. It is as if the centre of gravity in Indian Writing in English has shifted abroad."

Perhaps the most important book on Chitra Banerjee Divakaruni and other Asian American writers is a full-length study: *Locating Asian American Women Writers in the Diaspora* written by Nandini Bhadra. The book charts the narrative of migration and demonstrates how a comparative approach to the complex area of Diaspora Studies can lead to interesting and fruitful results. The writers selected for study are all women of colour who "live a hybrid life in an in-between zone, a threshold space where identity is endlessly constructed and tell stories of men/women with hyphenated identities, divided fissured selves, and the worlds they challenge are almost exclusively male-dominated." (23) The book takes up for detailed study four Asian American women writers, two of Chinese and two of Indian ancestry, and attempts to explore their in-between position as they belong to more than one history and one place. Chitra Divakaruni and Jhumpa Lahiri have produced a rich body of fictional work which provides valuable materials for us to look at the lives and experiences of the Indian diaspora in the U.S. In the age of globalization and postcolonialism, Nandini Bhadra argues, the significance of the voices of Indian American women writers has gone far beyond traditional boundaries. A reading of their works demands new approaches which would, in a way, expand the field of Indian American studies by incorporating cross-cultural, transnational and postcolonial inquiries. In the recent years, the boundary between Indian American and native American writing has blurred. It is not desirable anymore to draw boundaries and isolate the immigrants' history and their state of being as not part of the mainstream life.

Nandini Bhadra takes up for study the theme of 'emerging relationships' in the fiction of Chitra Divakaruni. She has critically examined Divakaruni's *The Mistress of Spices* and *Sister of My Heart* and some of her short stories. She bases her approach on Divakaruni's concept of feminism which is primarily a philosophy of action and engagement. She shows how by writing from the diasporic space, Divakaruni empowers the marginalized Indian American women of the diaspora.

Another book, *Rushdie, Kureishi, Syal: Essays in Diaspora* by Italian scholar Esterino Adami explores the world of diasporic fiction in Britain, especially critical issues such as the impact of ethnic communities, the role of diasporic cinema and the literary experience of hybridity.

Although there is a plethora of critical response to the writings of Chitra Divakaruni but no single book has yet come out giving a collective response to her writings, especially fiction. Divakaruni is undoubtedly a prolific writer who since her first collection of stories *Arranged Marriage* has been producing remarkable pieces of fiction like *Mistress of Spices*, *Sister of My Heart*, *Queen of Dreams*, *One Amazing Thing*, *Palace of Illusions* and *Oleander Girl*. A book devoted to the fiction of Chitra Banerjee Divakaruni is long due. The present book comprising brilliant articles, we hope, meets the aspirations of scholars, critics and admirers of Chitra Divakaruni and will be useful to all those interested in Women's Writing, Indian-English Literature and the Diaspora Studies.

Bibliography

Bala, Suman, ed. *Jhumpa Lahiri: The Master Storyteller*. New Delhi: Khosla, 2014.

Adami, Esterino. *Rushdie, Kureishi, Syal: Essays in Diaspora*. New Delhi: Prestige, 2002.

Bhabha, Homi, "Introduction: Narrating the Nation," *Nation and Narration*. London: Routledge, 1990.

Bhadra, Nandini. *Locating Asian American Women Writers in the Diaspora*. New Delhi: Prestige, 2013.

Dhawan, R.K. and Venu Mehta. *Literature of South Asian Diaspora*. New Delhi: Prestige, 2015.

Keya Majumdar, ed. *Diaspora Space: Emergence of Transnational Literature*. New Delhi: Prestige, 2014.

Mandal, Somdatta, ed. *Asian-American Writing*. 3 Vols. New Delhi: Prestige, 2000.

Raina, Anil and Manju Jaidka. *Multi-Ethnic Literatures of the World*. New Delhi: Prestige, 2010.

Said, Edward. *Culture and Imperialism*. London: Vintage, 1994.

Vinoda, T. and P. Shailaja. *Expatriate Indian Writing in English*. 3 Vols. New Delhi: Prestige, 2010.

Eloquence of the Poignant Self: The Select Fiction of Chitra Divakaruni

K. NARASIMHA RAO
Vikrama Simhapuri University, Nellore

> I've been writing more fiction because I'm interested in exploring relationships and showing the differences that develop in characters.[1]

The epigraph bears plainly the interest of Chitra Lekha Banerjee Divakaruni to make an admirable navigation of her fictional creations with ineluctable gaps that speak of the divergent concerns of the postmodern and postcolonial times to evolve into meta-narratives. Indian writers in English have a proud work behind them that speaks of their incredible eye for the social realities to rise to great heights in literary firmament. Writers such as R.K. Narayan, Raja Rao, Mulk Raj Anand, Nirad C. Chaudhuri, Anita Desai, Toru Dutt, and other eminent literary luminaries achieved global critical acclaim for their authorship. The shrunken globe has changed the interrogatives of approaching literature with several contemporaneous issues voicing the hitherto unvoiced.

Maxine Hong Kinston's The *Woman-Warrior (*1976) which won The National Book Critics Award led the way in upbringing the transformation in the Asian-American literature. The newly emerging writers who settled in the adopted nations charged up myriad voices through centring the eloquent subaltern in their texts that crossed the fluid geographies, and stern cultures. Among these writers, is a new generation of women writers whose unremitting quest for the multiple consciousness, the process of Diasporic Identity formation, mediating the historical discourses, tradition in exile and the cross-pollination of cultural symbolism, which among several others try to reconstruct the spaces they come to inhabit. This reminds us of the critical practice that John Maxwell Coetzee espouses in reading the absence and silence in the texts which exist as signs of ideological exclusion and oppression. In *White Writing*, he remarks:

> Our craft is all in reading the other: gaps, inverses, undersides, the veiled, the dark, the buried, the feminine, alterities. To a Pastoral novel . . . we give an anti-pastoral reading . . . alert to the spaces in the text. . . . Only a part of the truth, such a residing asserts, resides in what the writing says of the hitherto unsaid, for the rest its truth lies in what it dare not say for the sake of its own safety, or in what it does not know about itself: in its silences. (81)

The novels of the new-wave Indian-English writers Chitra Banerjee Divakaruni and Jhumpa Lahiri offer a fair possibility of reading these spaces. Padma Rangaswamy in *Namasté America* observes: "The post-1965 Indian immigrant [writers] are a different breed. . . . As articulate and organized professionals, they have expressed themselves in literature and recorded their immigrant experiences for posterity" (147).

Chitra Banerjee Divakaruni was highly honoured for her first poetical renderings and later received high critical acclaim for her novels and short stories. Born in Kolkata on 29 July 1956, she spent nineteen years in India and immigrated to the USA in 1976. She now teaches in the nationally ranked Creative Writing program at the University of Houston, Texas. The themes of her writings represent her life-size experiences as an immigrant. The protagonists exhibit tolerant cultural traits and a nostalgia for their cultural roots as they incidentally encounter the western life. Shamita Das Gupta in *A Patchwork Shawl* records the challenges of the South Asian women writers and their resort to resistance: 'It is an expression of our resistance, resistance to invisibility, "othering," and silence, resistance to being defined by others and being corralled into an artificial "culture" that renounces our diversity of experience and being. [The Book] is [an] assertion: We are, we are!' (15)

Divakaruni's website underscores her preoccupation with "Indian experience, immigration, the South Asian experience, history, myth, and the joys and challenges of living in a multicultural world"[2]. The characters are torn between the eerie discovery of the new and the quintessential denominator of the past memory. This understanding indulges the characters in recalling the past and makes them conscious of envisioning a future through an endearing transformation towards love.

Ambivalence marks the immigrant Indians as it bemuses them to break away with the long-associated customary inhibitions while at the same time lighting upon the superficiality of the new culture. The conflict between the preserved past and the high-ranked western culture is imminent as the characters of Divakaruni take a long march through their live-experiences of the exotic lands and set on exploring the unknown realms. The characters do not indulge in the preferential choice of one country over the other but tend to explore the possibility of a union with the new host as the way to returning home is always present. In radicalizing the strategies to overcome this dislocation, Divakaruni insists on a relocating self while redefining one's own cultural background on a new canvas. Her merit lies in the essential validation and the preservation of the immigrants' native background.

Divakaruni's *Arranged Marriage* is a short-story collection dealing with the issues of identity and negotiation of cultures. The private realm forms the locus on which indeterminate time and space cease to reflect any change. Divakaruni portrays the abiding faith of women in the tradition of marriage and her readiness to stay with her husband despite several trials. The stories portray the transformed lives of the protagonists both liberated and entrapped by the cultural changes. In "The Bats," the heroine victimized by the domestic violence flees away from her husband and goes to her distantly related uncle in a village. She cannot tolerate the words of the fellow women. She is still optimistic about making her home despite the repeated physical violence she is meted out by her husband. The social norms and mores play a key role as Indian traditions are upheld against the free will of mating and conjugality of the western world.

It is also the touching story of a young girl who verges on being initiated into the vagaries of life's experiences and she is perturbed to know the reason why her mother cried a lot. Father to the young girl is a diabolic apprehension whose "shouts . . . shook the walls of my bedroom like they were paper." The young child when inquires about the yellow blotch on her mother's cheek is denied allowance to know her mother's pain and shame. Marriage again ignites the subliminal thoughts, though placidly, in "Clothes" where Sumita is graduated to own the "psychic mimesis" by her mother that a woman's future lies with an unknown person and that *parampara* is to be carried on carefully. Sumita wonders how a girl after the magic moments of exchanging garlands will belong to a person who is unknown to her. She says: "I whisper my new name to myself, Mrs. Sumita Sen, but the syllables rustle uneasily in my mouth like a stiff satin" (*Arranged* 20).

Sumita after her marriage with the Indian American longs for stepping out of her meek image hoping for a new day "moving out of this two-room apartment where it seems to me if we all breathed in at once, . . . Where I must cover my head with the edge of my Japan nylon sari. . . . I felt caught in a world where everything is frozen in place, like a scene inside a glass paperweight" (25). Sumita while at home is tradition-bound, clad in a sari and a dutiful house-wife living "the Indian way" (26), while she thinks of liberating herself from this familial bond, she exudes her independence and confidence. The low-key battle affair in her mind conveys her psychological dilemma middling the disguised likeness of the traditional cloistered virtues of subservience and the unsported confidence walled in by the cultural bounds.

The story "The Disappearance" depicts a wife settling for disappearance to have a feel of individuality. She is denied of behaving like American women by her husband, "to go for a job or go back to school or buy American clothes" (172). He softly demurs with his "no's . . . like what for I'm here to take care of you or you look so much prettier in your Indian clothes, so much more feminine" (172). Leaving no chance for her to try the new, she finally chooses to pursue her deep needs and desires. To quote Patricia Waugh, she throws "off her guilt for being frigid and unmaternal, she leaves her husband and child to preserve her own individuality and seek her freedom" (320). This story also leaves us a point about man's feelings about the disappearance. To his perception, the wife never appears to be dissatisfied and he grows concerned with her absence as the crime rate is high in that area. When he realizes that she has disappeared with the jewellery shocks him which he never forgets even after his remarriage.

In "The Word Love" the heroine is torn between two cultures: the western represented by her boyfriend and the Indian, guarded closely by her mother. The heroine by the magic of love begins to live with a man. American culture accepts this living together beyond the mutual regard for marital honour. The story fairly presents the mother-daughter relationship as the girl often recalls her mother's pains in bringing her up after her father's death. She is ethically bitten whenever she thinks of her mother kept in the dark about her living together with a man. Her ideological sensuousness makes it hard to hide her affair from her mother. She cannot bear severing links with her mother and continue on her live-in relationship with her boyfriend. She recoils from her past to tread on a new path to undo the mistake she had committed by her live-in relationship with a foreigner, she muses: "What will you remember of him when it is all over" (63). She chalks out her own way of rooting herself in the past sustaining her present to assimilate the cosmopolitan culture. "Doors" opens vistas on western and Indian cultures. The American brought up heroine, Preeti, marries Deepak from India wherein the closing doors on herself making her person private and lonely unsettles her relationship. Hospitality, one of the cultural constructs has its own diversified practice in both the societies. This grows for confrontation between the couple. Preeti's shutting off the doors acquires a figurative meaning as this act disallows her even from her husband.

In "Silver Pavements, Golden Roofs," the protagonist Jayanti experiences the same as she moves from Calcutta and settles in Chicago with her Aunt Pratima and Uncle Bikram. Expectation and a romantic pull is writ large about the new culture and towards the new realm. To Jayanti their house is still stuck in Indian tradition while America outside the window is whizzing past. Jayanti finds it hard to assimilate certain English words in her speech: "Sorry," I say, "So very sorry," like the nuns had taught me in these old, high-ceilinged classrooms cooled by the breeze from the convent neem trees" (35). For the Indian immigrants, the past with its associated traditions bears a faithful promise. This realization goes profound as they experience the superficiality of the new culture they meet with. As Jayanti and her Aunt go on a walk in the neighbourbood, a group of young boys approach them with racist slurs: "Nigger." He says it softly, his upper lip curling away from his teeth. The word arcs through the empty street like a rock, an impossible word which belongs to another place and time" (50). This feeling of superiority is only hollow as the protagonists experience it while assimilating the two worlds—the past and the present. Befalling this balancing act is a conflict at the core that, at times, makes the protagonists schizophrenic and disillusioned.

Divakaruni's *The Mistress of Spices* is located in indeterminate time and space in an unbelonging world. The smoothly slicing narrative heads past exploring the changing face of Diaspora to stabilize the theme unsettled by the overpowering fantasized-imagination. The entire narration underscores a quest for identities coupled with the narrator's own predicament of a desperate quest for meaning and identity. Tilo, the mistress of spices, who arrives in America in disguise of an old woman, never pays a stray thought about her customers identifying her real identity which she has left behind walking in shampathi fire to enter the "city which prides itself on being no older than a heartbeat" (4). She bears her own witness of her disguise, "The eyes which alone are my own. . . . One more thing is mine. My name, which is Tilo, short for Tilotamma, for I am named after the sun burnished sesame seed, spice of nourishment. They do not know this, my customers nor that earlier I had other names" (5). Tilo introspects on her numerous fake identities as she contends with her assuming the present role of a mistress without any external imposition upon her to serve the people expecting no returns. At times, she wishes to be known by her real identity.

In America, Tilo, for no good reason, becomes incapable of self-perception while the characters around her bear witness of it leaving her self-bearing as secondary and unpaid for. This leads her to adopt the glasses of others to view the society leading her to conflicting visions about her identity. In her pursuit, it can be seen that she lacks a clear understanding about herself while she has the clearest map of the others so deeply. In fact, Tilo is forbidden to look in a mirror while in Oakland and attends the duties of a Mistress of Spices, "a Mistress has taken on her magic Mistress—body, she is never to look on her reflection again" (41). This distancing away from mirrors is a subtle example of Tilo's incapacity to perceive her own self. In wending her way through American culture, Tilo grows anxious to see herself rather than viewing through the eyes and perspectives of others.

This is evident when Tilo questions the prohibition of mirrors for Mistresses: "First Mother, why is it not allowed, what can be wrong with seeing yourself?" (66). Circumstances lead Tilo on to a quest for identity which can be realized only if she sued for her own change of her deepest nature tearing apart her disguised appearance. The same also holds good for Raven to reveal himself and accept his heritage identifying himself with the mythical references of raven in both Native American and Indian culture.

The novel also delineates a character of suppressed identity through Lalita, Ahuja's wife. Lalita stands for those Indian wives in America wriggling for an identity to come out of the caring eyes of their husbands. With a bank account and a boutique of her own, Lalita is not interested in getting married and in fact is broken about her abusive marriage. By Tilo's reminding of a woman's right to be happy and independent, Lalitha breaks her last hesitation of hurting her parents and the befalling shame. The Indian ethical dimensions become the calculus to examine how human deeds and actions attract appropriate fate during a calamitous occurrence of an earthquake. The novel ends with this calamitous incident which leads to a necessary shift in perception of how life is to be understood, as the writer places Tilo and her spices at the centre of mediating between races and cultures.

The novel *One Amazing Thing* draws on a direct link with this calamitous incident in *Mistress of Spices,* as a group of strangers hit by an earthquake confine to a common place to interrogate as to who they are and their expectations from life. With no character charted out to lead, Divakaruni brings them all on an equal plank, a new paradigm with horizontal connections, an interdependence overpowering the vertical hierarchy. This wells up from the formidable ethical stance of the writer to recognize other people's suffering and closely guarded secrets as equally important.

Queen of Dreams shows the struggle of Rakhi and Belle, two women—who have set all their hopes on their chai house to earn for themselves a sustained livelihood and individuality. It combines the Indian American experience with magical realism. The novel depicts a conflicting urban space of different ethnic groups in America in the aftermath of 9/11. Rakhi's chai house threatened by *Java* chain, a new café with aggressive commercial designs connotes the threatening ramifications of globalization. A stark contrast emerges with this engulfing voracity of commercialism as Rakhi draws inspiration from the eucalyptus grove to paint her picture to represent her mother's "dreamy world." She muses of the symphony of colours: "Deep-forest green, gold-gray green, green tinged with foggy silver of dawn, edged with the brittle brown of time passing. All the colours of the eucalyptus grove she walked to earlier this morning" (10). The novel also posits a longing for identity with Belle urging her parents to let her have the money reserved for her dowry to become self-reliant. In a way, this *chai* house opens a chance to escape from the marriage.

Circumstances set the tenor for natural human response as the characters react and act with inner strength and vision to set the models for the readers to emulate rather than imitate. *The Palace of Illusions* (2008), though is a retelling of the greatest and longest Indian epic parades a tide of human emotions and feelings of abstraction such as pain, overpowering anger, revenge, humiliation, pride, despondency among many on the general canvas of life which means philosophically to be "Maya" or illusion according to Hindu mythology. The major shift in Divakaruni's narrative is the novel centring on Draupadi or Panchali (the wife of the five) who is clairvoyant of her life's changing the course of history and her courage to rise with dignity when meted out with subordination and shame. The filial quality of fire flames in Divakaruni's Draupadi to exude the dignity born out of confidence. It is the wounded pride of Draupadi that leads to the cataclysmic decimation of the *kula vrukshas* (dynasties) on the *Dharmakshetra* (the justice-rewarding) Kurukshetra. Draupadi (Panchali) also suffers through the loss of her brother, five sons and her father. An intuition generates whether Draupadi can avoid this self-loss and self-waste transforming herself through forgiving her humiliation. Lord Krishna, her guide and mentor, enlightens her "wrongdoing in spite of good intentions" results from "anger and desire, our two direct enemies" (264). From the resulting carnage of the battlefield the truth dawns upon her that "the desire for vengeance" should not be "stronger than the longing to be loved" (194).

Cultural ambiguity and unbelongingness always stares in the face of the Indian Americans despite their unprejudiced assimilation of the new culture, which finds expression in Rakhi of Divakaruni's *Queen of Dreams*. They are disoriented about their sense of belonging and their locus. Rakhi who always considers America her home is made to realize that she is Indian not American. She feels diffident to put a flag outside her chai house to make known that she is an American despite her taking birth there. She is disoriented as her family is accused of planning the 9/11 attack and her identity despite Jespal assuring her of the American descent. Lilia, Gogol and Rakhi are the victims of hyphenated identities which Homi Bhaba dwells on as "the process of cultural translation . . . opens up a 'space-in-between,' an interstitial temporality, that stands in contention with both the return to an originary 'essentialist' self-consciousness as well as a release into an endlessly fragmented subject in 'process' (Chambers, 204).

Hence, it can be said that the cultural worlds open up numerous possibilities of exploration which at best can be done through fictive narratives conveying the mute realities through the powerful art of personalization. Divakaruni weaves her stories with a realistic base—stories that speak so eloquently of the poignant self. Despite the recurrent search for identity and the dilemma of Diasporic experience, she stands at the top of the crest to accept the challenges that stare in the face through the writerly ethics of relocating the self and vitalizing her protagonists to balance the cultural forces. This equipoise and her elegant literary transport make us revisit Homi Bhabha who turns to Levinasian ethics to evaluate, "the 'art-magic' of the contemporary novel lies in its way of 'seeing inwardness from the outside'" (Bhabha 15).

Notes

1. Chitra Banerjee Divakaruni in conversation with Erika Bauer. "A Discussion with Chitra Divakaruni." March 1993.
2. http://www.chitradivakaruni.com/

Bibliography

Bhabha, Homi K. *The Location of Culture*, Routledge: New York, 2005

Coetzee, J.M. *White Writing: On the Culture of Letters in South Africa*, New Haven: Yale University Press, 1988.

Chambers, Iain and Lidia Curti, ed. *The Post-Colonial Question*, Homi K. Bhaba, "Unpacking My Library . . . Again," Routledge: New York, 1996.

Dasgupta D Shamita, ed. *A Patchwork Shawl: Chronicles of South Asian Women in America*, Rutgers University Press: New Jersey, 1998.

Divakaruni, Chitra Banerjee. *Arranged Marriage*. New York: Doubleday, 1995. London: Black Swan, 1997.

_____. *Queen of Dreams*. London: Abacus, 2004

_____. *Mistress of Spices*. London: Double day, 1996. London: Black Swan, 2006.

_____. *The Palace of Illusions: A Novel*. New York: Doubleday. 2008.

_____. *One Amazing Thing*. New York: Voce/ Hyperion, 2009.

Rangaswamy, Padma. *Namasté America*, Pennsylvania: Pennsylvania State University Press, 2000.

Severed Roots and Clinging Soil: The Diasporic Conflict in the Works of Chitra Divakaruni

SAKUNTHALA A.I.
M.P.M.M.S.N.Trusts College, Shoranur

A gale of fresh air is blowing in the landscape of contemporary literature with the advent of globalization. Texts are now crossing the borders of nations and cultures, as newly emerging authors express myriad voices of those who were once considered as the marginalized and the minorities. In the present era, postcolonial studies are foremost in any programme of literature in English and postcolonial texts are preoccupied with issues of Diaspora, Hybridity, Creolization, the In-betweenness, Flux and Cross-overs of identities. The term 'diaspora' has been taken from the Greek, meaning 'to disperse.' As Robert Cohen stated, "From 1960s and 1970s, the classical meaning of diaspora was description of dispersion of Africans, Armenians and Irish. 1980s onwards the term was deployed as expatriates, expels, alien residents, immigrants and racial minorities. From mid-1990s diaspora stands for the people who live outside their national territories" (Cohan 9). Now the term 'diaspora' practically describes any population which is considered deterritorialized or transnational—that is, which has originated in a land other than which it currently resides.

Bill Ashcroft defines diaspora as 'the voluntary or forcible movement of people from their homeland into new regions" (Ashcroft 68). The severing of people from their homeland, their culture and language causes loss of identity followed by a deep effort to appropriate, transform and merge local cultures with their own traditional ones. The term can be considered a synonym of displacement, diversity, cultural clash and marginalized subjects who live in the border between two worlds. The transnational migration, the flow of the people among different countries, convergence of the heterogeneous cultures, creolization of language and hybridization of identities all result in a sort of fissured and fragmented identities.

Oscillating between the attraction of home and those from the new, the migrant wage a psychic battle, whether to remain in a ghetto of old values or break the barriers and get assimilated with the overwhelming new culture. "The individual living in the diaspora experiences a dynamic tension every day between 'here' and remembering 'there,' between memories of places of origins and entanglements with places of residence, and between the metaphorical and the physical home" (Agnew 19). Identity is lost as they are treated as Indian on the foreign land and as a foreigner on their homeland. This idea of dislocation is a very complex and traumatic feeling.

An immigrant carries with him to the host land the social, cultural and religious beliefs ingrained in his psyche by his homeland, "the socio-cultural baggage" (Jayaram 22). Because of the burden of this baggage, the person uses his parent culture as a defence mechanism against a sense of insecurity in alien settings. They try to stick to their identity of home and nation and this leads to the formation of diasporic and ethnic identity of the diasporic communities.

Loss and nostalgia constitute the key elements of any diasporic writing. At the same time, it gives vent to a certain alienation due to incomplete assimilation in the adopted society. John Hartley states: "It is this experience that is sought to be transmitted to readers through diaspora literature" (Hartley 66). The diaspora writers are obsessed with search for identity and their writing displays a poetics of exile and displacement. Diasporic identity can be defined as the identity of an immigrant living in a diasporic condition.

Migration and immigration have directly or indirectly affected several generations of contemporary writers in English engendering hybridism and culture complexity within them and urging them to grapple with multiple cultures and countries and tensions between them. A number of diasporic writers like Salman Rushdie, Amitav Ghosh have been dealing with the issue of diasporic identity in their works. Diasporic women writers also deal with this important issue in the present day in a different fashion than that of a male writer in a perspective distinctly different from that of their male counterparts.

With the rise of women's diasporic writing, the images of immigrant women have often been discussed in literature. Indian women writers in foreign lands are equipped with better themes than the perennially penned subjects like rights of women, injustice, gender inequality and so on. With the alteration in political, social and economical scenario, literature by women writers living in India and abroad have evolved to demonstrate some universal experiences like the contradictions of old and new values, conventions and change, ethics and freedom.

Women writers, those in India and those of the Indian Diaspora, are moving forward with strong and sure strides matching the pace of the world. In the 1960s, the delineation of women characters in novels underwent a remarkable change in Indian fiction. South Asian women writers are the newest voices in America's multiethnic literature, Bharati Mukherji, Anita Desai, Jhumpa Lahiri, and Chitra Banerjee Divakaruni to name a few. Among these writers Chitra Banerjee has distinguished herself as a ground-breaking novelist in the genre of South Asian diasporic literature.

The 'skilled cartographer of the heart,' the award-winning novelist and short story writer, Chitra Banerjee Divakaruni, proved her mettle as one of the most prolific and vociferous voices of the Asian American immigrant women. In almost all her novels she has explored the physical and psychological tensions and tortures caused by the angst of a transplanted life to which the immigrant women are subjected. Women are portrayed as the most visible symbols of the perilous incongruity arising out of the cohabitation between cultures.

In a short span of 15 years, Chitra Banerjee has received accolades for her novels, volumes of poetry and collection of short stories: *Arranged Marriage; The Unknown Errors of Our Lives; Neela: Victory Song; The Conch Bearer; The Mistress of Spices; Queen of Dreams, Sister of My Heart* and its sequel, *Vine of Desire*, and the latest *Oleander Girl.*

Chitra Banerjee focuses on the diasporic Indian women caught between two opposing worlds—the world of acquired values and adopted values. In her, gender specific representations of character development are explored. They find themselves in an in-between state, struggling with cultural shackles to carve out identities of their own, oscillate between self-fulfillment and the demands for self-sacrifice. "The novelist has chosen to use literature to dramatize the ordeal of wronged womanhood" (Showalter 405). Her novels *Mistress of Spices, Sister of my Heart, Vine of Desire and Queen of Dreams* all deal with similar themes. Her literary output treats all shades of identity crisis such as alienation, marginalization, despair, nostalgia, readjustment, assimilation, adaption or adoption.

In 1991 Chitra Banerjee began an organization called Maitri (which means friend) which offers counsel to South Asian women about domestic violence, depression, cultural alienation and other issues. It was her involvement with Maitri that ultimately led her to write *Arranged Marriage*—a collection of 11 short stories which deals with abuses and bravery of immigrant women.

Arranged Marriage, the literary representation of women's experiences of displacement, explores the cross-cultural experiences of womanhood through a feminist perspective. Here the writer skillfully tells stories about immigrant Indians, who are both modern as well as trapped by cultural transformation, and are struggling to shape out an identity of their own in an unknown land. Majority of the characters are caught in the web of dualism of convention versus modernization and as such they are in a dilemma either to break away from or to adapt to the changing socio-cultural scenario.

The collection chronicles the accommodation and the rebellion Indian born girls and women in America undergo as they balance old treasured beliefs and surprising new desires, which is an important theme in the mosaic of American culture. All her characters in this collection, be it Sumita in "Clothes," Shona in "The World of Love," Meena in "A Perfect Life" or Asha and Mrinal in "Meeting Mrinal," are women of potency and vigour, constantly trying to strive a balance between the old conventional beliefs and their new life in America, who have the capacity to be strong and make their choices.

Chitra Banerjee made an indelible impression on the literary world with her first novel *The Mistress of Spices*, a magical tale of love and herbs. It narrates the voyage of Tilo, an immigrant woman, from the established paradigms of the past to an uncharted future in America. Tilo, a true representative of diasporic identity, is the proprietress of Spice Bazaar in Oakland, California. Born in India, she becomes trained in spices and is called the Mistress of Spices and she is sent to Oakland to open a spice shop from which she administers spices as curatives to the local Indian community. She comes across many characters who visit her store, mostly first or second generation immigrants, displaying vivid identities of diaspora life like scattered identity, marginalization, rebellion, and the painful efforts to adapt their old world ideals to the unfamiliar world.

Sister of My Heart tells the poignant story of two young women Anju and Sudha. Though distant cousins, they regard one another as sister of their hearts as they were born a few hours apart from each other on the same day. Since the day they were born Anju and Sudha have been bonded in ways even their mothers could not comprehend. Urged into marriage, their lives take sudden unexpected turns with Anju in India and Sudha in America. The upheavals in their lives are the simple aftershocks of their cultural displacement and ambivalence, quite typical of postcolonial cultural shifts.

After three years of parting the cousins look forward to the joy of expecting their first baby and motherhood. But both experience tragedies in their lives, which make them reach out to each other. Sudha walks out of her unhappy marriage with Ramesh, when his mother urges her to abort the female foetus. Anju is miserable after a miscarriage and its untoward effects on her marriage. The novel ends with Sudha's arrival in America with her daughter Dayita, at the invitation from Anju.

Vine of Desire is a sequel to *The Sister of My Heart*. The novel picks up where Sudha, now a divorcee comes to America to visit Anju and her husband Sunil, who has an early crush on Sudha. The happy reunion of the duo is again marred by Sunil's passionate feelings for Sudha and by Sudha succumbing to his desire.

Sudha leaves Anju, works as a nursemaid to earn a livelihood. Anju seeks divorce from Sunil and starts a new life, shedding her old value system. Having gone through the story of the two sisters, it can be said that whatever be the cause of immigration, the diasporic community faces the problem of displacement, rootlessness and marginalization. Anju and Sudha demonstrate the female independence that women writers celebrate, although such independence is achieved not without too much trauma and pain.

Mrs. Gupta of *Queen of Dreams*, gifted as dream teller, tells the dreams of the local people, interprets their dreams and the effect on their lives. But the gift proves to be inescapable, causing her to help many persons, but she has to remain distant from her husband and daughter. The novel clearly depicts the Indian-American's experience of struggling with two identities or cultures.

In *Unknown Errors of Our Lives*, a collection of nine short stories, the protagonists are caught between the beliefs and traditions of the Indian heritage and those of their or their children's new homeland.

The *Palace of Illusions* is a retelling of the *Mahabharata*, the greatest Indian epic. The story is told from the viewpoint of Panchaali, the wife of the Pandavas.

One can see the brilliant story teller, the skilled cartographer of the heart, Chitra Banerjee, at her best in her most gripping latest novel *Oleander Girl*. It tells the story of Karobi Roy, orphaned at birth, but sheltered by her ever-loving grand parents. . The novel unfolds as Karobi undertakes a brave journey to America to find her true identity. The plot is simple but full of twists and unexpected turns.

These women are no doubt conditioned by the Indian upbringing but have risen above the traditional constraints. They think more rationally, but they mentally retain some of the traditional beliefs. They cope with the cross-cultural relationships, ultimately try to achieve self-esteem and autonomy denied to them within their own insular and bigoted community. The novelist has her finger accurately on the diasporic pulse, fusing eastern values with western ethos. Her writing course with her identification is with a brave new world forging to life. "Her sensitivity to contemporary voices, today's issues are threaded through with an ongoing search for identity beyond anthropology, beyond sociology and beyond academia" (Dhanum 62)

Chitra Banerjee astonishes her readers with her exquisite individualistic styles, themes and techniques. Being an expatriate woman writer, she vividly portrays the lives of immigrant women, their loss, their alienation, social inequalities and ideological structures of Indian and American societies, assimilation and acculturation in the diasporic realm. Her women characters emerge as new women who claim their own space. She is a representative of the Indian women's liberation, autonomy and independence in a new society. The questions of identity, recognition, self-construction and adaptability are given equal importance in her literary endeavours.

With her writing, whether in a novel, short story or poem, Banerjee casts a spell, her words flowing swiftly, sweeping readers along with the current. Her works are full of vivid vibrant caricatures, the microcosmic representations of the lives lived by women who are caught in the cross-roads of a cultural shift. By giving voice to these women, whether in California, Chicago or Calcutta, Banerjee redefines the age-old notions of woman hood making them perform acts of agency and resistance, adapt to their new and changing culture and, as a result, discover their own sense of self amidst joy and heartbreak. This awareness leads them to rethink about their own lives as women, and instills in them the confidence and strength to go ahead.

Works Cited

Agnew, Vijay. *Diaspora, Memory and Identity: A Search for an Identity*. Toronto: University of Toronto Press, 2005.

Cohan, Robert. *Global Diasporas: An Introduction*, W.A: University of Washington Press, 1977.

Dhanam, K.S. "Negotiation with the New Culture: A Study of Chitra Banerjee Divakaruni's *The Mistress of Spices*." *Critical Essays on Diasporic Writings*. K. Balachandran, ed. New Delhi: Arise Publishers, 2000.

Hartley, John. *Key Concepts in Communication, Cultural and Media Studies*. London: Routledge, 2004.

Jayaram, N. "Introduction: A Study of Indian Diaspora." *The Indian Diaspora: Dynamics of Migration*. New Delhi: Sage, 2004.

Showalter, Elaine. "Towards a Feminist Poetics." *Contemporary Criticism: An Anthology*, ed. V.S. Sethuraman. Chennai: Macmillan India, 1989.

Migration to Heaven or Hell: An Emigrant Perspective of Chitra Divakaruni's Works

A. PADMAJA
SRK Institute of Technology, Vijayawada

Globalization has produced new patterns of migration worldwide. Migrations are driven by some of the factors like "economic inequalities within and between regions, expanding mobility of capital, people's desire to pursue opportunities that might improve their life chances, political strife, wars, and famine" (Brah178). According to the Eurostat Statistical report the first decade of the 21st century has seen large waves of migration from both within the EU (European Union)and from outside it. The inflow in that decade appears to have peaked in 2007. In 2008, 3.8 million people migrated to and between the EU-27 Member States. As per Migration Information Source, immigration in the U.S. from Asia has increased considerably since the 1965 US Immigration and Nationality Act. In 1960, the Asian born accounted for just five percent of the foreign-born population in the U.S., while in 2000 they made up over a quarter of those born outside the United States. Today, the Asian born are the country's second largest foreign-born population by world region of birth behind those from Latin America. The above stated details only emphasize the growing phenomenon of migration that has resulted in bringing Indian professionals into contact with people of many races and nationalities absorbing them into a radically different multicultural and multilingual international white collar workforce.

This migratory group or "masala diaspora" a term used by Sudesh Mishra has contributed generally as well as concretely to the growth and dissemination of intellectual work across the international borders. It has also resulted in migration of a large number of educated Indian women, especially to North America. As Vinay Dharwadker mentions, this "community has produced many of the newest authors of Indian origin in English, besides serving as an extensive, enthusiastic international readership for contemporary Indian writing in English" (254). The contribution by emigrant Indian women to the Indian writing in English is immense, which in itself is yet another genre of Indian writing in English. They "create and inscribe 'alternate worlds' by exchanging one tradition for another, one culture for another, and one home for another" (Samad xiii). The writers' hyphenated-identity becomes the source of creativity. As Farbat Singh puts it in her article: "The experience of cultural transplantation lends new perspectives and creative possibilities for these writers and they have fashioned astounding artistic patterns. . . . They mix the past, the present and the future and the imperial and the colonial cultures in their fiction, dislocating time and subverting the imperial purpose in the process."

In this context, the works of Chitra Banerjee hold interest as she falls under the classification of first generation emigrants. She comes from traditional Hindu families settled abroad at a young age and took to writing after migration to the U.S.A. This article is a study of the fiction by Chitra Divakaruni as emigrant writer. Here, she is referred to as emigrant writer purely from the semantic point of view as the writer of the article is based in India and looks at them as emigrants of India. She portrays not only the emigrant experiences of Indians but also the experiences of other nationals as emigrants. Migrants are caught in the interstitial space between the home culture and the culture of the adapted world and their works capture the essence of it. The world of migrants thus becomes a contesting space for religion, culture, experience, home creating a hyphenated identity.

> Not only is the diasporic/ migrant's belonging split between a family/cultural experience (language), religion/culture of origin, and city/street experience (the culture of current location) but the past becomes a complex multi-layered and hybrid phenomenon. The outcome of this interaction between past and present, this reworking, is the production of cultural identities that in Stuart Hall's term, are in 'transition' and in negotiation and transformation. (M. Singh 12)

Chitra Divakaruni has transcended boundaries negotiating two different worlds—her country of birth, India and the adopted western country, America, from various perspectives. Through her writings, Divakaruni projects the emigrants' struggle to assimilate the culture of the adapted country and yet retain the cultural and traditional practices of the home country. Divakaruni also speaks from the perspective of immigrants living in India. In her novel, *One Amazing Thing* she shows the travails of Chinese settlers in Calcutta. The attitude towards the 'outsiders' is universal. In *Queen of Dreams*, she raises the issues of identity especially in post-9/11 scenario. Rakhi, a second-generation migrant suddenly realizes that her skin raises lot of unhappy questions about her nationality. In and as mistress of spices, Tilo observes the suffering emigrants from her store of spices. In fact, the store is like any other Indian store catering to the needs of the Indians in America, selling Indian groceries and spices. Therefore, throughout the text, very rarely, any other national enters the store except for Raven, the American Indian.

Her works are studied essentially under five heads namely: Racialism; Identity Crisis in Asian Americans after 9/11; Phenomenon of Ghettoization; Transculuration and Assimilation.

In Divakaruni's novel, *Queen of Dreams*, Rakhi and her friends are a witness to the racial attacks. The attack on the Kurma House in the aftermath of 9/11 is similar to what Raihana suffers in Denmark. Jespal, a second-generation Sikh, is mistaken for a Muslim. Muslims are often equated as terrorists the world over. He was attacked by the vandalizers despite his repeated pleas that he was also an American.

> But they grab him and say "Looked in the mirror lately?" You ain't no American. It's fuckers like you who have planned this attack on the innocent people of this country. Time someone taught you faggots a lesson. (267)

Rakhi is faced with the dilemma of hoisting an American flag at her shop to profess her patriotism. This act of exhibiting her nationality raises a few doubts in her. She found it odd that she has to convince somebody of her nationality and patriotic feelings while she has been an American throughout her life. Suddenly she is assailed by doubts at her reflection in the glass, "the brown skin, the Indian features, the dark eyes with darker circles under them, the black crinkles of my hair. It's familiar and yet, suddenly, alien" (271).

As 'the architect of the immigrant dream,' Tilo in *The Mistress of Spices* reads the thoughts of Indians, especially those who operate as truck drivers and unskilled labourers who are abused by the adopted countrymen and the cops alike with racist remarks.

Brutal racist attack on the food vendor, Mohan, by two youngsters sporting a swastika sign confirms the growing intolerance for the emigrants by the natives. "No one told us it would be so hard here in Amreeka, all day scrubbing greasy floors, . . . Yes, always smile, even when people say 'Bastard foreigner taking over the country stealing our jobs.'" (62)

Jagjit, a new immigrant Sikh boy, is humiliated by his fellow students at school. They abuse him by taking off his turban and letting loose his long hair and joking about his use of Hindi. In the tussle that ensues, his dress is dirtied for which he is reprimanded by his mother. Jagjit learns his first English words which are swear words. According to A. Sivanandan, a Sri Lankan novelist, in an article, "Racism manifests itself as a cultural phenomenon, susceptible to cultural solutions, such as multicultural education and the promotion of ethnic identities. . . . Racism is conditioned by economic imperatives, but negotiated through culture: religion, literature, art, science and the media."

In Divakaruni's *One Amazing Thing*, the Indo-American Tariq is so westernized that his mother used to apologize for her son's modernity. Suddenly, a reversal in behaviour pattern is noticed in him. "What made him change? Was it 9/11, or was it Farah?" (29). "The first sign of Tariq's change was arguments with friends (at that time, most of them had been white) about what led to the attack on the Towers, about the retaliatory bombings in Afghanistan, about what Muslims really believed" (28). The outward changes became evident when he gave up drinking and dressed in a salwar kameez outfit.

> The relentless marginalization by the white society also produces on Tariq a counter-productive effect. Instead of trying to publicly accord as much as possible to the norms of the white society, he learns to acknowledge and ponder over the 'differences' which make his identity unique. For instance, he educates himself (via extensive reading and email conversations) on the reasons behind the attacks on the Towers, about the retaliatory bombings in Afghanistan and about the true beliefs of Muslims. (Sarkar)

At the consulate, Tariq develops a strong dislike for the African American, Cameroon. Perhaps he sees him as "establishment," trying to take over (36). It is because his father suffers at the hands of the Americans. But the much misunderstood Cameroon wanted to share with Tariq "how it had been growing up with no money and skin that colour the inner-city Los Angeles" (36).

In contrast to their parents, the second-generation Asian American is less likely to tolerate racial stereotyping and racial discrimination and is more aware of their minority status and the disadvantages associated with it. In Tariq this trait is highly visible.

Divakaruni through the story of Jiang in *One Amazing Thing* gives the readers a picture of the Chinese ghettoes in India. The Chinese in India are no exception to the racist attacks. During the Sino-Indian War in 1962, "People stopped patronizing Chinese businesses. Stores were vandalized. A popular Chinese restaurant was set on fire because a group of customers got food poisoning and believed it was a part of a deliberate plot to kill Indians. Chinese banks failed." (78)

Thus, a keen study of the novels by Chitra Banerjee Divakaruni shows not only the racism as practised by the whites but also racism as practised by the Asians.

The terrorist attacks by the Al-Qaeda on the iconic World Trade Centre (WTC) in the U.S. on September 11, 2001 in which three thousand innocent people died shook the world. This inhumane and horrific act was condemned by all communities irrespective of any affiliations of religion, nation, caste, colour or class. But, this tragedy did not end with the death of its victims. It impacted the lives of Muslims in America and Europe in a big way. America's "war on terror" and its retaliatory action on Afghanistan and Iran fuelled by Islamophobic rhetoric in the post 9/11 created fissures in America known for its multiculturalism and freedom for all, Muslims have come to be represented as 'terrorist' and as a threat to the society. This has resulted in a significant dilemma among the American Muslims regarding their identity and their belief in the ideals of democracy of their adapted country. The discriminatory and racist attacks on Asian Americans seem to have intensified after this incident.

As per the survey report made by New York City Commission on Human Rights on anti-Arab and Muslim discrimination, the publicity about the countries where terrorist organizations originated seems to have alerted people to cultural or religious symbols on which they could pin their fears. In many instances, those fears may have been translated into hostile, vicious, or illegal discriminatory acts that prevented members of these communities from fully participating in education, work, recreation, or finding housing. In the report, one young Muslim woman from Pakistan summed it up: "I live in fear in the land of freedom." Many who avoided discrimination lived and worked in community settings and, with their culture in the spotlight, altered their behaviour and appearance.

In *One Amazing Thing*, Tariq who "wore dark glasses, a scowl, and a beard of the kind that in recent years made airport security pull you out of line and frisk you" (4) narrates his personal story which is like looking at the other side. At the end of the story, he gains acceptance and respect. This is evident when Sino-American Lily tells him that he reminds her of her own brother. "Signs like Muslim names, dress code, topi, Kurta pyjama, hijab/naqab, beard, and coal in their eyes which not only became signifier of terror but signified the identities of terror and terrorism in the post 9/11 era" (Sajuadeen). He and his family are victimized for being Islamic followers. In the wake of terrorist attack on the Twin Towers in New York, life for the immigrants of the U.S., especially for the Islamic community has been testing.

Just like Tariq, Rakhi and her friends also undergo the same dilemma soon after the attacks on 9/11. Jespal was mistaken for a Muslim because of his attire and beard. "The victims of Post-9/11 Islamophobic backlash are not only Muslims but also non-Muslims like Hindus and Sikh who share common racial and cultural features with Muslims. They became target of terror and torture of "war on terror," different phobias, and suspicions" (Sajaudeen). The nightmare changes the lives of Tariq's family overnight forever. Tariq's religion makes his situation more vulnerable than that of Rakhi. Tariq's words, "It was a bad time for Muslims in America" (137) reflects the lives of many American Muslims.

> Jalal's Janitorial Services, which my father built from scratch into a flourishing enterprise, had lost many of its biggest customers since 9/11. . . . People weren't comfortable having Islamic cleaners going into their offices when they weren't around. It didn't matter that the same men had been cleaning those offices for over a decade. Abba was too proud—may be too hurt—to try to persuade his clients to change their minds. (135)

The mob unrest and the government's vindictiveness against the Islamic community created a fearful environment disturbing the secular fabric of the society.

> Government agents, some said the FBI, would pick up people from our community. Sometimes there was a reason; often there wasn't—at least not anything that was explained to the detainees. Some were released within a few days. . . . We knew men who had been deported, along with their families. (135)

After his father's return as a broken man, Tariq and his mother, unable to face the suspicion and distrust, decide to deport to India on the advice of the few trusted friends. But, the decision raises many questions in Tariq about his nationality. He considered himself an American citizen. Yet, he felt like an outsider in the country in which he grew up. In fact, it is the only country that he knows. The sudden loss of identity looms large at him.

> The uncles and aunties were not sure what I should do. They felt I wouldn't fit in India after having been raised here. I had the same doubts. Apart from lifestyle differences, there was another issue: this was my country. I was American. . . . Conflicting loyalties warred in my head, keeping me awake at night. (139)

When Uma observes Tariq for the first time at the consulate, a stereo-typical thought assails her at once. "It was Tariq. A Muslim name. Uma wondered if that had anything to do with his violent outburst; then she was ashamed of such a stereotypical thought" (23). Though educated and Indian, Uma is also not free of the general stereotypical and paranoiac response that is fed in the minds of the public in general against the Muslims. The reversal of acculturation process as witnessed in Tariq is to express his solidarity with the people of the community who have been suffering like him.

> They have been stereotyped, tortured, harassed and humiliated since the tragedy of 9/11 in American society. They are treated as the other, the Saidean "Oriental Arab" and the outcast/the outsider in the society's so-called American Dream and Transcendental multicultural society. They became "subaltern" who 'cannot speak.' (Sajaudeen)

Rakhi and her friends were pushed into such a situation that they had to declare their loyalty to their adapted nation. Rakhi's quandary in fact stems from Divakaruni's personal experience. In an interview, Divakaruni declares:

> As an American, I wanted to show my support and my patriotism. I wanted to put up a flag. On the other hand, letters were being circulated in my community that said "Put up a flag for your own safety." Then I felt, why should I have to put up a flag for my own safety? Why should I have to prove I'm not a bad person, just because I look a certain way? And so it became a very ambivalent gesture. I did put up a flag, but every time I looked at it, I was visited by these very different feelings.

Both Rakhi and Tariq as second generation immigrants of the U.S. tackle their problems by adapting different solutions. For Rakhi, it leads to her rediscovering of her past and being at home with the multiculturalism offered by her nation. She is at once at ease with the fusion music created by husband which earlier caused in her confusion bordering on hatred. Tariq, on the other hand, joins fellow Muslim men in standing up for their beleaguered community in America.

In other words ghettos are about the 'gathering' of the dislocated as stated by Homi Bhabha in his seminal work, *The Location of Culture*: "Gatherings of exiles and émigrés and refugees;

gathering on the edge of 'foreign' cultures; gathering at the frontiers; gatherings in the ghettos or cafes of city centres; gathering in the half-life, half-light of foreign tongues, or in the uncanny fluency of another's language; gathering the signs of approval and acceptance, degrees, discourses, disciplines; gathering the memories of underdevelopment, of other worlds lived retroactively; gathering the past in a ritual of revival; gathering the present." (199)

Paranjape in his essay takes this idea further when he says, "He [Bhabha] reminds us how a time of scattering, which is what causes the diaspora, is also a time of gathering. Because those who are scattered here gather elsewhere."

The phenomenon of ghettoization is a solution adopted by any settlers in their adopted country. It helps them retain their culture and yet provides a kind of security in togetherness.

Even in India, the Chinese immigrants form into ghettos. They suffer from the societal demarcation and choose to live in ghettos, trying to preserve their own culture and tradition. Divakaruni in *One Amazing Thing* writes about this occurrence:

> No one gave the Chinese any thought—not until much later. Indians considered us below them because many of us were in the tannery business or owned leather-goods store. . . . We had our own people, and we got from them everything we needed. (71)

The identicalness of life in Chinese ghettos is reflected in the following lines: "There was no reason to tell the other Chinese of these things. They already knew, and many of the children's friends' houses mirrored theirs. And as for non-Chinese—the ghosts, as were called—the children were taught from the beginning to stay away from them. To keep family secrets safe." (72)

'Kurma House,' the coffee house run by Rakhi in *Queen of Dreams* and Tilo's Indian spice store in *The Mistress of Spices* which are the places of meeting for the ethnic people, especially from the Asian community mirror the aspirations, disappointments, pains and pleasure felt by them. In America, Indian grocery stores often become the flag mast of cultural identity keepers. Most of these stores stock all general grocery items used in Indian cooking like dals, spices, rice, flours, canned and pickled items, frozen Indian dishes, Indian sweets, utensils, etc. Some even sell a few fresh vegetables and video cassettes of the latest Hindi and regional movies not available at the regular supermarket. In fact, Divakaruni makes all the action happen in these places. In *One Amazing Thing*, the office of the Indian Consulate becomes the spot where the actions in the form of stories unfold. However, in contemporary immigrants, the preservation of ethnic identity rather than becoming one of them is the order of the day.

> In the United States, immigration scholars initially argued that to move up the socio-economic ladder, immigrants would have to abandon unique customs, languages, values, and homeland ties and identities. Even when remaining ethnic became more acceptable, most researchers assumed that the importance of homeland ties would eventually fade. To be Italian-American or Irish-American would ultimately reflect ethnic pride within a multicultural United States rather than enduring relations to an ancestral land. (Levitt 1: 156)

The assimilation among the migrants is initially confined to the external societal issues. They try hard to preserve their cultural identity at least at homes. One such aspect, especially among the first generation, is continued usage of mother tongue. However, in the next generation onwards, the model of bilingual is visible but often the mother tongue is limited to the spoken form: "many migrants continue to speak their mother tongue, and since usually they live and work among brethren, sometimes they do not even bother to acquire the host country's language. Moreover, even after acquiring the new language, there is a strong tendency to become bilingual and use the homeland tongue at home and among the fellow members of diaspora and the host country language at the school, market place and work." (Sheffer 1:56)

Rakhi, the heroine in *Queen of Dreams*, despite her urge to know the ethnic country her parents hail from, could master only the spoken form of the language. Therefore, she seeks her father's assistance in deciphering the Dream Journal written by her mother. Of course, the slowly disappearing proficiency of language eventually results in the widening of communication gap among the first and subsequent generation.

> Language is, however, more than just a tool as it connotes symbolic and cultural meanings. It can bring an immigrant child closer to the American mainstream while also detaching him or her farther away from the immigrant family. Likewise, the mother tongue is not simply a tool but has significant symbolism. Even though children of Asian immigrants tend to lose their mother-tongue proficiency rapidly, they still express emotional attachment to it and link it to family, heritage, and even self-identity. (Min Zhou)

This is true not only among immigrants in America but also among any other nation. Uma's parents in *One Amazing Thing* emigrate to the U.S. as educated professionals and as such are more adaptive. Yet, they try to preserve the cultural identity in their child.

> They loved their jobs, plunging enthusiastically into their weekends with similar gusto, getting together . . . with other suburbanite Indian families. They had orchestrated elaborate, schizophrenic meals and bemoaned the corruption of Indian politicians. (5)

Trans Borders which are geographic, national, territorial, and symbolic separate and distinguish not only countries, but also languages, classes, genders, and individuals. The crossings of these borders create a space where new identities are formed. According to Fernando Ortiz: "Transculturation is a set of ongoing transmutations; it is full of creativity and never ceases; it is irreversible. It is always a process in which we give something in exchange for what we receive: the two parts of the equation end up being modified." (GIRA)

The reciprocal of transculturation—that is, the dominant group also adopts patterns typical of the minority group—is called acculturation. Assimilation of one cultural group into another may be evidenced by changes in language preference, adoption of common attitudes and values, membership in common social groups and institutions, and loss of separate political or ethnic identification.

The process of assimilation among the first generation is very slow as they still carry the culture and tradition of their home country. However, in the next subsequent generations, they are not exposed directly to the cultural norms of the country of origin. Their exposure depends on the home environment only. Hence, their assimilatory process is directly proportionate to the home environment. Culture loss is an inevitable result of old cultural patterns being replaced by new ones. Within a society, processes that result in the resistance to change include habit and the integration of culture traits. Older people, in particular, are often reticent to replace their comfortable, long familiar cultural patterns. Habitual behaviour provides emotional security in a threatening world of change. Religion also often provides strong moral justification and support for maintaining traditional ways. In the early twenty first century, this is especially true of nations mostly guided by Islamic Law, such as Iran, Saudi Arabia, Afghanistan, and Pakistan. In other words:

> For immigrants, the challenges of exile, the loneliness, and the constant sense of alienation, the knowledge of and longing for the lost world, are more explicit and distressing than for their children. On the other hand, the problem for the children of immigrants, those with strong ties to their country of origin is that they feel neither one thing nor the other. The feelings that there was no single place to which they belong bother them in growing up. (Sharma 63)

Most Asian Indian families strive to preserve traditional Indian values and transmit these to their children. Offsprings are encouraged to marry within the community and maintain their Indian heritage.

The second generation kids have a problem in communicating with their parents. The parents being first generation have a difficulty in understanding the acculturation changes in their kids. They are averse to their kids participating in the cultural events of the colleges like proms. Angry Manu, who is graduating from school, seeks his father's permission. But for his father, prom is "All that drinking whisky-beer and dancing pressed up against cheap American girls in miniskirts" (*Mistress* 79). The words show the non- acceptance of the adopted country's culture as well as low opinion of the Americans.

One of Tilo's customers thinks of her teenage son who might be doing drugs. The impact of the western culture is high on the second generation. "He's been acting so strange, hanging out with boys who frighten her with their razor earrings and biker jackets and heavy boots as though for war, their cold, cold eyes and slits of mouths that are becoming his eyes, his mouth." (77)

The case of Rakhi in *Queen of Dreams* is different though she is a second generation migrant. Interestingly, her mother keeps her in ignorance about her culture and country unlike other Indians. Ironically, this leads to Rakhi being inexorably drawn towards the mystic and ethnic India. In her mother's words:

> I thought it would protect you if I didn't talk about the past. . . . I didn't want to be like those other mothers, splitting you between here and there, between your life right now and that which can never be. But by not telling you about Indian as it really were, I made it into something far bigger. It crowded other things out of your mind. It pressed upon your brain like a tumour (89).

Rakhi's mother, Mrs. Gupta, as a first generation immigrant to the U.S.A. tries to acclimatize herself to the life of America but without actually losing the essential Indianness such as preserving the dress sense and food habits and other visible manifestation of culture.

> Socially and culturally positioning herself as an immigrant Indian Mrs. Gupta neither acculturates nor assimilates but just adapts or adjusts with life around her, without changing or transforming herself. Her adaptation and her will to be an authentic Indian surfaces when Rakhi's Chai Shop was at the point of crumbling and Mrs. Gupta's valuable suggestion were called for. (Bharathi)

If Mrs. Gupta preserves Indianness, Rakhi, despite her mother's effort to see her assimilate the culture of America, awakes to the American life late. As a girl, she uneasily accustoms herself to the school friends and environment. As Bharathi and Kalamani state:

> Her problem of complete assimilation to the host culture and tradition is complicated and complex. Though born in America, America does not offer her the passport of being an American. Yet, the stamp of a true American is seen in her. . . . She makes acculturation her strength, as towards the end of the novel she learns to appreciate Indian instruments produce music that is not purely Indian but an American mix.

Often, the degree of transculturation and assimilation depends on the education. This only proves that in the contemporary society where "moving populations are the norm rather than exception, configurations of home, homecoming, identity, alienation, loss, forgetting, memory, rootlessness, become truly real and global issues" (Kumar).

To sum up, Divakaruni boldly takes up the issues of emigration in her works. She has chosen to write about the reversion in peoples' thinking after 9/11—assimilation, transculturation and acculturation process that are major aspects in any migration issue. She writes about the cultural preservation in the form of ghettoization. She depicts in her works how women face the double burden of preserving the home culture and tradition as well as learn new cultures and tradition in order to integrate into their newly adopted country.

Works Cited

Bhabha, Homi. *The Location of Culture*. Oxon: Routledge, 2004.

Bharathi, C. and S. Kalamani. "A Study of Family Relationships in Chitra Banerjee Divakaruni's *Queen of Dreams*." *Impressions: Bi-Annual Refereed ejournal of English Studies*, Vol VI: Issue I, Jan. 2012.

Brah, Avtar. *Cartographies of Diaspora: Contesting Identities*. London: Routledge, 1996.

Dharwadker, Vinay. "The Historical Formation of Indian English Literature." *Literary Cultures: Reconstructions from South Asia*, ed. Sheldon Pollock. Berkeley: Univ. of California Press, 2003.

Divakaruni, Chitra Banerjee. *The Mistress of Spices*. Great Britain: Black Swan, 1997.

_____. *The Vine of Desire*. London: Abacus, 2002.

_____. *Queen of Dreams*. London: Abacus, 2005.

_____. *One Amazing Thing*. New York: 2009.

_____. "The Imagined Homelands." Interview by Susan Comninos. Atlantic.

GIRA. "Transculturation and Cultural Hybridity." http://www.gira.info/en/about-us/research-questions-andkeynotions/transculturation-and-cultural-hybridity.

Levitt, Peggy. Nina Glick Schiller. "Conceptualizing Simultaneity: A Transnational Social Field Perspective on Society." *Sociology of Diaspora: A Reader*, Vol. I, ed. Ajay Kumar Sahoo and Brij Maharaj. Jaipur: Rawat, 2007.

Migrants in Europe. A Statistical Portrait of the First and Second Generation. Eurostat Statistical Book. 2011.

Mishra, Sudesh. "From Sugar to Masala: Writing by the Indian Diaspora." *A Concise History of Indian Literature in English*. ed. Arvind Krishna Mehrotra. Ranikhet: Permanent Black, 2008.

Paranjape, Makarand. "Interrogating Diasporic Creativity: The Patan Initiative—A Valedictory Address." The official website of Makarand Paranjape.

Sajaudeen, Chapparban Nijamodeen. "The Muslim Experiences in America and Bollywood Discourse after 9/11." *Galaxy: International Multidisciplinary Research Journal*. 10 March 2013.

Sarkar, Ananya. "Bracing the Shadows: A Study of the 9/11 Impact on Second Generation Indian Americans in Chitra Divakaruni's Novels." Muse India Archives. Issue 45, 2012.

Shaikh, Samad, ed. "Introduction." *Literature of Diaspora: Cultural Dislocation*. New Delhi: Creative, 2009.

Sharma, Monika. "Rootless Gogol-Quest for Identity in *The Namesake*." *Mapping Migrations: Perspective on Diasporic Fiction*, ed. Charu Sharma, New Delhi: Book Plus, 2006.

Sheffer, Gabriel. "The Emergence of New Ethno-National Diasporas." *Sociology of Diaspora: A Reader*, Vol. I, ed. Ajay Kumar Sahoo and Brij Maharaj. Jaipur: Rawat, 2007.

Singh, Farbat. "Indian English Novel Writing: Shifting Themes & Thoughts (with Special Reference to Salman Rushdie and Amitav Ghosh)." *International Research Journal*, Vol. I, Issue 10, July 2010.

Survey Report. "Survey of Anti-Arab and Muslim Discrimination. Survey of discrimination against Muslims and other South Asians in New York city since 9/11." New York City Commission on Human Rights 2003.

Zhou, Min, Yang Sao Xiong. "The Multifaceted American Experiences of the Children of Asian Immigrants: Lessons for Segmented Assimilation," *Ethnic and Racial Studies*, Vol. 28, No. 6, Nov. 2005.

White Feet in Black Sandals: A Study of Magic Realism as the Narrative Mode in Divakaruni's *The Mistress of Spices*

JAGDISH BATRA
O.P. Jindal University, Sonipat

Magic or magical realism, the narrative mode, employed by Chitra Banerjee Divakaruni in her novel *The Mistress of Spices* places her in big league of celebrated authors like Jorge Luis Borges of Argentina, Gabriel Garcia Marquez of Columbia, Gunter Grass of Germany, Salman Rushdie of India.

Ironically, the fictional tool of magic realism has gained popularity even as it deviates from the foundational premise of the genre of novel. Not long ago—in the 18th century to be precise—when the genre of novel developed in Europe, it was meant to be different from the foregoing epics, fables and romances which thrived on fantasy. It is believed that the German art critic Franz Roh first used the term 'magic realism' in 1925, to refer to a painting style. However, the term caught attention of the literary world in 1955 through an essay "Magical Realism in Spanish American Fiction" penned by the critic Angel Flores. Latin America has been home to the early growth of this kind of fiction. While the Spanish writer Miguel de Saavedra Cervantes' novel Don Quixote is considered to be the precursor of magic realist novel, the Argentinean author Jorge Luis Borges is accepted as the father of the genre by Angel Flores who finds his collection of short fiction titled A Universal History of Infamy as the first example of Latina Mexican writing "influenced by European literature" (Bowers 17).

Besides Marquez, whose work *One Hundred Years of Solitude* won acclaim, other leading practitioners of magic realism include the German playwright and novelist Gunter Grass (The Tin Drum), American novelist Toni Morrison (*Beloved*), Chilean writer Isabel Allende (*Daughter of Fortune*), African fictionist Ben Okri (*The Famished Road*). The mention of only one novel against their names should not mean that their other works do not have the element of magic realism. Salman Rushdie is the mascot of this kind of fiction so far as Indian English literature is concerned. Most of his works including *Midnight's Children*, Satanic Verses, Shame, etc. show the use of magic realism. While there are hundreds of novels produced in the magic realist mode in the world, in Indian English literature, its progress has been rather tardy. After Rushdie, a few writers like Amitav Ghosh, Michael Ondaatje and Chitra Banerjee Divakaruni have tried their hand at it.

It is indeed surprising that this oxymoronic expression Magic Realism should catch the fancy of writers and the reading public, but behind its back is the realization of the postmodern times that reality is not all rational or reason-based. The philosophical approach that justifies this kind of fiction questions the representation of reality through the Enlightenment tools of reason and logic. It is believed that this Eurocentric phenomenon denigrates other epistemologies followed in the so-called third world: "Texts labelled magical realist draw upon cultural systems that are no less 'real' than those upon which traditional literary realism draws—often non-Western cultural systems that privilege mystery over empiricism, empathy over technology, tradition over innovation" (Zamora et al 3).

In their support, the votaries of magic realism point out that Freud too found the working of the sub-conscious to be irrational. Deriving inspiration from him, the painters and literary writers started using the technique of surrealism. Magic realism is differentiated from surrealism as it does not depend upon the dream as the via media of representation. Instead, it is the material world which is shown altered through magic.

It may be pointed out here that magic realism as a narrative mode of representation is not for indiscriminate use of the fantastic. The use of fantasy, it is believed, lands the reader in a state of doubt as to whether what is narrated in the text falls in the category of the real or fantastic. Magic realism does not create such a predicament for the reader; rather it clearly shows that its fantastic aspect is well accepted in human society. In Brenda Cooper's words, "Magical realism attempts to capture reality by way of a depiction of life's many dimensions, seen and unseen, visible and invisible, rational and mysterious. In the process, such writers walk a political tight-rope between capturing this reality and providing precisely the exotic escape from reality desired by some of their Western readership" (32).

The critic Wendy Faris finds magical realism as a 'liberating poetics' for the colonized writers, for whatever a realist text may say, the fact that realism purports to give an accurate picture of the world based on empirical evidence which is a European import and which, therefore leads the writers in colonized societies to experience it as "the language of the colonizer. From this perspective, to adopt magical realism, with its irreducible elements that question that dominant discourse, constitutes a kind of liberating poetics." (Faris 103). Indeed, being a postcolonial development, the magic realist texts are mostly subversive texts in which the voice of rebellion gets easily camouflaged through the use of magic.

However, Stephen Slemon looks at the mode of magic realism in a different way. According to him, "due to its dual narrative structure, magical realism is able to present the postcolonial context from both the colonized peoples' and the colonizers' perspectives through its narrative structure as well as its themes" (qtd. Bowers 97). Such an explanation should not create the binary: colonized-magical/colonizer-logical, for both the colonizers and colonized of yore are attracted towards this literary technique for reasons as varied as escapism from reality to carnivalesque heteroglossia. The magical/logical binary, therefore, tends to be undermined through metonymic association. It may be that sometime in future, this technique loses its popularity because the twin discourses do not lead a focussed truth and can, at best, be seen as deconstructive play.

It may be noted here that the art of magic realism is nearer to the Indian art of story telling. The magic realist text is told in the form of a modern fable and serves as a means to synthesize divergent conceptions of the world. In this kind of contradictory narrative, the realistic story takes magical turns at times. Divakaruni's use of magic realism, arguably an import, sits comfortably with Indian myths and legends. One must examine the European standpoint which downgrades magic realist text on the ground that the irrational and the illogical belong to the non-European cultures. While reference has already been made to Freud and the paranormal movement that is a respectable field of study in the west today, we should not forget that myths belonging to any nation are full of impossible tales. The problem with the western world is that it has transformed itself so much that it has lost touch with its own past—something that is now stored in museums only, and if museums do not satisfy man's curiosity, then there are the mummified locales like Williamsburg in USA. It is man's fascination for the fantastic that is evidenced in the success of movies like *King Kong*, *Godzilla*, or the comics starring Superman and Spiderman. The problem is the approach of the western mind that takes its own fancy as valuable and derides others' as idiotic.

An Indian diasporic poet and novelist based in USA, Chitra Banerjee Divakaruni, has successfully employed the technique in her novel *The Mistress of Spices* (1997). She is a prolific award-winning novelist, who teaches creative writing at Foothill College in California. She is also president of MAITRI, a helpline for South Asian women in distress. In all, she has written some sixteen books till date.

The Mistress of Spices is the story of Tilo, born Nayan Tara in a poor family in India, where she is regarded a liability. As the child grows up, her parents realize that she is blessed with some special powers whereby she can find lost things as also forecast calamities. The word of her oracular faculty spreads far and wide and people from different villages come to her to know their future. Some bandits also come to know of her special gift, and wanting to make use of her rare gift to hit jackpots abduct her. Life with the bandits is indeed very difficult, but a brave person that she is, Nayan Tara overthrows the pirate captain and becomes the pirate queen Bhagyavati.

Later, with the guidance of an old snake (the snakes speak here), she manages to escape. Regarding the symbolism of snake, it is observed: "All fertility goddesses, including Kali, are associated with snakes. Snakes are symbols of renewal—they shed their skin regularly and rejuvenate themselves just like the earth restores its fertility each year. Snakes are also symbols of Kundalini, the seed of occult wisdom that lies coiled in all beings, waiting to be aroused by various Tantrik practices" (Mohanty, qtd. Chakravarti, 209). Thus, the magic world and the real world meet here.

The mysterious sea-serpents also tell Bhagyavati of 'kala-pani' a primeval place where an old woman called First Mother trains women in a sort of cult of spices. In Tantric tradition, the role of women has been very significant since ancient times. In present India also, the women, due to their educational and financial backwardness are seen influenced more by notions of magic than the comparatively better off menfolk. The name 'kala-pani,' though not specified in the novel, is normally taken to refer to the two islands Andaman and Nicobar which were called 'kala-pani' during the period of Indian freedom struggle because the revolutionaries were sent there with the stipulation that they will die there and would never return to the mainland to create problem for the British colonizers. The term can also be taken as a reference to the diasporic situation of the first settlers who were taken as indentured labourers to different colonies of Britain—to Fiji, Guyana, etc.—as plantation workers. They lived and died there because of their poverty and the limited means of transport to reach back home. Divakaruni obliquely refers to the immigrants to America who mostly spend their entire life there even as their economic status is far better than that of their ancestors.

While it is known that the spices, herbs and condiments used in the Indian dishes have medicinal value, there is no denying the fact that some of these like black til (sesame seed) are used in magical rites also. Divakaruni has, however, extended the magical property to most spices. Etymologically, the name Tilottama given by the First Mother, can be divided into 'til+uttam,' i.e., the best til, which suggests that she is the magic incarnate herself. This is an old name which finds mention in Padma Purana, in which Tilottama appears as apsara or a beautiful dancer. It is stated that in her earlier life, she was an ugly widow named Kubza but she performed penance and was born a beautiful woman in the next birth. (Bhadra 281)

In the novel, Tilottama has two types of attributes: "most elegant of dancers, crest jewel among women" and also "the essence of til, life giver, restorer of health and hope" (42). However, Divakaruni has created a reverse parallel to the mythical tale in her novel in which Nayantara, a beautiful young girl gets transformed into an old woman and is named Tilottama. In the movie made on the basis of this book, Aishwarya Rai plays Tilo's role. However, she is shown young and captivating throughout the movie, in order, perhaps, to cater to popular taste.

Tilo is the mistress of sesame seeds, and like all others must follow the three commands, which are: look after desires of others; never leave the spice store; and, never touch anyone else's skin. The atmosphere on the island is thoroughly magical which gets accentuated through Divakaruni's poetic prose. After her training is over, the First Mother gives her the gift of a knife ostensibly "to cut my [Tilo's] moorings from the past, the future. To keep me always rocking at sea" (51).

She is asked to serve people with whom she has affinity: "To help your own kind, and them only. The others, they must go elsewhere for their need" (68). There is a mental reminder to her when she serves Kwesi, an African-American and Raven, the American with whom she finally falls in love, much against the rules laid down for the mistresses of spices. This leads one to conclude that the Old One wanted Tilo to serve only her compatriots because they too were diasporic like her and needed special care due to their marginal status in the American society. This injunction is in sync with the secret primitive rites practised in most ancient societies. Some critics believe that Divakaruni inserts such a command because she is herself deeply involved in activism aimed at helping the Indian diasporic community.

Tilottama has rare power to use spices to cure the physical and mental problems of her clients. Spices occupy the centre-stage in the novel in the form of chapter headings like Fenugreek, Fennel, Kao Jire, etc. Serving the diasporic Indians as also others becomes Tilo's life-long ambition. She helps a number of people. Geeta is a second generation member of an Indian diasporic family. She does not want to go in for an arranged marriage as suggested by her parents and grandfather. She is attracted towards Juan, a Chicano (of Mexican-American stock). Her grandfather visits Tilo for a magical cure which can bring Geeta to accept his choice for her. Similarly, Lalita who got married to Mr. Ahuja through latter's fraud when he sent an old picture from his college days, while the matrimonial negotiations were in progress. Now in the US, he would torture his wife regularly. She is able to escape her rapacious husband with Tilo's help.

Another diasporic couple Mohan and his wife Veena see themselves as different from other minority communities and wonder why they are the targets of racism. Tilo experiences their pain as if it were her own:"My limbs ache as after a long illness, my sari is damp with shiver-sweat, and in my heart I cannot tell where your pain ends and mine begins. For your story is the story of all those I have learned to love in this country, and to fear for" (44). Other beneficiaries include Daksha, the nurse, Dr. Lalchandani's wife, Jagjit and Manu, though Jagjit takes to the ways of American gangsters later.

When she meets the handsome American architect Doug (Raven), Tilo feels attracted towards him, much against the first rule. He is also a victim of circumstances. She seeks advice from the spices but they, for once, are silent: "Then: so be it for now. We are patient. We know you will come to us soon. Once you have heard our song, have paced the rhythms of desire whose seat is deep in the body's core, you cannot resist." (190)

The all-knowing magical spices know Tilo inside out. Soon, she calls upon spices to beautify her for just one meeting with him and the spices willingly oblige: "Use us for love, for beauty, for your joy, because that is why we were made," the spices say (212). It was the magical shampatti's fire which had aged her and the magical spices would bring back her youth.

When Raven hugs her, she feels the woman in her. He suggests to her to run away with him to a remote place—an earthly paradise—away from the urban jungle, that is, America. But then an earthquake changes Tilo's mind. Even though she has lost her magical powers as she had violated the First Mother's code for the mistresses of spices, yet she feels that she should not give up helping the American people in their hour of need. The new resolve is indicative of the solution that Divakaruni suggests for the diasporic—to involve themselves in the community life of the host society. Tilo rightly declares: "India and America, for I belong to both now" (313).

Not long back, Simon de Beauvoir had faulted western literature for dishing out stereotypical images of woman as either a goddess or a vamp. Critical surveys have pointed out that writers have depicted Indian woman as exotic though oppressed; as demure, delicate and docile. In *The Mistress of Spices*, we find several roles that women play. They appear as daughter, sister, wife and mother. Tilo's character, however, is singular in that she is a brave-heart from the very start. She charts her own course of life. She dedicates her life to empowering women so that they do not suffer injustice. Of course, she has magical powers to support her lone existence in the US.

Even though she is a coloured person, Tilo has a special place as the giver of mental and spiritual solace to people of all faiths and communities—something for which she had not been ordained. She rebels against the diktat of the Old One. Tilo is also for a fluid identity; she changes her own name from Nayantara to Bhagyavati to Tilottama, and finally to Maya. In fact, she represents "the journey of a woman not only from innocence to maturity but a voyage that criss-crosses the realm of reality and magic, and transcends the confines of geographical borders and cultural specifications" (Chakravarti 208).

It would not be inappropriate to conclude that by mixing the real with the fantastic, *The Mistress of Spices* has assumed form to a cross-cultural experience of the Indian community in the United States. Divakaruni presents the image of a woman which goes against the stereotypical docile and subservient type generally found in diasporic literature. Of course, she employs the tool of magic realism to achieve it. We do have realistic images of woman as daughter, sister and wife. If anything is common in Tilo with the typical Indian female, it is the sacrificing and self-effacing aspect that finds expression here. Needless to say that such a character must succeed in winning the approval of the host society. The charge that an ancient culture is dished out as a primitive one through exoticizing and commodifying will not curry favour with a reader who is aware of the possibilities and limitations of the narrative mode of magic realism.

The use of this technique should also not be interpreted to mean the propagation of superstition. She fails at times to cure the maladies of her clients as the magic remedy does not bring in the desired result. The reason advanced is the violation of the code laid down by the First Mother. This code lays stress on charitable work for society without any selfish motive. Through the character of Tilottama, alias Tilo, Divakaruni shows that neither the East nor the West is complete in itself, so instead of acrimony and hatred, love and cooperation should mark their relationship.

It was Franz Fanon who used the title Black Skin White Masks for his book which became seminal to the postcolonial movement. The use of magic realism appears like black sandals on white feet, both the colours acting as foil to each other. The feet here denote the western rational epistemology and the sandals the postcolonial mystical knowledge systems. Both produce a new and attractive complex. However, the realistic novel, as it has been known prior to the emergence of the magic realist narrative, continues to reign supreme. There are indications that the magic realist novel may not survive for long.

Works Cited

Bhadra, Nandini. *Locating Asian American Women Writers in the Diaspora*. New Delhi: Prestige, 2013.

Bowers, Maggie A. *Magic (al) Realism*. New York: Routledge, 2004.

Chakravarti, Devasree & G.A. Ghanshyam. "Shifting Identities: Re-Invention of the Self in Chitra Banerjee Divakaruni's *The Mistress of Spices*," *The Indian Journal of English Studies*, Vol. XLIX 2012, pp. 207-13.

Cooper, Brenda. *Magical Realism in West African Fiction*. London: Routledge, 1998.

Divakaruni, Chitra Banerjee. *The Mistress of Spices*. 1998. London: Random Black Swan, 2005.

Faris, Wendy B. *The Question of the Other: Cultural Critique of Magical Realism*. Arlington: The University of Texas, pp. 101-19.

Zamora, Lois & Wendy B. Faris. *Magical Realism: Theory, History, Community*. London: Duke University Press, 1995.

Crafting Reciprocation and Womanhood: A Study of Chitra Divakaruni's *The Mistress of Spices* and *The Vine of Desire*

BOLLAVARAPU RAJU
Andhra Loyola College, Vijayawada

The search for identity has emerged as a major concern in much of the postcolonial writings. America, like any other newly emergent commonwealth country, tried to define and establish itself as a nation with its distinctive national and cultural identity. The country has witnessed the flowering of many ethnic writers with their emphasis on the marginalized, resulting in the meeting of many races and cultures trying to assert their identity. Multiculturalism in the United States has given impetus to various ethnic writings today. The ethnic and cultural diversity of America is reflected in the literature dealing with immigrant experience, which has come of age and has found a separate space for itself.

South Asian American literature today has been defined in terms of the mainstream discourse. The meeting of many cultures in America has resulted in the writers resorting to different modes to give expression to their unique voice and vision.

In recent times, South Asian writers have made significant contribution to the growing body of American literature and a few of them like Chitra Banerjee Divakaruni have received critical attention. Divakaruni has come to occupy a prominent place in South Asian American Writing with the publication of her poems, short stories and novels. Today for that matter major contemporary women writers with Asian origin have raised their voices against these gender based inequalities through their writings in Canada, and America, especially fiction writing seems to have taken a new turn in the 1960s with the appearance of women novelists into the literary scene like Margaret Atwood, Margaret Laurence, Bharati Mukherjee, Chitra Banerjee Divakaruni, all who tend to write more as women than as patriots, social critics and crusaders. A close study of their novels reveals that their focus is on the world of their feelings and sensibilities. Divakaruni in one of her novels titled *The Vine of Desire* draws attention to the dimensions of gender system through her fictional world. She projects in her novels how the concept of gender has transcended all barriers between man and woman. Anju for instance takes up the job of writing by going to college even after her marriage with Sunil. Through her novels, Divakaruni makes a plea and expresses the fact that gender system be demolished because it is possible for a female to be creative like her male counterpart and envision a new world in which men and women are equal at every level of existence. So like all feminist writers, Divakaruni's texts deal with the issues of gender and claims that 'human quality' and 'human freedom of choice' should be given to women as they are born as human beings first.

Divakaruni in her fictional works depicts the problems faced by Indian and other third world immigrants who attempt to assimilate into North American life styles. In *The Mistress of Spices*, Divakaruni explores the immigrant experience through her central character-narrator, Indian born woman Tilottama, in America. She uses her laser like insight and skilful use of a story, plot and lyrical description to give the readers a many-layered look at her character and her respective worlds which are filled with fear, hope and discovery. We understand that Tilo makes her decision to be in love with him that she changes her name to Maya, which means the world of illusion, a place of inevitable sorrow. Tilo discovers that she has not a single being to whom she can turn. She pleads with the spices that she will accept their decrees to look this way as long as she must; though love and power were lost to ashes. The guilt in her is that for one person to be happy, another must take the suffering. So she begs the spices to give her sleep and oblivion that she may not want her body twist back into misshapenness and the spices do not say no.

Tilo lies down for the last time in the centre of the store of which she is no longer the mistress. The voice calls Tilo, Tilo, the floor tilts and she hears sounds of her heart tearing but ironically it is the shop that cracks like egg shell. She could feel the red stars (may be the red chillies) explode. As she plunges into pain, Tilo realizes with hopelessness that it will not kill her. Awareness comes to Tilo that she has to adopt herself to ugliness having known beauty already. She feels that life is a game beyond understanding. She wonders if all this is the doing of the first mother who is kind to her, an unforgiving daughter despite her mistakes. Tilo hears the voice of raven for an answer, so that they can head towards the paradise. Tilo feels that it is time for her to relax into her density all her life, but one thing is unresolved to Tilo, whether she is an Indian or American, she is caught between two different cultures and the clash results in a dilemma. She wonders if she belongs to the native Indian Culture.

In Divakaruni's works, women occupy the central role and they are treated equally on par with men, though she is vociferous in voicing her fears and concerns regarding the future of women in an alien land. Her female protagonists are sensitive, self-conscious, brilliant, creative, independent beings with their own unique and individual identities. Tilo, in *The Mistress of Spices* is an immigrant from India who runs a spice shop in Oakland California. While she supplies the ingredients for curries and kurmas she also helps her customers to gain a more precious commodity: whatever they most desire. For Tilo is a mistress of spices, a priestess of the secret magical powers of spices. Anju and Sudha in *The Vine of Desire* are also women with strong determination, will-power and self-centredness. Thus the women in both the novels bear testimony to the fact that they are depicted as strong and empowered women though they encounter lots of trials and tribulations in their journey towards self-discovery and realization and identity.

From the reading of the novel, we understand that the immigrant encounters with the new world forms the core of Divakaruni's fiction and the 'woman' as immigrant dominates her works. Much of her fiction is informed by her own personal experiences. More often than not, Divakaruni creates characters who lack a stable sense of personal and cultural identity and float gleefully in the multicultural society of America. She tries to dig deep into the problems of immigration and its impact especially on women. Regarding immigration Bharati Mukherjee has disclosed her views in one of her interviews: "We immigrants have fascinating tales to relate. Many of us have lived in newly independent or emerging countries which are plagued by civil and religious conflicts. We have experienced rapid changes in the history of the nation in which we lived. When we uprooted ourselves from these countries and come here either by choice or out of necessity, we suddenly must absorb 200 years of American history and learn to adapt to American society. Our lives are remarkable often heroic" (*Jasmine* 99).Thus all immigrant women writers focus on female experience and explore the subtle psychological dominance and the plain physical brutality frequently directed toward South Asian women whose subjugation is sanctioned by India's patriarchal system. This traditional bias, Divakaruni suggests in her narratives, too often carries over into the immigrant experience as both the women and men struggle to adjust in a new society that makes demands they are unprepared to meet. Both Sudha and Anju in *The Vine of Desire* are unprepared to adjust themselves because of emotional bonds and the love triangle that exists between Sunil, Anju and Sudha. While Sunil continues to do his job, Anju and Sudha face problems. So it is clear that too often women bear the brunt of masculine frustrations and are the victims. *The Vine of Desire* (2002) is the third novel of Divakaruni. It is a moving and satisfying sequel to the second novel titled *Sister of My Heart* which is about the lives of two women Sudha and Anju and how they are changed by marriage, as one woman comes to California, and the other stays behind in India. *The Vine of Desire* stands on its own as a novel of extraordinary depth and sensitivity. The title expresses the story of two immigrant women, Sudha and Anju, enmeshed in the making of American lives and in the work of living with passion and commitment with parents, children, and men, with one another and most importantly of all in their own skins. It speaks of desires and dreams that all human beings keep closer to their hearts like Anju and Sudha and how sometimes life disappoints us, but we keep striving to find that deep joy we once knew as children. The very story of desires and dreams of the two heroines Anju and Sudha teaches a lesson that life is a journey full of changes and transitions and that nothing is permanent. The book is not just about transformation and growth but also about expectations versus reality. It depicts a lot about the Indian culture and what it is like to be immersed into a completely foreign culture. Sudha experiences a lot of changes as she realizes the freedoms that come with a culture so different from her own.

Injustice has been experienced by the women all through the ages. Whether it is in India, America or Canada, women have been persistently suffering and silently sacrificing themselves as candles. But South Asian immigrant writers acclimatized themselves to the new atmospheres in Canada and America and portrayed the conditions of women in their writings.

Divakaruni's novels depict women entangled in the mesh of their own psyche born out of the pressures of a society which is both patriarchal and cloistered but at the end, all of them break strongholds of their society and explore new avenues. In a remarkable terse and evocative language, Divakaruni tells the story of a pronouncedly individual woman who emerges as representative figure with her brave attempt to find an identity of her own. She makes us realize that all human relationships are in fact, a gamble, a throw of dice, a matter of chance and destiny. In other words, we can say that the 'refashioning of the self' in America and the search for new identity for immigrants in general and women in particular, in Divakaruni's fiction, is an odyssey which requires sacrifices on the part of those who aspire for it. This remoulding of self is realized upon both body and the spirit and in most cases it leaves the aspirants traumatized, lost, confused and pathetic, losing the vitality of their former life and warmth of the new.

Works Cited

Divakaruni, Chitra Banerjee. *The Mistress of Spices*, Great Britain: Blackswan, 1997.

_____. *The Vine of Desire*, New York: Anchor, 2002.

_____. *Sisters of My Heart*, Great Britain: Blackswan, 1999.

_____. *The Unknown Errors of our Lives*, Great Britain: Blackswan, 2002.

Harvey, David, *The Conditions of Postmodernity*: Cambridge University Press, 1989.

Tradition and Modernity in Chitra Divakaruni's *Sister of My Heart*

C. BHARATHI
K.S.R. College of Engineering, Tiruchengode

In every age a tussle between tradition and modernity goes on. What is current at a particular period is considered modern; what has gone by and is a part of the past becomes traditional. Champions of modernity criticize traditions. Tradition suppresses modernity. Both tradition and modernity are necessary for a society. Tradition or modernity alone is inadequate as a living philosophy of life. In all stages of human development, both tradition and modernity have played a significant role. Only tradition binds people in chains while modernity makes them hollow. Therefore, it cannot be either tradition or modernity. It has to be a combination of both. In modern Indian English novels, many writers have tried to underline modernity, or significant changes, by creating illustrative situations and characters in different contexts.

Across the world women writers from Indian Diaspora have carved their distinct niche. Indian English women novelists realised and synthesized tradition and modernity in their novels. Their mindset is deeply rooted in Indian tradition and culture. It is not that Indian women have suddenly become writers, they have been writing down the centuries across time and tradition. The voice of Indian woman speaks in many languages, each having a rich regional flavour of its own. The thoughts of women, writing in regional Indian languages and in English, significantly from post-independence times, have guided the shaping of modern India. They have been opting to have the best of both the worlds of Tradition and Modernity. Thus, their thoughts and words brought modernity into traditional India.

From time immemorial, throughout the world, there has been a fixed image of man and woman. Traditionally, the image of woman has been what men have thought it should be. A "good" woman is one who is meek, docile, passive, obedient, virtuous, humble, kind and self-sacrificing. A bad woman was one who was bold, adventurous, active, articulate, intelligent and questioning conduct of such a woman was not appreciated by society—a society which was shaped by men who laid down the norms of behaviour. This image of woman is found in the cultural attitudes of the world, and departure from this has come to stand for the dividing line between tradition and modernity.

Contemporary authors like Chitra Banerjee Divakaruni are groping for ways in which to depict the South Asian immigrant experience and possible appropriation by mainstream discourses has significant consequences. Readings of her work produce new meanings and new sites of contestation. Therefore she cannot claim to be outside of the power struggle that revolves around the authenticity of voice. Within the Indian community in the diaspora there are many versions of history being produced and the questions of what's being said, by whom and who is representing who, have become pertinent. Divakaruni, writing about gendered identity politics, needs to be careful of the ways in which her work can be used.

Writing in one of the territorial extremes of the United States, Chitra Divakaruni in San Francisco, represents the current crop of writers, who are concerned with crossing over from one culture to another without compromising either, negotiating new boundaries and remaking themselves. In her writings, the diaspora with its shifting boundaries and conflictual encounters between different cultures is an important focus where nationalisms and literatures need to re-define themselves. The de-stabilization of identities that occurs in the daily confrontation with the hegemonic discourses of United States compels re-conceptualization of identities and re-presentation in the corpus of literary works. Divakaruni locates her texts at the troubled intersection of female subjectivity and national identities. Although she captures different aspects of the cultural encounter, the ways in which identities are ordered forms a common matrix in her writings.

Divakaruni approaches the themes of tradition and modernity in innovative ways. She projects varied themes in her works like inter-racial marriages, mobile parents or preference for alternative sexualities, home and family, ethnicity and identity, body and sexuality through which she articulates a perspective of women's experience of exile in particular and women's alienation in general. She brings her ideas into the story, which makes the reader feel about the character, and the reality with which she interweaves the story is really appreciable. The characters are very close to reality and find a balance between old treasured beliefs and surprising new desires.

Divakaruni writes about the transformed lives of the women both liberated and trapped by cultural changes. The additional charm of her novels resides in the graph that she has tried to chart out in the advancement of women from tradition to modernity in family situations. If modernity, as defined by Stuart Hall, can be considered "the experience of living with rapid, extensive and continuous change" (qtd. Wadia 216) then that is amply illustrated in Chitra Divakaruni's *Sister of My Heart*.

Chitra Divakaruni manufactures the story that reflects an ordered perfection of her life and it is co-related with her efforts at adhering to traditional values. This creation of a "historical identity of culture as a homogenizing, unifying force, authenticated by the originary past, kept alive in the national tradition of the people" (qtd. Banerjee 14) is an attempt at imposing a unitary national identity using cultural signs as a rubric of generalization. Such an understanding of national identity belies its multiplicity and blocks the perception of cultural practices as living process that can be challenged, modified and transformed. The strategies of national identification that function in the name of the people hinge on an artificial binary of tradition and modernity. Tradition is good, essentially indigenous and uninterpellated by western influence while modernity is evil, degraded and a western ethos.

For the female protagonists in Divakaruni's *Sister of My Heart*, clothes, education, thinking about their own rights and pleasures become a signifier of modernity. The identity of modern women is associated with an elite "westernization," and a repudiation of ancient and ostensibly timeless traditions; the force of the rhetoric of nationalism conceals the fact that these traditions are selectively resurrected, posited as trans-historical and woven into a coherent narrative of religion. In her essay, "Contentious Traditions: The Debate on Sati in Colonial India," (88) Lata Mani has shown that the re-constructions of women's experience can thus be fundamental to the invention of "tradition," and "modernity," both of which, Mani argues, are colonial constructs.

Descriptions of tradition are significant in the diaspora while defining a community in flux. In *Nation and Narration*, Homi Bhaba writes about the moment when discourses of nationhood re-write themselves in the diaspora. Here:

> History may be half-made because it is in the process of being made; and the image of cultural authority may be ambivalent because it is caught, 'uncertainly' in the act of 'composing' its powerful image. . . . The marginal or minority is not the space of a celebratory, or utopian, self-marginalization. It is a much more substantial intervention into those justifications of modernity—progress, homogeneity, cultural organicism, the deep nation, the long past—that rationalize the authoritarian, 'normalizing' tendencies within cultures, in the name of the national interest or ethnic prerogative. (3-4)

Chitra Divakaruni's fiction politicizes the process of using inculcated and internalized ideologies as resistance. The novel *Sister of My Heart* is formed by patriarchal structures and modernity with available privilege. However, the woman who is looking to define her subjectivity outside of the traditional paradigms of family and modern identity never had any discourse of nationalism made available to them in equivalent ways as to men. The diaspora, where the rhetoric of nationhood of the "nation of origin" and other traditional mores become distanced and precarious, functions as the strategic terrain on which to re-formulate diasporic female subjectivity as a contingent rather than as essential identity. The ways in which Divakaruni's characters grapple with and refute an essential identity linked to cultural roots forms the backbone of my analysis.

Sister of My Heart opens with the Chatterjee family already deprived of its male figures and its former economic status. As the three widows (Pishi Ma, the cousins' paternal aunt, and their mothers) and two young girls (Anju and Sudha) of this family meander their way through the drama of life, facing marriage, motherhood, divorce, widowhood, etc., each stage brings into focus a certain aspect of the upper-class Bengali culture and tradition, which is cherished or criticized from the uniquely feminine and diasporic perspective of the author.

The novel depicts their gradual loss of financial status as they are forced to relinquish their riches and amenities of comfort, one by one. First, they cannot afford a paid chauffeur. Then, they have to sell the bookstore which had been meticulously run by Gauri Ma for years and has been one of their major income sources. The final blow comes when the old inheritance, the grand mansion and childhood abode of the cousins, has to go in order to make both ends meet. So when Pishi Ma, the otherwise strong upholder of traditions, sounds adamant regarding her decision to sell the generations-old patriarchal property and move to an apartment, even the sisters are appalled. Yet, with only the family name and the skeleton of its old fame to their credit, these women have no other choice. And for the first time the widows of the Chatterjee family learn to live their lives with a girlish lightness.

Traditional Indian society has carefully segregated its men and women, has equally carefully nurtured the social stereotypes that prevent female bonding: the mother-son relationship has been valorized, the brother-sister one privileged, but the mother-daughter one overlooked, and women's friendship marginalized. In the artifacts of popular culture—fiction, films, television serials, commercials—the feminine mystique is a suitably Indianized version of Betty Friedan's account; mother and daughter or sisters come together only to counter the threat posed by a new daughter/sister-in-law or to reinforce the stereotypes of the Sati-Savitri syndrome, and women's friendships, when they do survive marriage or are formed after marriage, must be subservient to and certainly underscore the rights and the demands of the husband and his family. Women's relationships in contemporary Indian fiction, then, are governed by the power politics of patriarchy.

The novel *Sister of My Heart* portrays a woman's world, this time of middle-class urban women, confined to houses in which their domain is strictly demarcated but which enables them to reach out to each other in sisterhood, and in so doing achieve far greater success as human beings than the men who straddle the outside and bigger world. Rendered in an often sensual and poetic language, the story primarily weaves around the magnetic love that pulls these two women together, though with birth, marriage, and pregnancy all occurring for the two Chatterjee sisters at about the same time, not to mention the fact that they also lose their fathers under the same malicious star. Psychological healing and memory-mending are orchestrated by the characters in the novel through the device of story-telling. And in spite of the mild allegorical overtones concerning the inscrutability of the human heart, this is a scathing critique of the patriarchal and religious institutions of Bengali Brahmins and the socio-cultural traditions of postcolonial India.

In Divakaruni's fiction sisterhood is always a deeply rooted, instinctual relationship that brings together women who are very different from one another in every way. This is especially so in "The Ultrasound" and its novelistic version, *Sister of My Heart*. Anju and Sudha Chatterjee are very different in appearance, temperament and achievements, and grow up together under similar yet very different conditions: their fathers, cousins themselves, died together in the same accident, but where Anju's father was the master of the house, and her mother from an equally aristocratic family, Sudha's father was a poor relation, her mother's background non-descript, lower middle-class. Sudha and her mother continue to live in the family mansion not out of ancestral right but because Indian family ties would not have it otherwise.

Anju's mother, Gouri Ma, or Rani Ma, as her servants and battalion of lower-caste workers love to call her, is the main earning member of the family. With her bunch of household keys tied to her cream-coloured, toshar silk saree, her pearl broach on the shoulder, and her generous, calm, and calculating personality, she reminds one of the pomp and splendour, the grace and intelligence often attached to the "bou thakurans" or the leading ladies of the zamindar households. However, at the tail end of the zamindari system, the Chatterjees are no longer the awe-inspiring, lavishly wealthy family they once were.

The girls do everything together and love one another fiercely, demanding to be known not just as sisters but as twins, and not just because they were born on the same day: sisterhood to them is not just a matter of ties of blood but of love. As Anju tells Sudha, "I would love you because you love me. I would love you because no-one else knows us like we know each other" (61). They may be separated by fate and marriage once they reach adulthood, but they let nothing stand in the way of their love for each other, even jeopardizing the love of the men in their lives for each other. It is perhaps this that makes Divakaruni call *Sister of My Heart* a novel of women's friendship, not of sisterly bonding.

The girls, Sudha and Anju, live in a patriarchal home in which there is absolutely no male control. The only male alive in the family is disguised as Singhji, the driver and exerts no authority over the household. What was originally conceived of as a restrictive boundary for the women is recreated into a female universe. The rules that are upheld in this world are laid down by the patriarchal society. It is only later that the world of the Chatterjee women is completely transformed into a modern world.

Divakaruni exposes women freedom, humanity, and the right to life. She also judges the often superstitious, planet-gazing conservative Bengalis through the highly critical eyes of a postcolonial commentator who scrutinizes the far-reaching impact of British colonialism on the Bengali psyche. Thus, the Chatterjee cousins go to English-medium convents, like most children of upper and middle-class Bengali families, and Anju looks forward to getting enrolled at Lady Brabourne College's English Honours program, both of these institutions being the fruits of British rule. Also, Anju's excessive fascination with Virginia Woolf, or her craze for Elizabeth Barrett Browning are examples of modern education trends.

The writer through Anju gives us a clear picture of the need of economic stability for emancipating women. Sudha's father left nothing other than debts. This has been one of the reasons for her inability to perform academically well even if she is as intelligent as Anju. On the other hand, Anju gets a lot of encouragement from her mother and she goes on to win spelling bees and debate contests and good academic achievements in college. Sudha, nevertheless, also does well with her cooking, knitting and crocheting even if she can't excel like Anju. She chooses to be traditional which also demands a lot of courage and tolerance.

> I want to design clothes. Salwaarkameezes. Pleated wedding ghagras with mirrors stitched in. Kurtas for men, embroidered white on white silk. Baby frocks in satin and eyelet lace. I want to have my own company, with my own tailors and my own label, so that customers at all the best stores will ask for the Basudha brand. People in Bombay and Delhi and Madras will clamour for my work. (90)

Divakaruni expands the story with additional details that the cousins may not actually have been cousins at all, that Bijoy's father had been deceived by Gopal, Sudha's father, about their relationship. (That this is proved wrong in the end is beside the point.) This should have helped to establish the fact that their love is far deeper than the ties of blood. Anju, who knows nothing of the tenuousness of their kinship or of what Sudha's father had done, his treachery and complicity in Anju's father's death, is sure that their sisterhood can never be broken; but it is clear that much of her certainty is due to her ignorance. Besides, as the social superior and the more intellectually gifted of the two, it is easy for her to be generous. But Sudha remains consumed by guilt for what her father has done and by her conviction that she must atone for his sins by always putting Anju first; when, therefore, she decides to sacrifice her own happiness for Anju's sake it is uncertain whether she does it out of a sense of filial duty or out of love for a sister of the heart. Indeed, when she has to choose between her mother and her cousin when it comes to consenting to an early marriage instead of going to college with Anju, she chooses her mother, although, of course, it is a painful decision for her. Besides, she is always a very passive person, as contrasted to Anju's energy and initiative, and her reluctance to elope with Ashok, the man she loves, seems as much due to her fear of action and her preference for going with the tide rather than her love for Anju, which makes her worry that this elopement might break up Anju's engagement to Sunil.

In *Sister of My Heart*, Divakaruni rejects conventional myths and creates new ones. The first book in the novel is titled "The Princess in the Palace of Snakes." In this part both the protagonists attempt to conform to the traditional feminine roles allocated by the male hegemonic society. This is symbolized by the traditional fairytale of the princess in the palace of snakes waiting for her Prince Charming to rescue her. The second book titled "The Queen of Swords," is not a traditional fairytale.

When Anju is upset over her miscarriage, Sudha tells her this tale and Anju recovers. Then she relates what happened to the three mothers. Then Pishi, the usual teller of tales, asks her about the story she told Anju.

> 'I told her a story.'
>
> 'Ah, a story,' nods Pishi. More than any of us, she knows the power stories hold at their centre, like a mango holds its seed. It is a power that dissipates with questioning, so she merely asks, with an odd, wistful look, 'Was it a story I had told you, Sudha?'
>
> I am sorry to disappoint her. 'It's a new story. One I made up, sort of, on the spot.'
>
> 'Does it have a name?' asks Gouri Ma.
>
> I start to shake my head. Then it comes to me.
>
> 'The Queen of swords,' I say. (312)

This new myth symbolises the new feminine world that Divakaruni envisages. It is a world across the rainbow (ironically a conventional symbol of hope) where women rescue other women and do not wait helplessly for the men.

This change is seen not only in the story that Sudha narrates but also in her attitude and her actions. During their childhood, the girls used to enact the fairytales that Pishi told them. Sudha always played the princess in danger and Anju the prince who rescued her. Even while they were playacting, Sudha would never reach out to the prince and help him help her. She always said that it was the duty of the prince to do all the hard work and rescue her. Later when she falls in love with Ashok and the mothers decide to get her married elsewhere, she waits for Ashok to make all the moves and rescue her.

The extent of the woman's oppression within the marriage is obvious. After her marriage to Ramesh, Sudha enters a household ruled by her tyrannical mother-in-law. She is not allowed to pursue her financial independence. In many ways, she is the prototypical victim of an arranged marriage. In arranged marriages, an attempt to schedule an expression of female sexuality to coincide with institutional structures of marriage renders impossible an articulation of women's desires. Her commodification is complete within the imbrications of patriarchal structures and economic systems. She puts up with the ill-treatment there for a long time, still the conventional princess of the fairytale, waiting for her husband, the prince, to rescue her. When she conceives and it is established by tests that her baby is a girl, her mother-in-law tries to force her into an abortion and treating her as a baby machine. "You probably agree with all those Indian men who see a woman as nothing more than a baby machine." (213)

In traditional relationships women are not expected to have the power to leave home; in fact, to have agency is to transgress beyond normative feminine behaviour. But now Sudha decides that she should do something to protect her baby. She leaves her husband's home and returns to her parental home in Calcutta. Sudha leaves with her jewellery, possibly "gifted" by her parents during the marriage, to set up her own economic unit within which she can re-formulate her own identity. "I have five hundred rupees. I took them from Ramesh's desk drawer. And all my jewellery that wasn't in the safe. Just in case." (261)

Amidst the different settings and ideologies, the writer brings home the similarities of the tradition and modernity through psychological and physiological changes accompanied with the experience of pregnancy of the two cousins. Sudha, who was bearing everything, now wants to stand up to defend the life of the child inside her. She is forced to run away from her husband's house but she knows that nobody will entertain her and bear the stigma she carries. Even her mother will not understand her predicament as she has more to worry about her society than her daughter's plight. Moreover, she can never come out of the belief that a married woman should always live under the shelter of her husband, no matter what the condition is.

The mother is the person most directly responsible for curbing the daughter's independence, for facing her to adjust and accept the patriarchal norms she has internalized herself, even though she may do it out of love and fear for her daughter. The daughter in turn channelizes all her resentment of patriarchy towards her mother. Nalini, the mother of the more beautiful Sudha, primarily comes across as a woman doubly handicapped in attitude, first by a patriarchal tradition, and second, by the modern need for reinforcing identities. She does not hesitate to sacrifice her own daughter's happiness, or even her first granddaughter's life, when it comes to saving face in her honour-conscious, prestige- and scandal-obsessed society. Thus, when Sudha is unable to kill her yet unborn daughter and, instead, runs away from her married home, risking a divorce, her mother is furious: "I told her to grit her teeth and put up with it, and try for another pregnancy. A woman can have many children, after all, but a husband is for ever . . . what will we tell our relatives? Uff, she's smeared kali for ever on the Chatterjee family, to say nothing of my ancestors." (266)

The upholder of family tradition, Pishi comes to rescue Sudha. She renders support and says Sudha is old enough to make her own decision. The women in the Chatterjee family do not allow Sudha to kill the girl baby to save the family's face in the society, instead they bless her to be like the Rani of Jhansi, the Queen of Swords. In spite of her mother's lamentations she wipes off the sindur powder and puts off wedding bracelets and accepts the divorce proceedings sent by the Sanyals. Pishi mourns for the tyrannical rules of the society for a widow at the age of eighteen and says: "Why should she care any more what people say? What good has it done her? What good has it done any of us, a whole lifetime of being afraid of what society might think? I spit on this society which says it's fine to kill a baby girl in her mother's womb, but wrong for the mother to run away to save her child." (268)

Divakaruni's women, however, face a different situation. They love their men, or believe they do, and they suffer agonies of jealousy and misery when they feel they have been betrayed by friend with husband; but they quickly realize that they love their women friends more than their men, a love that surpasses all other relationships. It is in her *Sister of My Heart* that Divakaruni most obviously explores this theme.

Even after marriage Sudha is the most important person in Anju's life, not Sunil, her husband. When, therefore, she learns that Sudha's in-laws want her to abort her baby because the prenatal sex-determination test has shown it is female, in spite of Sunil's evident disapproval she urges her to leave her husband and go to her (Anju's) mother in Calcutta—apparently Sudha's mother is not sufficiently supportive to start a new life there, promising herself that she would somehow bring her cousin over to America no matter what the cost to her, financially and emotionally.

> Tomorrow I'll think of all the prickly details: how to get them here, the visas, how much it'll all cost. I can get a job and save for their tickets. That way I won't have to ask Sunil for a single penny. Tomorrow itself I'll go to my college library—I know they're looking for an assistant. I won't even tell Sunil about it. It'll be my secret, mine and my baby's. (276)

Western influence and Westernization of Indian society, especially in the upper classes stand in sharp contrast to the traditionalism of the middle and lower classes. However, if the Eastern world is delineated at times in a rather negative light in this book, then the Western world is presented not without its own evils and shortcomings. Freedom and riches in the West are often bought, particularly by the immigrant, at the expense of the love and support provided by the extended family or the community. This is proved while Anju doubts herself: "Did I push Sudha into making the wrong decision, misled by my American-feminist notions of right and wrong? Have I condemned her to a life of loneliness?" (272)

Hence the same Anju, who used to complain about the noise and lack of privacy in her mother's home back in India, because of the host of servants and gossiping aunts, yelling neighbours, and shouting road vendors, now misses the din and bustle in her desolate apartment in America. Indeed, America provides "the advantage of anonymity," (qtd. Khan 106) but it also adds the burden of responsibility and loneliness. No doubt America adds to the self-confidence of the Indian male, endowing him with a certain light-heartedness and ease that allow him to trust his partner's vivacity and enterprise, which come in place of domesticity and docility, but America may also turn him into a reckless philanderer, as seen in the character of Sunil, Anju's Americanized husband. But he is not supportive to Anju and argues with her regarding Sudha's arrival in the Chatterjee house. He also warns her that she is safe in America. Anju doubts and asks him: "Maybe you'd have wanted me to have an abortion too, if we'd been in India and my baby hadn't turned out to be a boy. . . . Does it mean he'd be the same way towards me if ever I got into trouble? Does he love me at all? What if something happened to our baby? Would he love me still?" (274-75)

The woman in the mirror is none other than she herself, but in a novel manifestation. She is that woman who has emerged victorious over all dilemmas, all oppositions, all crushing sensibilities, and is as bright and radiant as a bird, ready to fly into the exotic skies. Sudha refuses to go back to a tormenting past, she is ignorant of what the future holds for her, yet her eyes look forward, and the spirit of fire burning within her convinces everyone that none can now dare to stop her in her upward and onward journey. Sudha indeed, emerges as a triumphant woman. She transforms herself, from the princess in the palace of snakes to the queen of swords. She refuses to return to Ramesh. When Sudha is given a second chance of happiness, when Ashok reappears in her life and wishes to marry her, she is once again faced with the choice between her own happiness and Anju's, and chooses Anju's. She also turns down the conditional offers of Ashok to marry her. The rejection of male-allotted stereotypical roles is complete. Anju wants her in California, and so she will go to California. But she doubts that this would have been a real friend's decision. Both she and Anju know that Sunil was really in love with Sudha and had never been able to forget her; indeed, their friendship had almost broken up when Anju had discovered her husband's feelings for her cousin. Not only will she be a financial burden on Anju, as she and her parents have always been on Anju's family—a fact that she cannot forget and feels she must be grateful for—in a sense, in fact, Sudha is responsible for Anju's miscarriage, for Anju feels obliged to pay for Sudha's fare to the USA, since Sunil cannot afford it, and takes up a job, overworks, and loses her baby. It was not as if she would not have been able to make a fresh start in life in Calcutta; indeed, she had already begun to do so. Above all, she knows that her presence in Anju's marriage will inevitably cause problems and unhappiness, something that Sudha had anticipated long before in an old dream: "If only Anju and I, like the wives of the heroes in the old tales, could marry the same man, our Arjun, our Krishna, who would love and treasure us both, and keep us both together." (131) Sudha's journey to America is really the beginning of her journey to a new world of women.

Anju is a true sister of the heart for Sudha. Divakaruni makes Anju and Sudha speak alternately in their own voices, constantly shifting perspective, the narrative technique itself underlining their twinning as much as the events of their lives and Anju's voice is always clear and unambiguous. The richer, the cleverer and the more talented of the two, but perhaps the less imaginative and sensitive, she has always stood by Sudha, doing what she thinks is best for her, being willing even to sacrifice her relationship with Sunil in her obsessed belief that she must have Sudha by her side if her sister-friend is to thrive. It is appropriate, then, that, a novel of sisterhood should end with Anju's thoughts:

> We've formed a tableau, two women, their arms intertwined like lotus stalks, smiling down at the baby between them. Two women who have travelled the vale of sorrow, and the baby who will save them, who has saved them already. Madonnas with child . . . for now the three of us stand unhurried, feeling the way we fit, skin on skin on skin, into each other's lives. (347)

Despite the innumerable headaches that an American lifestyle entails, Divakaruni's characters seem convinced about its ultimate superiority. This is well expressed in these words of Sudha, who is planning to leave for America with her fatherless, newborn daughter in search of a respectable life for both: "Best of all, no-one would look down on her, for America was full of mothers like me, who had decided that living alone was better than living with the wrong man" (274).

The solace faced by Sudha in the novel is similar to the postmodern woman faced by all souls stuck between the crossroads of tradition and modernity. When certain aspect of conventional pattern of life becomes morbid and tormenting, one wishes to tear apart all boundaries and escape into a world where everything is replete with novelty, glory and adventure.

The mothers also enter this new world of women. This is symbolically shown when they sell their dilapidated, ancestral house and move to a new flat. The change in them after they move to their new home is amazing.

> Along with the old house, the mothers seem to have shrugged off a great burden of tradition. Perhaps, ironically, I helped it happen. For now that I have come back neither wife now widow, now that I have let go of all that society considers valuable, what is left for them to fear? Away from those ancient halls echoing with patriarchal voices which insisted that foremost of all they must be widows of the Chatterjee family, for the first time they can learn to live their lives with a girlish lightness. (296)

The mothers begin to lead a fulfilling life with a social purpose. They listen to the music that they like and take walks where they please. They no longer worry about the social stigma attached to a divorcee and keep Sudha with them. They lovingly take care of her daughter. The final gesture of the rejection of patriarchal norms and the acceptance of the rules of the new female universe is the gifting of the ruby left to them by Sudha's father to Dayita, Sudha's daughter.

> The mothers have joined book societies and knitting classes. They go for walks around Victoria Memorial. They volunteer at Mother Teresa's Shishu Bhavan and—chaperoned by an insistent Singhji—attend all-night classical music concerts from which they return, cheeks flushed with the early morning cold, humming a song in the bhairav raga. They take day trips to Dakshineswar and bathe in the Ganges. . . . Already they are talking of a trip to Darjeeling in the summer. (296)

Divakaruni's protagonists aspire to adapt to their newfound world. Though firmly rooted in tradition, female characters find it hard to break the bounds set by patriarchy, to experience what has so far been restricted in their life, and resolve the psychological conflict that is accompanied with the new situation. She presents very vividly the dilemmas of Indian women in traditional society. Her women characters represent the sentiments of women within and outside traditional bounds.

When Divakaruni declares, then, that she has made sisterhood her theme, she has clearly put herself squarely in the tradition of the West rather than of India. Certainly her fiction is part of the growing corpus of Asian American women's writing, whose major theme is the lonely outsider, the first- or second-generation Asian immigrant in an often hostile, uncomprehending and incomprehensible environment, struggling to assimilate and to keep her ethnic identity alive at the same time, suffering the double yoke of colour and gender even more than the African American, for whom the USA has always been the only home she has ever known. For Asian or African American women, sisterhood is a strength and succour, enabling them to discover themselves as persons and to nurture their ties with their community; friendship with other women becomes, therefore, central to the fiction of all American "women of color."

Divakaruni's texts are powerful and significant; they are particularly effective in mapping the contours of the new South Asian community in the United States. They provide a lens with which to view the struggle for identity amongst women and to develop a critique to patriarchal structures that organize the life of Indian diasporics.

Chitra Banerjee focused her writing on friendships with women and trying to balance them with the conflicting passions and demands that come to women as daughters and wives, lovers and mothers. She believed that friendship with women is a unique one because of life-changing experiences that they share—menstruation, childbirth, and menopause. In an interview she states that the force behind her writing "is the desire to put women in the centre of stories, to have their voices be the voices of interpretation, their eyes the ones that we see through. There just hasn't been enough of that in the world, if you look back at literary history" (qtd. Lalita 23).

It is Divakaruni's professed manifesto to celebrate the courage and humanity of suffering women who have rebelled against oppressive patriarchy and have joined a universal sisterhood. Her writings are efforts in the direction of creating a world of women. The effort is certainly rewarding both for the author and her readers. The novel, despite defects and discrepancies, rings a fervent note of sincerity and that is where their appeal lies.

Chitra Divakaruni not only shows us how contemporary society makes an individual but also portrays how man's greed has wreaked havoc and horror in the world we live. She enlarges the enormity of consequences. She recognizes the social, economic and psychological forces behind colonialism and strives to show how they dehumanize both the colonizer and the colonized. These worlds are also imbued with a moral vision that emphasizes social interaction, growth and carrying out responsibilities. Divakaruni expresses her own idiosyncrasy, one that is composed of tradition and modernity where a vision of life and love is valued.

Works Cited

Banerjee, Debjani. "'Home and Us': Re-defining Identity in the South Asian Diaspora through the Writings of Chitra Banerjee Divakaruni and Meena Alexander." *Asian American Writing*, Poetry and the ed. Somdatta Mandal. New Delhi: Prestige, 2000.

Barat, Urbashi. "Sisters of the Heart: Female Bonding in the Fiction of Chitra Banerjee Divakaruni." *Ibid.*

Bhabha, Homi K. *Nation and Narration*. New York: Routledge, 1990.

Curtis, Sarah. "Rev. of *Sister of My Heart*." *The Times Literary Supplement*, 5054 (Dec 10, 1999), 21.

Divakaruni, Chitra. *Sister of My Heart*. Great Britain: Doubleday, 1999.

Khan, Hafiza Nilofar. "Rev. of *Sister of My Heart*." *The Toronto Review of Contemporary Writing Abroad*, 18.1 (Fall 1999), 103-7.

Lalitha, R. "Chitra Banerjee Divakaruni: A Rising Star in the Diasporic Literature." *The Commonwealth Review*, 17.2 (2009): 21-26.

Mandal, Somdatta. *Asian American Writing*, 3 Vols. New Delhi: Prestige, 2000.

Mani, Lata. "Contentious Traditions: The Debate on Sati in Colonial India," *Recasting Women*. New Delhi: Kali, 1989.

Nalini, M. "Sharpened Sensibility in an Exiled Woman Novelist: A Study of Bharati Mukherjee." *Indian Women Writing in English: New Perspectives*, ed. S. Prasanna Sree. New Delhi: Sarup, 2005.

Selvam, Veena. "Mistresses and Sisters: Creating a Female Universe: The Novels of Chitra Banerjee Divakaruni," *The Commonwealth Review*, 17.2 (2009): 9-20.

Wadia, Hutoxi. "Shades of Indian Modernity in the Novels of Rohinton Mistry." *Makers of Indian English Literature*. ed. C.D. Narasimhaiah. New Delhi: Pencraft International, 2000.

In the Voice of Panchali: Maya and Catharsis in *The Palace of Illusions*

V. VISHNU VANDANA DEVI
Vijaya Institute of Technology for Women, Vijayawada

N. USHA
Krishna University, Machilipatnam

Reimagination of classical literature in the contemporary scenario and its reinterpretation informs the audience of the epic's popular reception today. Modern writers revisit ancient texts to reinterpret them from different perspectives. Eugene O'Neill's *Mourning Becomes Electra* (1931) reinterprets Aeschylus's ancient Greek tragedy *Oresteia* through psychological theory. John Gardner's *Grendel* (1971) is a reinterpretation of the Anglo-Saxon epic poem *Beowulf* of 1000 AD from Grendel's existentialist perspective. In *The Penelopiad* (2005), Margaret Atwood rewrites Homer's *Odyssey* written in the 8th century BC, and focuses on Penelope, one of the major female characters in Odyssey. Jeanette Winterson's *Weight* (2005) retells the myth of Atlas and Heracles as part of the Canongate Myth series where contemporary writers imagine ancient myths. Similarly Chitra Banerjee Divakaruni retells the life of Panchali, from the ancient Indian epic *The Mahabharata* and renders it in her feminist narrative *The Palace of Illusions* (2008). She presents a humane version of the fiery Panchali, also known as Draupadi, who was often portrayed negatively in earlier versions of the epic.

With sixteen works to her credit, which include *The Mistress of Spices, Sister of My Heart, Arranged Marriage, Oleander Girl* and *The Palace of Illusions,* Chitra Banerjee Divakaruni is an award-winning author, poet, activist and teacher. Indian immigrant experience, women, history, myth and multi-culturalism are the major themes of her creative work. She broadens her interpretation of the epic and presents first-person narrative through Panchali's eyes. In the Author's note, she writes:

> [A]lways, listening to the stories of the *Mahabharata* as a young girl in the lantern-lit evenings at my grandfather's village home, or later, poring over the thousand-page leather-bound volume in my parents' home in Kolkata, I was left unsatisfied by the portrayals of the women. It wasn't as though the epic didn't have powerful, complex women characters that affected the action in major ways. . . . But in some way, they remained shadowy figures, their thoughts and motives mysterious, their emotions portrayed only when they affected the lives of the male heroes, their roles ultimately subservient to those of their fathers or husbands, brothers or sons (vii).
>
> If I ever wrote a book, I remember thinking . . . I would place the women in the forefront of the action. I would uncover the story that lay invisible between the lines of the men's exploits. Better still, I would have one of them tell it herself, with all her joys and doubts, her struggles and triumphs, her heartbreaks, her achievements, the uniquely female way in which she sees her world and her place in it. And who could be better suited for this than Panchaali? (xiv-xv)

The novel is an innovative imitation of the original epic from the psyche of Panchali, the stubborn and independent princess. This paper tries to establish Panchali's illusions (maya) about herself and life and her catharsis as important markers in Divakaruni's narrative and Panchali as the Aristotelian protagonist. Aristotle's philosophic treatise *Poetics* greatly influenced the western aesthetic philosophy. His analysis of tragedy is relevant today as tragedy is considered to be a representation of life and it has necessarily a societal function involved in the ethical utility of art. According to Aristotle, tragedy comes to the protagonist of a drama not through either some misfortune or evil shade in the attitude, but because of making some irrational or unwise judgment. Catharsis is defined as the *purging* of emotions, especially of pity and fear which are experienced by the audience, when they watch a tragedy. The principles stated by Aristotle should take a critical look at a work of art in its psychological as well as social context and purpose. According to the German philosopher Hans-Georg Gadamer in his *Truth and Method*:

> What is experienced in such an excess of tragic suffering is something truly common. The spectator recognizes himself [or herself] and his [or her] finiteness in the face of the power of fate. What happens to the great ones of the earth has exemplary significance. . . . To see that "this is how it is" is a kind of self-knowledge for the spectator, who emerges with new insight from the illusions in which he [or she], like everyone else, lives. (132)

According to Aristotle, a tragedy should rouse the feelings of pity and terror among the audience after watching the drama. A novel also can rouse the same kind of emotion and the character of Draupadi in *The Palace of Illusions* gives way to catharsis, finally aiming at the purgation of souls. In a tragedy, it is the audience whose hearts are cleansed and purified, and in a novel when the readers also are able to feel the same, the effect of catharsis is achieved. The emotional relief thus gives the readers an aesthetic enjoyment. The readers feel pity for the tragic fate of Draupadi and also terror as they read the lines about the protagonist's suffering. They also experience other antagonistic feelings towards the same character like dislike and delight; indignation and admiration. Chitra Banerjee Divakaruni has achieved success in creating the feeling of catharsis as the readers witness Panchali's suffering through their mind's eye. Readers learn about human weaknesses and failings, the play of destiny and also about the strength of the character, thus making it a legendary one. A drama should have a well-structured plot with a beginning, followed in logical sequence by middle and a definite end where there is no further continuity of action. The thread of action should not lose the connection, thereby giving the plot a unified structure. The universal themes can be presented powerfully, with an introduction of the element of surprise. It involves peripetia or reversal of fortune; and anagnorisis or discovery.

In a tragedy to experience the feelings of pity and fear, the readers should find a hero from a noble family who journeys from happiness to misery, all because of a fault/weakness in his character. It is the chief character's own members of the family who hurt or brings misery into the former's life. A character tries to avoid the killing of another relative of his or hers, as through anagnorisis the family relationship is established. The hero should possess noble qualities which suit his rank and should be depicted in a credible manner from time to time. There should be a logical connection between the hero and the plot, and the ending must be in accordance with the action or the story-line. Aristotle's philosophy of a drama makes us reflect on life and there is an undeviating interaction between the characters and the audience. Though the drama is real to life, at one point or the other, the audience experiences a sense of detachment. The audience is well-aware of the mimesis involved in art and as such, they become wise and knowledgeable after watching the drama. It gives an opportunity to the audience to ponder upon the causes and effects of a violent and calamitous situation, thereby making them to be more reflective and sensitive over such issues.

Catharsis, mentioned by Aristotle, does not clearly suggest that it is the purpose of the art or an outcome after watching a drama; it aims at the purgation of the soul. On a symbolic level, it refers to the release of the emotions of pity and fear at the end of the drama, as the release of tension is quite necessary. Art is thus equivalent to therapy, as it intensifies the thought-process and deepens and rather changes the outlook towards life and its situations. It gives way to the inculcation of compassion and love in the lives of human beings.

The Palace of Illusions fulfills this criteria and Divakaruni's portrayal of Panchali is no lesser than that of Aristotle's Greek hero as she is from a royal family, the princess of Paanchal and she is strong, dominant and independent. Out of her own choice, she invites her destiny, claiming pride and vengeance to be two fatal flaws in her character. The readers identify with the travails of the character as a human being and more of a woman. The character stirs the feelings of the readers throughout their reading and thus the narrative is captivating and enthralling. Panchali remains with the readers forever, though they finish the reading of the novel. The portrayal of the character stimulates and influences the reader's mind. Vyasa in his prophecy to Panchali about her destiny observes:

> But in your case, your own nature is going to speed its process.
> What do you mean?
> Your pride. Your temper. Your vengefulness. (40)

The readers find an element of *hubris* in the protagonist, excessive pride and ego in her beauty and wits, which ultimately lead to the fall, shame and humiliation of the character.

The moment she learns that she is merely a *pawn* in the *Great Design*, she grows more confident of herself and her wits:

> I can! I said, with the confidence of the untested. I knew I was intelligent—wasn't Dhai Ma always complaining about how overly smart I was? I knew enough to control passion. I visualized myself as a great queen, dispensing wisdom and love. Panchaali the Peacemaker, people would call me. (66)

Destiny moves her forward in life, and she gets ready for the swayamvara, and though her heart longs to marry Karna, the great warrior, it is again the fate which decides her life, and Draupadi's inquiry about the caste of Karna makes him withdraw from the contest. Panchali's conscience pricks her throughout her life, for doing so in the court, but she could not act otherwise, so as to prevent destiny. Her judgment of Karna, and leaving his hand, remained an unwise decision on her part, as it throws her into further troubles: "If I'd been wiser, I might have been able to call forth that love and, in that way, deflected the danger of the moment—a moment that would turn out to be far more important than I imagined. But I was young and afraid, and my ill-chosen words (words I would regret all my life) quenched that light forever." (97)

As the great tragedy involves an element of surprise in its course of action, in *The Palace of Illusions* also, Panchali's marriage comes as a surprise to the readers. Eventually, she is won by Arjuna in the guise of a Brahmin warrior and follows him to the forest only to get tied up in wedlock to the rest of the Pandava brothers. Without her consent, she is declared the wife of all the five brothers by Kunti. Initially, Panchali could not receive or interpret the words of Kunti and she wanted to oppose the decision, as she felt that she was the wife of only Arjuna, but of no use: "I stared at her, my brain trying to take in what she had said. Was she joking when she said they must all marry me? No, her face made that clear. I wanted to share, five husbands? Are you mad? I wanted to say, I'm already married to Arjun! But Vyasa's prophesy recoiled upon me, robbing me of my protests." (108)

Thus the events are logically connected, the storyline moves at a greater pace and meanders through various life events. It is also Panchali's reference to Karna and her secret love for him, even after her marriage strikes as an astonishing fact to the readers. As the queen of Indraprastha, Panchali enjoys all the fame and fortune. Her dream is fulfilled as she witnesses her dream-home, The Palace of Illusions, constructed by Maya. The beautiful palace is built according to the wishes of Panchali and she wants to have water everywhere. Maya grants her wish by constructing floors looking like rivers, waterfalls looking like a wall: "But running water inside a home! Kunti would gasp when she saw it. 'Fool of a girl, didn't anyone teach you that it washes away good luck?'" (145)

Destiny plays with her life that she becomes a victim to the Palace of Illusions. After the Rajasuya, the Kaurava party stays back at Indraprastha. When Duryodhan walks through the garden, especially designed by Draupadi and falls into a pool, stepping on an illusory bridge, it evokes laughter among the attendants of Draupadi and encouraged by their mistress' smile cries out, "It seems the blind king's son is also blind!" (173)

If only Panchali could have reacted immediately by offering her due apologies, the story would have been otherwise. But Karna's angry countenance and her self-pride evade her from doing so.

> Had I acted immediately, calling out my apologies, sending down maids with dry clothes, and publicly punishing the girl who had spoken I might have minimized the damage. But the cold fury on Karna's face paralyzed my tongue. I couldn't bear to humble myself in front of him to Duryodhan, to admit that I had been at fault, to listen in silence, with bent head, as he blamed for my palace's trickery. What could I have said, in any case, in my defence? That Karna had distracted me from noticing what Duryodhan was doing? And so I stood struggling with my ego until the brief moment of opportunity vanished. The two friends stalked off, whispering angrily to each other, leaving me to wonder what would come of this. (173)

Thus the ultimate agency regarded as predetermining the course of events dominated the life of Panchali throughout. This important event accelerates the series of events that follow. It becomes evident that the protagonist Panchali cannot escape the preordained, however hard she tries. The readers also turn out to be fearful of the impending danger, as they are quite aware of the vengeful attitude of Duryodhan. Subsequently, the readers are appalled at the humiliation and disgrace faced by Panchali at the

Kaurava court and startled by the hatred she develops towards diminishing the Kaurava clan.

> I lifted up my long hair for all to see. My voice was calm now because I knew that everything I said would come to pass. "I will not comb it, until the day I bathe it in Kaurava blood." (194)

Therefore, it is her own member of the family, her husband's cousin who plays a dominant role in her reversal of fortune, peripetia. Every minute of her later life is filled with powerful detestation and vengeance against the grievance she faced. She makes up her mind not to yield to the softer emotions in life, as she fears that it would fail "to achieve the destruction that had become the goal of my life?" Twelve years of exile and one year of hiding at King Virat's court make her stronger and tough to face the battle with the Kauravas. She also tries to instigate her husbands to face the battlefield.

> "I didn't expect such superstition from the foremost heroes of Bharat!" I taunted them. "Of course, there will be blood. Of course there will be death. As kshatriyas, isn't that what you've trained for all your lives? And are you afraid now?" (239)

Suddenly, as Panchali receives the gift of witnessing the war from a distance, she also then realizes the challenges she has to encounter and there is a discovery in her mind, a doubt about instigating her husbands to plunge into destruction for her own petty satisfaction. There is anagnorosis in the character of Karna at the end of the novel that all the Pandavas are his brothers and gives a word to Kunti not to slay Arjuna, his enemy, and succumbs to all the fatal flaws in his life. Panchali witnesses the horror of the war and the death of all her kith and kin. She loses her five sons and Abhimanyu. She ponders:

> Constant, pitiless, ever-increasing, the stench assaulted us as we made our reluctant way to the battlefield to deal with our dead. I pressed my lips together to keep from vomiting. Where earlier soldiers had built their cook fires, now funeral pyres were being

> lighted—so many that the vista in front of us was covered in a haze of smoke. I blinked my stinking eyes. The chandaals whose job it was to burn bodies rushed from fire to fire, shaking their cudgels and yelling at mourners to keep their distance. (311)

Thus the plot of the narrative revolves around horror and gives rise to negative emotional feelings among the readers. Fear, which is an outcome of the macabre scenes, is vividly depicted in the chapter 'Pyre.' Aristotle believes that our pity is awakened by undeserved misfortune and our fear by that of someone just like ourselves. Slowly, the horror is followed by pity as Panchali discovers the truth that she has been the cause of the war and Duryodhan's last words to Yudhisthir echo in her ears: "I'm going to heaven to enjoy all its pleasures with my friends. You'll rule a kingdom peopled with widows and orphans and wake each morning to the grief of loss. Who's the real winner, then, and who the loser?" (309)

Panchali, as the queen of Hastinapur apologizes to the crowd for being a major cause of the war. If it is not for her pride and vengeance, the war would never have occurred. This *anagnorosis* in the character draws her close to the readers, as they start feeling pity over the character's psychological status for having lost her loved ones. In the last chapter, 'Fire,' Panchali is on her final journey of the Mahaprasthana. Her monologue in which she speaks about her craving for love and the feeling of guilt she carries, evokes sympathy in the minds of the readers and pity as defined by Aristotle in his *Rhetoric:* "Let pity, then, be a kind of pain in the case of an apparent destructive or painful harm of one not deserving to encounter it, which one might expect oneself, or one of one's own, to suffer, and this when it seems near" (96).

Panchali as she meets her destiny, learns through Krishna that she had been a part of the game and she played it perfectly. Death resolves the conflict of Panchali as she is shown dying, holding the hands of Krishna and Karna. The readers also take a deep sigh of relief as their emotions are cleansed through tears rolling down their eyes. The gravity and solemnity of the character leaves an indelible impression on the reader's mind. The emotions are powerful and there is an interaction of the character with the reader. The character's emotional response to an event, especially in the challenging and stressful situations leads to conflict, tension, and anxiety and finally grows into fascination towards the character. Thus Divakaruni's Panchali becomes exemplary and true instance of the Aristotelian theory.

Works Cited

Divakaruni Banerjee Chitra, *The Palace of Illusions*, 2009, Picador, London.

Das, Gurucharan. "Draupadi's Question: Lessons for Public and Corporate Governance." Web.

Trikha, Pradeep. *Textuality and Inter-textuality in the Mahabharata*. New Delhi: Sarup, 2001. 99-133.

Hiltebeitel, Alf. *Rethinking the Mahabharata: A Reader's Guide to the Education of the Dharma King*. New Delhi: Oxford University Press, 2002.

Mishra, S.D. "*Mahabharata* and Its Textuality." Trikha, *Textuality and Inter-textuality in the Mahabharata*, pp. 1-4.

Werbner, Pnina, ed. *Anthropology and the New Cosmopolitanism: Rooted, Feminist and Vernacular Perspectives*. Oxford: Berg, 2008.

Chitra Divakaruni's *The Palace of Illusions*: The Struggle for Feminine Identity in a Mythological Context

RAMESH BABU A
Government Degree College, Jammikunta

The *Mahabharata* is the story of the Pandavas who were five brothers and their wife Panchaali and Kauravas who were hundred brothers. Pandavas and Kauravas were cousins who were continuously fighting for the throne. Finally it leads to the Great War at Kurukshetra where thousands of people lose their lives. Pandavas are good and virtuous whereas Kauravas are evil and wicked. The epic deals with gods, demi-gods, kings, princes, warriors, and other noble men. Divakaruni's *The Palace of Illusions* provides a humanistic touch to the epic and makes it more realistic and relatable. It refers to the gorgeous fortress that the five brothers built and the only place where Panchaali felt at home and also refers to the Hindu concept of Maya. It also explores Panchaali's lifelong secret attraction for Karna, an enemy of the Pandavas. Manivannan says about the work that it is an "ambitious project, and not without predecessors, choosing as its medium one of world mythology's most idiosyncratic women." (B3) The novel has prediction, love, revenge, passion and feminine internal struggle for identity. Hoydis rightly says that the novel highlights a "crucial relation established between womanhood and vengeance. It displays the struggle for identity in a mythological context, which is distinctly Indian, yet transcends cultural borders, all the while showing the illusionary nature of those imposed by history and gender." (2) The plot, indeed, remains true to the original but the writer Divakaruni offers a vivid and creative companion to the famous poem. She has given a rich tale of passion, love and lust, honour, respect and humiliation of female characters.

The novel has been appropriately titled *The Palace of Illusions* based on the renowned palace that the Pandavas built for her. It opens with three narrators—Panchaali, her brother, and her nurse. It presents dissimilar versions of the tale of Panchaali's birth and fate. Her life as a child, her pride, her resentment, her expectations, her love, her passions, her dreams and her inquisitiveness are obviously explained by the writer. She declares that she does not want to support the men around her. Vyasa Rishi warns her that she will not be able to control anything in the future.

As the days roll down, she grows into a young lady and the time of her marriage comes. Unlike other women, she is married to five men, all of whom love and respect her. When she sees her husbands for the first time, she observes: "I was a woman. I had to use my power differently" (99). In spite of being granted independence from her mother's house and especially her father and the status as queen, "her unconventional polyandrous marriage bears the risk of being seen as an insatiable whore" (118). She spends a year for each husband and her virginity restored each time when she enters bedroom of a new husband. She says that "I had no choice as to whom I slept with, and when" (120). She describes a soothsayer's verdict: "I would be wife to each brother for a year at a time, from oldest to youngest, consecutively. During that year, the other brothers were to keep their eyes lowered. In a postscript added that he would give me a boon to balance the one that had landed me with five spouses. Each time I went to a new brother, I'd be a virgin again" (120). In the beginning, she has thought too much about other women, especially those who have one husband. But later on she changes her mind and thinks less about the surrounding women. She tells herself: "For better or worse, I was a woman" (139). She longs for her identity. Although she was married to five brothers, she loves her husband's enemy, the famous warrior Karna. It is that she wants to be from her internal and passionate struggle for sexual freedom but she is not supposed to make known whatever she feels about Karna.

Yudhisthir, one of her husbands, loses the kingdom in gambling. Panchaali and her husbands are banished from the kingdom for twelve years. Duryodhan takes possession of the kingdom including Panchaali's palace. She comes to know that she has been gambled away like property, "no less so than a cow or a slave" (190). When her palace has been captured, her emotional state is in Divakaruni's words: "She's dead. Half of her died the day when everyone she had loved and counted on to save her sat without protest and watched her being shamed. The other half perished with her beloved home. But never fear" (206). Soon she is dragged into the hall like a dead dog, the people in the court gaze at her. When taking off her sari, the only item of clothing protecting her from "a hundred male eyes burning through me" (191), nobody in the court is ready to save her. Their eyes are about to watch her naked body. Throughout the story, there is one constant in Panchaali's life—the generous presence of Krishna. When she prays, Krishna appears and saves her from shame by astoundingly extending her sari.

II

Like other women writers such as Arundhati Roy, Githa Hariharan, Shashi Deshpande, Jhumpa Lahiri, Kamala Das, Shobha De and Bharati Mukherjee, Divakaruni too deals with the problems of women in her works. Her works make us think and rethink about the contemporary predicaments and troubles of women. Buley-Meissner Mary Louise says: "formal literary criticism addressing her work is rare, a situation likely to change as her books are given more attention in educational circles" (43)

Divakaruni gives a "voice to female Asian immigrants and portrays the struggle with hybrid identities in her fictions" (Mandal, 2006: 115). Once she says that she really wanted "to focus on women battling and coming out triumphant" (Mandal, 116). Though she has written about the problems and troubles of women, she personally wants to pen down about the winning women over men. Her works have the themes of women struggling for freedom and her female characters disparaging power and stunning beauty. She declares: "they remained shadowy figures, their thoughts and motives mysterious, their emotions portrayed only when they affected the lives of the male heroes, their roles ultimately subservient to those of their fathers or husbands, brothers or sons. If I ever wrote a book . . . I would place the women in the forefront of the action. I would uncover the story that lay invisible between the lines of the men's exploits" (Divakaruni, xiv-xv).

Divakaruni holds that women are as equal as men in the society. She shows them to be more than just daughters, mothers and wives of great heroes of the epic *Mahabharata*. Although the story happened three thousand years ago, similar incidents have appeared in the society and there is no change in treating women as slaves in the present scenario. Draupadi who is known as Panchali is a powerful, strong and independent woman. She is very silent and mute character. She is seen as a victim of patriarchy. When Panchali's husband loses everything, he and his brothers gamble her. His opponents try to harass her by removing her sari. No one in the court tries to save her from this act of sexual harassment but she is saved by God. The comparable episodes recur in many places. After so many years, women are still suppressed by the male dominated society. There are hundreds of rapes and sexual harassments happening today. Suppression and oppression of women are very common in these days as in those days. Technically Indians are advanced and innovative for many things. But psychologically men follow the myth—treating women as slaves. Panchali's life's events are parallel to the many trials and tribulations faced by today's women.

Divakaruni has included other major and important female characters from the epic. She describes the story of Kunti, Panchali's mother-in-law, who devoted her life to educate her own sons and also the sons of her husband's second wife. She treats them all equally and prepares them to become kings. The writer also mentions the story of Gandhari, the wife of the blind king Dhritarashtra, who blindfolds herself at her marriage. She chooses to live as an equal to her husband and surrenders her power as a queen and mother. Like Panchaali, her sister Shikhandi is driven by revenge against men's greater freedom of action. Panchaali knows that the men want women in the bedroom. She says: "The air is full of men—but not men exactly, nor women, for their bodies are sleek and sexless and glowing. Their faces are unlined and calm, devoid of the various passions that distinguished them in life" (358). A woman gets liberation when she dies. She is suppressed by her parents before her marriage. Of course she is sometimes loved by them but most of the times she is not given preference anywhere. After her marriage, her husband and children take her freedom so that she can't get liberation until the end. Panchaali's death appears as liberation and resolve of the contradictions of her identity. She happily says: "I am beyond name and gender and the imprisoning patterns of ego. And yet, for the first time, I'm truly Panchaali" (360).

Works Cited

Buley-Meissner, Mary Louise. "Chitra Banerjee Divakaruni: A Bibliographical Review of Resources for Teachers." *Asian American Literature: Discourses and Pedagogies*, 1 (2010): 42-53.

Dasa, Bhrigupada. "Review of *The Palace of Illusions*." www. harmonist.us 15 May 2009.

Divakaruni, Chitra Banerjee. *The Palace of Illusions*. London: Picador, 2008.

Doniger, Wendy. *Splitting the Difference: Gender and Myth in Ancient Greece and India*. Chicago: CUP, 1999.

Hoydis, Julia. "A Palace of Her Own: Feminine Identity in the Great Indian Story." *Gender Forum*. 38. (2012): 1-6.

Mandal, Somdatta. "Chitra Banerjee Divakaruni." *South Asian Writers in English*, ed. Fakrul Alam. Detroit: Thompson Gale, 2006. 112-22.

Manivannan, Sharanya. "*The Palace of Illusions* by Chitra Banerjee Divakaruni." *The New Sunday Express*, 13 April, 2008. B3.

Tandon, Tariqa. "*The Palace of Illusions*: A Book Review." *Alternatives International Journals*, 2 July 2013, 1-4.

Re-inventing Myth: A Study of Chitra Divakaruni's *The Palace of Illusions*

BANANI CHAKRABORTY
Assam University, Silchar

A trend has developed among the Post-Independence Indian English litterateurs to utilize the Indian epics as their source for ancient myths to construct their own fictional world. Living in this high-tech world, they find the mythical stories fascinating, magical and yet relevant to the present situation. India has a rich treasure of mythological stories having admirers across the countries. Mythological stories of the great epics like *the Ramayana* and the *Mahabharata* are not merely tales of Gods, demons, demigods, miracles and mysteries; these also provide us knowledge about the social structure and cultural beliefs of the ancient time and people. Retelling of the Indian mythological stories re-establishes their significance in the modern Indian social context. This article aims at analyzing the mythological novel *The Palace of Illusions* from perspectives like the strategies involved in narrating the novel and its applicability to the modern context in relation to the war-effected situation. This objective will be pursued mainly through the theoretical perspective of myth criticism.

Ashok K. Banker is a prominent literary figure in retelling the myths of the *Mahabharata* and the *Ramayana*, the stories of Krishna and so on. Amish Tripathy, a young Indian writer is so much inspired by the stories of ancient India that he has penned down the myth of Shiva totally from a new outlook, so much so that his debut novel *The Immortals of Meluha (*2010) followed by *The Secret of the Nagas* (2011) have become bestsellers luring the readers of every age-group. However, it is Chitra Banerjee Divakaruni's re-invention of the *Mahabharata* in her novel *The Palace of Illusions* published in 2008 that has enthralled the East-West readers and made them re-think of the events and incidents and issues of the great epic.

Chitra Banerjee Divakaruni is an Indo-American writer well-known for her collection of short stories, poems and fiction. Divakaruni now teaches creative writing at the University of Houston. Despite living in America for a long time, she has not lost her connection with and admiration for Indian tradition and culture; rather she attempts to give this ancient Indian culture a global face. In *The Palace of Illusions,* Divakaruni does not tend to invent a totally new world out of Veda Vyasa's *Mahabharata.* The novel honestly pursues the story-line of the epic without introducing any new character. But, she re-invents those aspects of the mythical epic which otherwise seemed to remain unnoticed so long by the readers. She attempts to focus on those aspects which didn't get much attention in the original narrative. From a different standpoint, she narrates the story and through her simple language and style, Divakaruni appeals to the imaginative as well as the rational mindset of the modern readers. Thus, the mythological story is given a fresh look so as to use the same as a metaphor to interpret the present-day situations.

The *Mahabharata* has been translated from Sanskrit to many different languages. In this respect, Divakaruni's attempt is not new but her uniqueness lies in narrating the story in first person. Here Draupadi whom she calls Panchaali is the narrator. To make her the narrator of all the events, Divakaruni had to empower Panchaali with some special vision and perception. The narrator of the original epic, Vyasa, has also a role in the narrative structure guiding Panchaali build up her narrative through his prophecies. The story begins with Panchaali's birth from fire; it maturates reflecting on the life of Panchaali and ends with her final departure. Telling the story of birth through one's own voice requires a witty craftsmanship and Divakaruni chooses a grandmother as narrator to tell Panchaali the incidents of her childhood days: "Through the long, lonely years of my childhood, when my father's palace seemed to tighten its grip around me until I couldn't breathe, I would go to my nurse and ask for a story. . . . This winter afternoon, sitting cross-legged in the meagre sunlight that managed to find its way through my slit of a window, she said." (1) Thus both Panchaali and the readers are informed about the story of her birth.

As Divakaruni gives a mythological account in her novel, she employs certain facets which are largely applicable to the narrative structure of a myth. According to Frazer, myth should be read literally and be treated as an explanation of certain phenomena (Segal, 35). Ernst Cassirer points out that myth is one way of using language for expressive purposes with the help of some symbolic devices. He argues that mythical thoughts is a mode of symbolically structuring the world and that myth should be treated as relating to the process of mind as projected on to the world. This idea of projection makes one think logically of the psychoanalytic theories of myth (Segal, 36). The basic tenet of the psychoanalytic theories of Freud and Jung is the assumption that the symbols of myth as well as the themes of its plot are constructed in the unconscious. According to Jung, the symbolic structure of the unconscious is a reality which cannot be totally reduced to any other level of experience. However, the Freudian theorists treat myth as the expression of mental forces. This treatment possesses the idea that myths are like day-dreams. It involves the process of dream-work that symbolically reconstructs messages emitted from the unconscious. The message here is not explicit but disguised and the body of message is condensed.

In *The Palace of Illusions*, Divakaruni gives a series of messages through her protagonist's dreams. With the help of her unusual dreams, Panchaali is conscious of many of the events which otherwise would have been unknown to herself as well as to the readers. One of the most significant dreams that can be mentioned in this respect is her dream of Karna and Kunti. In her dream, Panchaali could not immediately recognize the shawl-wrapped lady as Kunti but she recognized Karna even before she could see his face. This dream arouses suspicion in Panchaali's mind as to why Kunti would go to meet her sons' enemy by the river side so secretly. Soon Panchaali discovers the truth about Karna and Kunti's real relationship. The device of dream has been skilfully employed as an agent in the narrative structure of the novel by Divakaruni to communicate what would remain otherwise inexpressible. In Chapter 34 of the novel Panchaali re-calls her dream hearing Karna's conversation with Bheeshma: "Suddenly, everything that had puzzled me began to make sense" *(*273).

Other than this dream, Panchaali's dream of the 'palace of lac' in Chapter 15 of the novel and her last but most painful dream of Aswatthama killing her most beloved children and brothers also render important messages in a condensed manner. The dreams apparently appear to be a representation of the un-conscious; however, these dreams have been given a good space in the narrative structure and are weighed with significant mean-ings. According to the psychoanalytic theory of myth, these dreams are utilized as mythical symbols. These symbols express a universal concern for themes such as the process of physical and psychological incorporation and expulsion, the fear of aban-donment and destruction, rivalry between parent and child and between parent and siblings etc. Rendering such voluminous connotations, the dream narratives fashion Divakaruni's re-writing of the epic in the form of a novel in a unique way.

Though an adaptation of the *Mahabharata*, Chitra Banerjee Divakaruni's narrative technique is quite different from the orig-inal epic written in verse-form. She has woven myth in the structure of the novel. This strategy can precisely be said as the technique known as story within a story. Within the structure of one story, another story is told, thereby giving the narrative a multilayered structure. Whereas the same stories in Veda Vyasa's *Mahabharata* can be studied as a story within a story intended to depict philosophical knowledge or knowledge about Dharma, Divakaruni's can be studied as a structural device that does not impose any didactic lesson but let it open to the readers to interpret and appreciate the same and relate them to the main story.

A story within a story is basically a literary device in which more than one narrative is interwoven simultaneously. One action is presented during the course of another action. This literary device can be used in different literary forms like novels, short stories, plays, poems, philosophical essays and so on. A writer can use this device as a tool of entertainment or to act as an example to the characters outside the inner story. The stories often carry psychological as well as symbolic significance for the characters of the inner story. One such inner story Chitra Banerjee Divakaruni takes from the *Mahabharata* is the tale of Nal and Damyanti. Divakaruni sets the background for the narration of the story with a sort of introduction: "To divert our minds from our misfortunes, they told us stories of people whose sufferings were far worse. . . . My favourite was the story of Nal and Damyanti, perhaps because of its parallels to our life. . . . This is the story, in the bareness of bones." (208)

The story of Nal and Damyanti was told by one of the sages who used to visit the Pandavas during their exile in the forest. The sage's intention to tell the story was to give a lesson to the Pandavas so that they learn to bear their misfortunes valiantly. Whereas Yudhistir's perception of the story was from one symbolic angle, Panchaali's perception was from another angle which is more akin to her deep insight: 'Yudhistir didn't seem to see' (208) the parallel to the story of the Pandavas. Nal, the Nishad king had lost every single bit of his possession and even his kingdom to his brother just as Yudhistir lost his own. Despite losing the last piece of cloth, Nal did not wager his beloved wife. Damyanti also supported her husband in his adversity. But, Nal left the sleeping Damyanti in the forest, thinking it to be the best for her to get rid of the calamities brought upon her because of him. It is because of Damyanti's conviction and determination to search for and get her husband back that they were united after a long span of years. After the narration of this inner story, Divakaruni elevates her story to the level of an impressionistic narrative. The virtuous Yudhistir brought out the symbol of righteousness from the story, saying: "Look, how Nal never swerved from righteousness, no matter what happened. And Damyanti never rebuked him for his losses but gave him all the support a man needs when in trouble" (209). However, Panchaali interprets the story through her psychological perception in a different way: "How did Nal repay her? By abandoning in a forest? How was that righteous?" (209) The answers are not given in the structure of the narrative and the readers are equally free to interpret the story as per their own perceptions.

Thus, the story woven inside the main story bears a symbolic and psychological significance to the characters. Such an impact had the story on Panchaali that she could not keep Damyanti out of her mind. She was amazed to think of the courageousness of Damyanti: "How frightened she must have been—and how brave. Because she didn't go back to her parents right away. Instead, she searched for Nal for years. Once she was stoned to death as a witch—she, a princess who had been famed the world over for her beauty." (209) And from there, the narrative captures the intellection of Yudhistir, the other character, as Panchaali travels from the thought of Yudhistir to that of her own: "I was no ideal wife. . . . She was better than I" (208)

In the construction of the novel, Chitra Banerjee Divakaruni narrates the past lives of some of the characters, like that of Bheeshma and Shikhandi. However, the myth of the past lives of these characters is not directly narrated by the main narrator herself. She is twice disconnected from this narrative to play either the role of a listener or of an eavesdropper. She gets aware of Bheeshma's past life by eavesdropping on the conversation between Karna and Bheeshma. The narrative of one's past life would definitely arouse questions in the mind of any rationalistic modern reader. However, Divakaruni skilfully incorporates these questions in the narrative structure, which are asked by none other than the narrator herself. The power and truth behind every myth is questioned time and again by the inquisitive scholars throughout the world. As readers, we seek answers to the questions that are raised in our minds regarding the myths related to our social, cultural and religious life; so does Panchaali, a mythological character and the narrator of the novel. She questions the truth about Shikhandi's past life repeatedly: "Could he really be Amba in a previous incarnation?" (49)

James Frazer in *The Golden Bough* observes the death-rebirth myth as the representative of the growing envisions and agriculture, whereas Carl Gustav Jung envisions the death-rebirth archetype as symbolic expression taking place not in the world but in the mind. That process, according to him, is the temporary "return of the ego to the unconscious—a kind of temporary death of the ego and its re-emergence or re-birth from the unconscious. This concept of Jung leads to the idea of collective unconscious" (Segal, 4). This theoretical concern can be applied logically to Divakaruni's narrative on the theme of re-birth which she employs on Krishna's comment made in reply to Panchaali's question regarding the truth of Shikhandi's past life: "He believes it to be so. Isn't that what truth is? The force of a person's believing seeps into those around him—into the very earth and air and water." (49) Allan W. Watts in his *Myth and Ritual in Christianity* (1954) observes: "Myth is to be defined as a complex of stories—some no doubt fact and some fantasy—

which for various reasons, human beings regard as demonstrations of inner meaning of universe and of human life" (7).

How far the meaning of the universe and of human life is demonstrated is questionable; but these myths and stories interwoven in the main narrative of the novel provide hopes and lessons to many. Bheeshma's past life, as he admits, taught him a lesson for lifetime, whereas Shikhandi's knowledge about his past life gave him a sort of hope or more precisely cause to ignite his thirst for revenge.

Chitra Banerjee Divakaruni, through *The Palace of Illusions* aims at attracting every twenty-first century modern reader across the world. For this purpose, narrating the story in an epic form would have been too ambitious a project. As she shifts from one literary genre to another, so does she shift from the typical narrative technique of the *Mahabharata* in verse form to her own multifarious techniques. The verse narrative of the *Mahabharata* consists of 48,000 lines but Divakaruni's re-invention of the epic is totally in prosaic form and concisely it records the important aspects of the epic. Like Vyasa, she does not divide the novel into Eighteen Parvas; rather she divides the novel into forty three chapters keeping thematic relevance to the original epic. Divakaruni pursues the oral narrative technique, the revelation of the reason behind King Drupad and Drona's enmity is one such example where different assumptions are made by Dhri and Panchaali through argument and counter-argument. As Panchaali starts the story like a professional story teller, Dhri interrupts saying, "No! No! The story must start early. You are looking at the story through the wrong window" (15). However, such interruptions do not stop Panchaali and she proceeds with her story: "You are too partial. . . . I am taking back the story. (15-16)

Thus, the mood of storytelling becomes an integral part of Divakaruni's narrative strategy in *The Palace of Illusions*. Though one narrator, that is, Panchaali has been given the most prominence in the course of the novel, multiple voices come to play their roles, thus conforming to the principle of heteroglossia. The narrative strategy of a literary product is a very important facet for its success. Laxmi Venkatesh in her review of *The Palace of Illusions* writes, "Divakaruni has managed to bind all the characters and the story together through the bold and enticing narrative style."

Divakaruni's re-invention of the myth of the *Mahabharata* focuses intensively on the destructive consequences of war. War is a product of vengeance and the issue of vengeance can be traced in *The Palace of Illusions* from the very beginning. King Drupad performed the great sacrificial yajna to be blessed with a son *who* could avenge him. Thus, the birth of Dhristadyumna along with Draupadi sets off the journey of war. It was prophesized by Vyasa much before the greatest war of the *Mahabharata* that Panchaali would be remembered for causing that greatest war. However, a reading of Divakaruni's reinvention of the Great Epic brings out the fact that the seeds of war were sown even before her birth. King Drupad, who was defeated by Drona, wanted to defeat him in turn. Shikhandi wanted a battle in which he could kill Bheeshma. The Kaurava brothers, at enmity with the Pandavas, wanted just a scope to call for a battle and to drive them away from the kingdom. All these repressed intentions found a way of ventilation when Panchaali cursed the Kauravas in the Sabha and vowed to bathe in their blood. Thus, everybody wanted the war, but very few thought of its after-effect. "War is like avalanche. Once begun, it cannot cease until it has wreaked all the destruction it is capable of" (263).

Whereas Vyasa's *Mahabharata* glorifies the Great War that destroyed the evil and helped to establish a righteous Kingdom, Divakaruni's rewriting of the great story makes a commentary on the devastation caused by war. While reading the painful account of the war, the readers don't feel like having an account of the unknown mythical past, rather they feel its impact, because every reader of the modern generation, who is the product of the war-torn world can identify herself with the situation. The premonition of the situation that would follow the Great War recurs throughout the novel. Thus reference of war becomes a recurrent myth as human beings have witnessed the misery and misfortune after every war since the ancient time. Whereas primitive men fought battles to bring back natural order of life and mythological war signifies the victory of good over evil, the modern wars are fought to assert power and impose supremacy of one nation over the other. For whatever reasons the war may take place, the post-war situation is almost the same.

In the essay *Theories of Myth,* Percy. S. Cohen discusses that the myth-making mind uses any material that it instantly gets. But this activity involves drawing materials from hidden places, and this process of drawing materials has a magic quality about it. If myth is the way of anchoring the present in the past, then it will draw to it the symbols of past which resides in most human minds. War, thus becomes a symbol taken from myth that Chitra Banerjee Divakaruni employs to connect to the present condition of human minds of the twenty first century. The devastating effect of the war of the *Mahabharata* can be identified with the impact of the First World War, Second World War and many other wars like that of the America-Iraq war. The world wars spread death and destruction throughout the world to a great extent. Innumerable people lost their lives, homes, lands and became refugees. The world economy also collapsed as a result of this. The impact of the world war carried forward generation after generation, so much so that children are still born with deformities in Japan as a result of the impact of atom bomb. The Second World War had filled the world with hopelessness, despair and spiritual degeneration. Eliot's *Waste Land* (1922) which is full of mythical references captures such degeneration in a symbolic way. The loss, destruction and violence of war could be felt by different countries several times. The America-Iraq war is a burning example of this. The long-drawn war not only affected those who died fighting the battle, but also left an ever-lasting mark on those who are living with the memory of loss in the war. If this is taken to be the modern context, then it comes in perfect confrontation with the war-torn situation of the mythical past. Divakaruni records the meaninglessness of war, which becomes appropriate in the context of any war, in the following words: "The land stretched sick and disrobed, great, gaping holes torn into its side by the blasts of astras. The few remaining trees were lifeless skeletons . . . only vultures sat on dead branches, waiting in eerie silence. This was what we had done to our earth" (300).

The account of the *Mahabharata* battle that Divakaruni gives through her spokesperson Panchaali is comprehensive. This account encapsulates the war from its preparatory period to the end. If men and Gods were busy with their own diplomacies to fight the battle, women were no less bothered with challenges: "We women—no less than the men—were going to be faced by challenges we'd never imagined. . . . Who we were as individuals was receding to the background. What mattered more was that our dear ones were going to fight beside each other. From now on we would be united in our anxiety, in being torn between pride and concern, in our prayers for the safety of them all." (247-48)

When the war ended, women were left with no reliable dependence. Whereas some women sacrificed themselves in the funeral pyres of their husbands, some went on to live the burden of life with their painful memories. No veneration but condemnation of war has been emphasized persistently in *The Palace of Illusions.* The violence and pain of war, the physical battle and conflicts within the warriors, the terrible outcome of war are the issues in the novel that appear to be a story of the mythical past. In Chapter Thirteen of the novel, the writer expresses the helpless condition that followed the Great War which has resemblances with the modern predicament of war: "Hastinapur after the war was largely a city of women, widows who had never dreamed that the survival of their families would depend on them . . . they were without male protection, they found themselves exploited. . . . Women became unpaid servants. Sometimes they were turned out. . . . There were others that I didn't but I heard of the street corners they frequented at night, selling the only thing left to them. It was a terrible situation" (322-23).

Even a myth gives the reference that no war between good and evil can be fought with perfect righteousness. The question of righteousness which recurs in the novel time and again has many times been seen to succumb to the power of immorality. Thus, the process of killing Abhimanyu was against the rule of war and this was followed by a series of unlawful killings like that of Jayadrath (the illusion of a false sunset created by Krishna betrayed him), Drona (the false news of his son being killed made him let down the weapons), Karna, the most helpless victim (killed when he was without armour), Duryodhan (he was hit with a mace on his thigh). War is thought to be a Kshatriya pride, but the pride becomes an irony in such cases. But justification to such dishonesty in mythological wars too is given. The evil must be destroyed by any means. Even after the evil is destroyed, can the good remain untouched or unaffected by the calamity and suffering of war? This is the question that underlies Divakaruni's handling of the narrative of war.

The myth of war as an agent has been employed by Divakaruni in a distinctive manner to give a sense of futility of it to the modern readers. War turns man into a butcher and insinuates the "drama of hate." The irony of war is that it is not as "civilized," "glory giving" and "great" as it is supposed to be. The war poems of Siegfried Sassoon and Wilfred Owen uncover the hidden disgust behind war. The soldiers and warriors were forced to fight in the name of patriotism and nationhood. The passivity of common soldiers who fought the Mahabharata war has been portrayed in *The Palace of Illusions* as well: "those soldiers had chosen to join my husbands because they supported our cause. Now I realized that for many of them, it was merely a job, an alternative to poverty and starvation. Or maybe they'd been forcibly conscripted by their overlords" (257).

It is not that the Kaurava-army had only been swept away in the battle of bloodshed, but the second generation of the Pandavas too was brutally killed in the battle. But for the unborn child of Abhimanyu, the Pandava clan would have been obliterated. Panchaali is left with the realization that 'she who sows vengeance must reap its bloody fruit' (306). As Devdutt Patnaik points out, "Myth is essentially a cultural construct, a common understanding of the world that binds individuals and communities together" (xvi).

This mythical perception of Panchaali can influence the minds of the modern people to keep them away from war and develop a sense of brotherhood and comradeship to bind the individuals of the societies together. The absurdity of war is a recurrent myth in many literary pieces. Rosencrantz in Act III, sc. iii of Shakespeare's *Hamlet* makes a very significant comment that is applicable to the war in the epic or in the novel and to war taking place between the nations of modern days. He asserts that majesty does not die alone but like a gulf, it draws everything that is close to it. A war can never be fought only between the rulers (Shakespeare, 135). Thus, the Mahabharata war was not only fought between the Pandavas and the Kauravas, not only the fate of the royal descendents was decided by the war, but also thousands of common people were sacrificed. Women became widows, children became fatherless. The land of Hastinapur and that of its neighbouring territories became waste and barren lands of the dead and the destitute. It is in the *Stree Parva* of the *Mahabharata* that Vyasa comments how the women mourned the deaths of their kinsmen and in *The Palace of Illusions,* the Thirtieth Chapter *Pyre* records the miserable situation of the mourners: "Constant pitiless, ever increasing, the stench assaulted as we made our reluctant way to the battlefield to deal with our dead. I pressed my lips to keep from vomiting. Where earlier soldiers had built their cook fires, now funeral pyres were being lighted—so many that the vista in front of us was covered in a haze of smoke" (310).

Duryodhan's last words to Yudhistir are philosophical in nature that reveals the true state of the post-war situation. No matter who wins, the misery of war would haunt the ruler: "You'll rule a kingdom peopled with widows and orphans and wake each morning to the grief of loss. Who's the real winner, then, who the loser?" (309) Such post-war situation is a bitter truth in any society that has gone or will undergo the experience of war—be it past, present or future.

Percy S. Cohen in the *Theories of Myth* observes that myths perform several functions. They contain layers of meanings that achieve an intuitive experience. Myths are narrated with time anchored structure, because they deal simultaneously with the socially and psychologically significant aspects. They link a sense of deeper level of reality of the past to the present (Segal, 49-50). This is why man makes myths as these contain significance and hence they also share myths. This re-invention of the myth of the *Mahabharata* by Chitra Banerjee Divakaruni can be a sharing of myth and the account of the post-war situation of the Mahabharata battle links the past to the present, as the present world is also a war-torn one.

Devdutt Patnaik claims that "there is no evidence of a perfect world, a perfect man or perfect family anywhere on the earth. Perfection, be it Rama Rajya or Camelot, exists only in mythology. Yet everyone craves for it. This craving inspires art, establishes empires, sparks revolutions and motivates leaders. Such is the power of myth. (Myth = Mithya, xvi)

It seems to be the inspiration gathered from the mythology of the *Mahabharata* that motivated Chitra Banerjee Divakaruni to represent this Great Myth in a new way. So she deals with the problem of an individual regarding her identity in *The Palace of Illusions*, which in the original narrative did not seem to have so much attention. In the middle of the novel, Panchaali seems to be puzzled regarding her identity: "The princess who longed for acceptance, the guilty girl whose heart wouldn't listen, the wife who balanced her fivefold role precariously, the rebellious daughter-in-law, the queen who ruled in the most magical of palaces, the distracted mother, the beloved companion of Krishna, who refused to learn the lessons he offered, the women obsessed with revenge—none of them were true Panchaali. If not, who was I?" (229)

However, it is at the end of the novel that Panchaali finds herself above the gender-biased identity in the patriarchal world. Divakaruni has provided her a new heaven. Draupadi was initially rejected to climb the stairs of heaven as a result of her partiality to love for Arjun. But, Panchaali in *The Palace of Illusions* is above such patriarchal laws. She enjoys the divine blessing of Krishna and is raised beyond the bindings of gender: "I am beyond gender and the imprisoning patterns of ego. And yet, for the first time I'm truly Panchaali" (360).

Many critics have argued that *The Palace of Illusions*, though a retelling of the *Mahabharata,* lacks a detailed study of many events and characters which, if included, would have been wiser on the part of the novelist. In this regard, it can be said that all the aspects of an epic may not be reflected in a novel with great details and so Divakaruni didn't aim at going through the details of the *Mahabharata* and record a personal account of all the characters of the epic. Chitra Banerjee Divakaruni does not only bring the ancient culture into existence, but also gives a new perspective to the mythical epic. Instead of a simple retelling of an ancient text, her work becomes a re-invention in the sense that she endows Draupadi with the characteristic of what can be called a narrator-heroine or *Sutradhari*; she has renewed the epic by encapsulating it in the novelistic genre with the help of lucid language and simple style of narration. Being a modern writer, she also tends to make the readers of her era find parallels of their present condition to that of the mythical past. Thus, to read *The Palace of Illusions* is to re-read the *Mahabharata*.

Works Cited

"Archetypal Literary Criticism." Wikipedia, the Free Encyclopaedia.

Bhattacharya, Tania. "Retelling of the Legends," *The Telegraph*| Graphiti. Kolkata, 6.3. 2011. www.telegraphindia.com/110306/jsp

Divakaruni, Chitra Banerjee. *The Palace of Illusions.* New York: Picador India. 2011.

Patnaik, Devdutt. *Myth= Mythya, A Handbook of Hindu Mythology.* New Delhi: Penguin India. 2006.

Sagal, Robert A. *Myth, Critical Concepts in Literary and Cultural Studies*, Vol. 2. Routledge. 2007.

Shakespeare, William. *Hamlet,* Delhi: Oxford University Press, 1999.

"Story within a Story." Wikipedia, the Free Encyclopaedia. Dec. 2007.

Tripathy, Amish. *The Immortals of Meluha.* Chennai: Westland, 2010.

Tripathy, Amish. *The Secret of the Nagas.* Chennai: Westland, 2011.

Venkatesh, Laxmi. *The Palace of Illusions*, A Review. Blah. 10 Mar. 2011. http:/blahmagazine.in/2011/03/9.palace-of-illusions

Watts, Allan W. *Myth and Ritual in Christianity.* New York: Grove Press, 1954.

Wilfred, L. Guerin. *A Handbook of Critical Approaches to Literature.* New York: OUP, 1992.

Negotiating Identities in Chitra Divakaruni's *Queen of Dreams*

N. PADMANABHA RAO
Lal Bahadur Shastri College, Warangal
&
P. MALLIKARJUNA RAO
Kakatiya University, Warangal

The importance of identity has been a major focus of current literature and search for identity is a pervasive theme in our society. While identity development is a complex task, it is particularly complicated for women belonging to ethnic groups in an alien culture. However, the identity of the South Asian diasporic woman cannot be categorized as simply Eastern or Western as it is contingent upon many factors, individual and social, personal as well as collective. As these women live in between the push and pull of opposing cultural forces, the result is the creation of an identity that is as multiple as the different components that helped to comprise it.

In Chitra Banerjee Divakaruni's *Queen of Dreams* (2004), the creation of identity emerges as a continuous process, forever transforming and never truly complete. However, the author depicts this transformation and transition as a positive and an optimistic journey. Unlike the female characters, in most of the diasporic novels, whose experience of the culture of the Other is traumatic, the protagonist in *Queen of Dreams* represents second-generation female immigrants who, being born and submerged by the culture of the Other, have fashioned such diasporic identities which let them survive and succeed in the liminal space.

The text is a bildungsroman about Rakhie, yet it is a story that moves outside of this conception, for Rakhie does not so much grow into her identity on her own. Her surrounding environments also influence her in the formation of her new identities, reminiscent of Lacanian theory. Lacanian theory, thus, complicates the bildungsroman structure of this text; for it suggests that, the formation of identity is a process whereby others create the self, where external forces rather than internal experiences determine the development of the individual, and where identity does not necessitate an obvious developmental path.

As Frantz Fanon says, "if I were asked for a definition of myself, I would say that I am one who waits; I investigate my surroundings, I interpret everything in terms of what I discover." (66) Like Fanon, Rakhie possesses an evolving identity that is unpredictable and filled with possibilities, forever growing and changing with her every new environment and each passing moment.

Perceiving both her race and sexuality through new and different lenses throughout the course of the text, Rakhie comes to realize that the notion of a singular identity is a fallacy and the reality of the diasporic experience is the indeterminacy of multiplicity. However, she does not fight with her multiplicity but rather accepts it as part of her progressive capacity.

Rakhi is the daughter of an immigrant couple, who try to "turn her attention from the long ago and far away (India), to get her to focus on her American life." (49) Thus growing up in America, Rakhie never sees herself as an immigrant. "I don't have to put up a flag to prove that I'm American! I'm American already. I love this country—hell, it's the only country I know." (264) However, at this point in the novel, Rakhie is oblivious of the complexities of racial and ethnic identities in America.

Meanwhile, Rakhie's life gets complicated with the arrival of Java, "the fastest-growing cafe chain in the country" (26) opposite her Chai House. The Chai House is important to Rakhi because the custody of her daughter depends upon her earnings from this place. "I love this place—and I'm fortunate to have it. Because if it weren't for this store, I might not have Jona today either" (22). Therefore, Rakhi turns to her mother, who advises her that she must "create a special attraction, something that means more to people than money." (46) And something 'authentic,' "that satisfies a need in them that's deep and real" (48). Unfortunately, her mother dies in an accident. However, with the help of her father, the Chai House is resuscitated as "Kurma house," an authentic Indian restaurant to the immigrants, with the tastes and smells of the old country. It almost becomes a symbol for one's family and heritage, for ones roots and rootedness, where the immigrants are able to travel back in space and time and relive their shared histories of their country of origin, thus re-membering it. Vijay Mishra's 'diasporic imaginary' suggests "people who identify themselves as part of a diaspora are creating an 'imaginary'—a landscape of dream and fantasy that answers their desires" (Fludernik, xi) which is reminiscent of Benedict Anderson's concept of 'Imagined Communities.'

Benedict Anderson, in his insightful comment on how Nations evolve, conceptualizes the notion of imagining a community into being. He says, "Nationalism has to be understood by aligning it, not with self-consciously held political ideologies, but with the large cultural systems that preceded it, out of which . . . it came into being." Nation is then essential a cultural community and is created and sustained by the customs, traditions, and experiences of a people who may never meet most of the fellow-members, or know them but come together in an "imagined community," "because in the mind of each, lives an image of their communion" (Anderson 12) Thus, diasporic situation is said to entail "dwelling, maintaining communities and having collective homes away from home" (Clifford 221).

This communion may, in the form of shared experiences of events, food habits, cinema, clothes, or forms of speech, unconsciously become material markers of a shared sense of community. For instance, when Rakhi sees her father talking to an Indian immigrant, she notices that the two of them have similar body language in the movement of their hands and head as they talk and she remembers that she and her friends in the West did not have them. For the first time, Rakhi finds 'authentic' Indian-ness in the shared sense of community that her father and his friends bring to the Kurma house.

Khandelwal discusses the importance of maintaining culture for diasporic Indians: "Culture symbolizes both group identity and survival for Indian immigrants. The high priority placed on transplanting their cultural traditions to foreign soil is also connected to a deeply rooted belief in the indestructibility of Indian culture—even removed from the home country in which it arose, it must and will have a life of its own. . . . Thus, Indians have made major efforts to celebrate their cultural traditions in the United States" (Khandelwal 35).

As an American born, Rakhie initially feels excluded during these events. To her, these experiences seem exotic and fantastic productions of a land that is "far, far, away," (196) yet she feels a sense of kinship with them. She is, nevertheless, surprised and unsure as to how to react but is strangely drawn to this unfamiliar scene where her two worlds had collided and mingled so easily unfolding the mystery of her past and a culture that she has been distanced from. "They're my countrymen. We share the same skin colour" (194). Moreover, for the first time, she desperately wants to claim some of this magic as hers. This interaction between past and present, this reworking, leads to the production of cultural identities that are in transition and in negotiation.

Thus, the people in diaspora live in a complex space between two worlds and two cultures, a situation, which is reminiscent of "Janus, the Greek god with two faces, one looking backward and the other forward." (Said 1994 240) As such, Rakhie comes to terms with the idea that she never will have a single identity but rather is dispersed between being Indian and American. She does not fight with her new identity but rather accepts it as part of her progressive capacity.

This situation, of being suspended between two worlds, changes for better. Rakhie understands the importance of a strong connection to one's family, its traditions, and the memories connected with it. It provides her, in fact, with roots, with something to hold on to and feel whole and complete. This new perception of her race is an essential portion of her identity. Finally, as she grows close to her family, she learns to negotiate her identity, living in two worlds and feeling at home in both of them.

Thus, for Rakhi, "re-memorizing" her roots through the immigrants is therapeutic. Her overpowering desire, to be a part of the experiences that her father's generation seems to have carried from their lands of origin, underlines Rakhie's hybrid identity-in-the-making, however, suggesting that she does not have an agency in the creation of her new self since Indian community constructs it for her. Here Divakaruni is depicting identity formation in Lacanian terms, as a complex process that is dependent not solely upon the agency of the individual, but rather also upon the agency of others. Nevertheless, the condescension that Rakhie feels is reminiscent of Said's concept of Orientalism.

However, while Rakhi is trying to order her chaotic life of hyphenated identity, failed entrepreneur, failed mom, divorced woman, mother-fixated daughter, into a unified whole through imagining her identity in a certain way, suddenly she finds herself in the midst of an inexplicable situation that highlights certain complexities for the people with hyphenated identities.

Thus, September 11 disrupts Rakhie's life. While the new political crisis challenges the multicultural image of America, it also triggers off a critical look at what shapes culture, sense of belonging to a place. Strangely, in the beginning, Rakhie reacts to the news in terms of an American who is unable to believe that anybody could hate America so much. "It makes me want to drop a bomb on these people (of the Middle East) and end their hellish celebration." (256).

It is important to note that there is a shift of consciousness. Rakhi has forgotten her hyphenated identity and thinks of herself as an American again, an inevitable lot of the second-generation immigrants. The author addresses the experiences that result from such changes in self-perception and presents the related paradoxes that emerge from the process of diasporic identity formation. Thus identity becomes ambiguous, with self-perception changing as one's perspectives on the surrounding environment and culture evolve. This condition, common to all diasporic communities, is created by the constant oscillation between contradictory conceptions of race and culture, time and geography.

What needs to be taken into account here is that the notion of identity in general and diasporic identity in particular is not a set, fixed and essential whole but is rather "constructed, fluid and multiple" (Brubaker 1). According to the recent anti-essential theorizing about subject, and the view that identity is in fact a cultural artifact, "identities are conceived as a process, as performed, and as unstable." (Pratt 154)

However, a vicious attack on Rakhie, her family and her friends calls their notions of citizenship into question. The encounter becomes crucial in Rakhie's understanding of her being different. The unjustified hurt inflicted, by the people (Americans) she thought were her compatriots, only because of skin colour, is an immense strain on this young woman. "But if I wasn't American, then what was I?" (271). She sadly realizes that America, in fact, has made her a nowhere woman.

Thus, during racial attack, her American identity is deeply disconcerted and disoriented creating chaos in her life once again. She feels terribly lonely and rootless dispossessed of India and disowned by America. It triggers a change in her perception of herself, her subjectivity, as well as her belongingness. However, this experience marks yet another change in her identity—position as she connects herself more with her ethnic roots.

Describing the plight of the immigrants, Manju Jaidka says, "The loss of one's homeland is invariably the consequence of having consciously opted for another . . . having made a choice [the immigrant] is doomed to accept and suffer it, to hang out there for better or worse. And yet the loss is unignorable: the feeling it brings with it is that of an exile" (Manju Jaidka 121).

In his essay, *Reflections on Exile,* Edward Said, has described the notion of exile as "the unhealable rift between a human being and a native place, between the self and the true home: its essential sadness can never be surmounted. The achievements of exile are permanently undermined by the loss of something left behind forever. The sense of alienation, homelessness, expatriation and state of exile, an immigrant experiences, in a foreign space have been constantly pondered upon and such issues raise the necessity to question the concept of identity for the immigrant" (2000 101).

However, the end of the novel suggests that Rakhie, who had suffered racial attack, will create yet another identity for her new environment. Though, she does not feel fully at home in America, she knows that it is her home, the world for which she is responsible, which, she is born into and which is everywhere around her. Hence, she decides to stay and explore the challenge of belonging, despite disappointments, broken expectations, and unease. This awareness, however, reinforces the notion that Rakhie's identity is forever evolving in relation to her surroundings, as the in-betweenness of an immigrant is a space of possibilities.

Works Cited

Anderson, Benedict. *Imagined Communities: Reflections on the Origin and Spread of Nationalism.* U.K: Verso, 2006.

Brubaker, R. & Cooper. F. "Beyond Identity." *Theory and Society*, 29 (1), 2000.

Clifford, James. *Diasporas: The Post-Colonial Studies Reader*. Ed. Bill Ashcroft et.al. New York: Routledge, 2006.

Fanon, Frantz. *The Fact of Blackness, Identities: Race, Class, Gender, and Nationality*. Ed. Linda Alcoff. U.K: Blackwell, 2003.

Fludernik, Monica. "The Diasporic Imaginary: Postcolonial Reconfigurations in the Context of Multiculturalism." *Diaspora and Multiculturalism: Common Traditions and New Developments*. New York: Rodopi, 2003.

Khandelwal, Madhulika S. *Becoming American, Being Indian.* Ithaca: Cornell University Press, 2002.

Jaidka, Manju. "The Writer as Trishanku: Indian Writing in a Foreign Space." Ed. Somdatta Mandal *The Diasporic Imagination: Asian American Writing, Theory, Poetry And Performing Arts.* New Delhi: Prestige, 2000.

Pratt, G. "Grids of Difference: Place and Identity Formation." Ed. M. Ryan. *Cultural Studies: An Anthology.* Singapore: Blackwell, 2004.

Said, Edward. '*Resistance and Opposition' Culture and Anarchy*. London: Vintage, 1994.

_____ *Reflections on Exile and other Literary and Cultural Essays,* London: Granta, 2000.

The Unfolding of Karobi: The Gradual Growth of the Central Character in *The Oleander Girl*

SUBHRA ROY
Women's College, Agartala

He who binds to himself a Joy
Doth the winged life destroy;
But he who kisses the Joy as it flies
Lives in Eternity's Sunrise. (288)

These are the treasured lines of the poem etched out on the book that Korobi had hidden under her wedding pillow, only to be read to Rajat in their flower-filled bedroom. The poem is not an ordinary one; it's the one that "My mother has sent to us" (288). Korobi, the central character in Chitra Banerjee Divakaruni's *Oleander Girl,* must not have expected a more valuable gift than the anthology of poetry containing the poem which was often read by her mother. Moreover, it was sent to her on her wedding day by her father, to find whom she had left no stones unturned. The search for her father which took her to America, had metamorphosed Korobi into a much stronger woman: "beautiful—but also tough" (253), like the Oleanders. When she started her journey, cut away from the cocooned world of 26 Tarak Prasad Roy Road, she must not have imagined the harsh facts that would turn her world upside down for a while! With gradual experiences in a foreign land, far away from Kolkata, Korobi turns out to be a courageous woman who had learnt to make peace with her past, as well as her future. In this article, I would be highlighting on this process of transformation which Korobi has gone through, while searching for her father in post-9/11 America which is alluring but unwelcoming at the same time.

The surreal existence of Korobi's mother at the very beginning of the novel gives us the cue about some impending tryst with the past which holds some secrets in the dark! Korobi, who is going to get engaged with Rajat very soon, is oblivious to the existence of her father who is equally unaware of his daughter's existence. When the household at 26 Tarak Prasad Roy Road is abustle with the preparation of Korobi's engagement, the oleander girl is visited by her mother, Anu Roy who was dead eighteen years ago. Korobi had tried hard to get a glimpse of her mother when she was in her boarding school, away from her grandparents: "All through my years of growing up, I longed for a visitation from my mother. . . . I prayed for it in secret, and, when that didn't work, tried to put myself in calamity's way. . . . But only ended up with bruises, sprains." (2)

These facts reveal Korobi to be quite stubborn and headstrong. But her grandfather's disguised pamper and strict guidance have made her gain a conventionally obedient poise. But deep inside, she is the befitting daughter of Anu Roy, and love for adventure lurks within her. And, this sudden visit by her mother leaves behind a trail for her, to be followed later on.

The docile grand-daughter of Bimal Roy can't afford to hurt or disobey her grandfather and her love for her grandfather makes her accept his decisions, though a bit grudgingly sometimes. But Korobi is an amalgamation of contradictions—docile but confident at the same time. When she buys an "off-the-shoulder kurti in maroon chiffon with slim-fitting pants" (18), she is unwittingly trying to be adventurous in her own way. But, nonetheless, she is afraid of her grandfather's reaction, "From time to time, I imagine with a mix of horror and pride—what Grandfather's reaction would be when he saw me in it." (18)

Korobi ends up having an argument with Bimal Roy who likes her to wear saree and disapproves her new dress. Soon we come to know that Bimal Roy has suffered heart attack, which according to Korobi, must have been triggered by her argument with him. In a fit of guilt, she tears the kurti apart! Korobi's mourning for her grandfather continues to be strong enough to make her lovelife get eclipsed for a while. But soon she comes face to face with a shocking truth which slips out accidentally from her grandmother: "Your dear grandfather lied to you—and forced me to do the same. Your father's alive." (52). The words hit her hard, but she is strong enough to recover to begin her search for her father who was thought to be dead long before!

Nina Sankovitch, in her article, "*Oleander Girl*: Coming of Age," has said, "Korobi starts out young and sure of herself, but it is the confidence of youth and not of experience. Once she commits herself to finding out who her father was, experience come fast and furious and Korobi is forced to grow up."

Once in America, experiences get flooded on her way; when Korobi lands in America alone with none but Mitra to receive her, her spirited self turns into an observant one. Her first challenge in America is to be with the schemer, Mitra. Korobi gets a whiff of Mitra's intention of maligning her in-laws and from then onwards she takes extra caution, so that Mitra cannot get to know the reason of her being in America. While going to meet Desai, the private detective who is going to help her find her father, Mitra accompanies her, not to protect her in this unknown part of the world, but to collect some news which can be instrumental in blackmailing the Boses. When a man, possibly a tramp, with shaven head and tattoos approaches her with hands outstretched, Mitra lets her stand alone, vulnerable to the situation! But Korobi is not the type of girl to act like a damsel in danger; instead she yells, "Go away! Stop harassing me!" (114).

To reinforce her voice she claps her hands and it works! The man stops advancing, and, Korobi's frightened self gets a boost when she notices an appraising look in Mitra's face—"I am happy to have disappointed him." (114). This little victory is powerful enough to make Korobi learn how to stand on her own, fearless and confident. Korobi disappoints Mitra twice; she can't be beguiled into exposing her family matters to any stranger, particularly if the stranger is someone like Mitra. When Desai was about to blurt out the details of his investigation in front of Mitra, who is "peering with far too much interest at the computer screen" (115), Korobi declares that privacy should be restored, and this is enough to infuriate Mitra, who is close enough to find out the secret with which he has planned to blackmail the Boses.

Apart from Mitra, there are other characters in the novel who have been instrumental in transforming Korobi into a stronger person. Even the failures and disappointments that she faces while searching her father, change her to be a brave and strong Korobi, ready to take life in her stride. Her first failure comes when Rob Evanston doesn't turn out to be her father! The valuable short period of time in America, along with the meagre money she is left with, and above all her heart-felt desire and hope to meet her father make her failure sting her bitterly, "Failure has carved a pit in my stomach; I can't gauge how deep it goes." (154)

During this time of distress, she finds a little solace in Vic, Desai's nephew and associate. Vic's easygoing manner, contradictory to that of Korobi, manages to keep the sunshine in Korobi's gloomy days in America. But soon she is torn between her attraction for Vic and her vow of faithfulness to Rajat. When Vic holds before her the prospective of a new life in America with him, Korobi gets excited about the possibility of a new life: "Here I could become a new Korobi. Vic—easygoing, good-humoured—wouldn't try to mould me into his concept of sweetheart or wife." (218)

When Korobi broods over such thoughts, the readers get the hint that the adventurous part of Korobi is getting control over her. She doesn't prefer the cushioned life of Kolkata anymore; staying protected under the overbearing shelter of the male members of the family. We can't stop wondering if Sarojini didn't break the news of Rajat and Pia's accident to Korobi, would Korobi have chosen her predestined life in Kolkata or would she go for the alluring free life of America!

Korobi's meeting with her probable father, Rob Mariner, turns out to be a disaster, but it doesn't go without teaching her a lesson. The way she protects herself from Mariner's predatory advances, catches him off-guard, and he has to accept his defeat. But Mariner is not such a person to accept defeat so easily; he destroys Korobi's chances to talk to her next probable father who happens to be a writer. When she has lost all hope to meet her real father, Rob Lacey comes in her life and along with that come two shocking facts that make her see life in a new light. The truth about her Afro-American heredity doesn't hurt her much, but the fact about the illegitimacy of her existence shakes her entire being. She is shattered; but soon she gathers herself, as she can't afford to spoil those treasured two days that she has planned to spend with her father. In an anguished outburst, Korobi throws her mobile away; but Vic is there on time to restore her mental stability. Soon, she goes back to the motel to continue her meeting with her father. She is so happy to meet her father and to taste paternal care, that she forgets everything. Korobi can give almost everything away to know the man whom her mother used to love so dearly. Moreover, she can also get to know many details about her mother whom she can never meet in her lifetime. Korobi is not melodramatic; she only needs love, respect & trust. Any girl of her age must have cried her heart out; and Korobi also does the same thing, but she recomposes herself very quickly, though not without a vent: "I'm furious with everyone—my mother, my father, my grandfather." (246)

Initially, she finds it difficult to come to terms "with this new, shameful me" (245). But after having an emotional reconciliation, with apologies on both sides, Korobi comes closer to her father. She knows very well that after the secrets get divulged, there will be no wedding in India. The way Korobi takes the reality in her stride highlights her to be a girl of mettle. Soon the day comes when Korobi is ready to leave America; she is accompanied by her father who has come to see her off. When they are about to get parted, Korobi asks him, the question that has plagued her all her life—why she has been named Korobi. She gets to know that her mother wanted her to have the qualities of the Oleanders—beautiful, yet tough enough to protect itself from predators. "Anu wanted that toughness for you because; she didn't have enough of it herself." (253)

Korobi returns to India as a better person who knows what's right for her, who knows how to resist temptations. When she arrives at Kolkata airport, Bahadur is unable to recognize her for her short hair; she cut her hair short to sell them to get some money for her sustenance in America. When the long mass of hair was snipped away from her head, she felt light-headed and "untethered" and this new avatar gave Korobi a modern and slightly dangerous look. When she reaches India, her first concern was to inform Rajat about the two secrets of her life. But before she can reveal them to him, the beans are already spilled by Mitra, who tries to blackmail the Boses for money. Though she is not welcome at the place of the Boses, she has the guts to face Rajat and Maman as she has no malice or duplicity in her mind. When she sees that even Rajat has no faith in her, she breaks off the engagement and returns the engagement ring with dignity.

Her broken engagement with Rajat or her new-found identity fails to curb Korobi's spirit for a new beginning. She is happy with Sarojini, her grandmother, in their old house; she starts her college again to keep herself busy. Now, she is a different Korobi who understands the nuances of every relationship and can handle them better than before. On the day of her wedding, she is a fully blown oleander—beautiful but tough, ready to take challenges. Thus at the end of the novel, we find that Korobi has grown into a balanced person—the perfect Oleander girl.

Works Cited

Divakaruni, Chitra. *Oleander Girl*. New Delhi: Penguin, 2013.

Sankovitch, Nina. *Oleander Girl*: Coming of Age.

www.huffingtonpost.com/nina-sankovitch/oleander-girll-coming-of-a_b_3108396.html

From Submission to Assertion: The Politics of Resistance in Chitra Divakaruni's "The Word Love" and "Clothes"

SUMITA PURI
Dyal Singh Evening College, University of Delhi

> There are many strong voices; there are many kinds of strong voices. Surely there should be room for all. Does it make sense to silence women in the name of woman? We can't afford this silencing, or this fear. (Margaret Atwood)

Introducing Chitra Banerjee Divakaruni as a writer of the Indian Diaspora presently settled in America would only serve as a cursory sketch of the creator whose literary oeuvre includes diverse genres of fantasy, poetry, fiction that have received many accolades. Her renowned works include *The Mistress of Spices, The Palace of Illusions: A Novel, Sister of My Heart*. *The Mistress of Spices* was also made into a film by Gurinder Chadha starring Aishwarya Rai and Dylan McDermott. Chitra Banerjee Divakaruni's collection of short stories *Arranged Marriage* has won the American Book Award in 1995 along with the PEN Josephine Miles Award and the Bay Area Book Reviewers Award for Fiction. *Arranged Marriage* raises serious questions of identity, diasporic dilemma and cultural transformation and is a fine reflection upon the predicament of women facing the challenges of assimilation in the new worlds and leaving the old ones behind. Her stories depict the silencing of women, their conscious struggle to get rid of this logocentric patriarchal discourse that makes them subordinate to men and liberate them to change the existing social order.

The present paper discusses the politics of resistance empowering women from submission to assertion in the two stories "The Word Love" and "Clothes." The narratives are Chitra Banerjee Divakaruni's endeavour to portray the dual dilemma of women who not only cross national boundaries and enter into the diasporic problematics of identity crisis, cultural disparity and the 'imaginary homelands' left behind, as Salman Rushdie would put it, but also resist and challenge their ascribed gendered space. Unlike many literary heroines who meet a tragic end, the writer locates a unique female experience, by deconstructing the stereotyped image of woman—as the angel or the monster, the 'Sati-Savitri' or 'Kali' to unshackle her and give her the basic right—the human right. In the 'Introduction' to *A Vindication of the Rights of Women,* Mary Wollstonecraft writes, "the first object of laudable ambition is to obtain a character as a human being, regardless of the distinction of sex, and that secondary views should be brought to this simple touchstone."[1]

"The Word Love" explores and unfolds the varied dimensions and definitions of the word 'love.' The short narrative and the word 'love' become a girl's journey from learning the traditional value system, to traversing and unlearning the accepted norms and conclusively, reaching the goal of self-discovery. The author begins her story by contrasting two worlds—one of the mother, who has lived an orthodox, conservative, confined role of a woman in a patriarchal hegemonic set-up; one who has "seen her husband's face for the first time at her wedding"[2]; who lived the life of a widow when the protagonist had just turned two and could neither dare nor imagine to step out of the conformity. The other world is of the daughter, brought up in the established Indian value system, but becomes 'The Lady of Shallot' and steps out of her 'four grey walls and four grey towers' and chooses her Sir Lancelot, an American named Richard, with whom she falls in love, 'moves in' and makes love eventually. The protagonist's love for her mother as well as for the boy-friend, at times, becomes 'protective' and at other times becomes suffocating, making her apprehend the dangers of transcending the said norms of the society. The mother obviously disapproves, is scandalized and breaks the umbilical cord, once and for all.

'Love' becomes an intense emotion—that makes life beautiful on the one hand, being wooed by the hero with 'violets' outside her Shakespeare class, the long drive followed by "watching the sunset spreading red over the Bay" or when she took her "hands in his warm strong ones." Love, unwillingly, saddens her heart, for having defied the role of a traditional daughter by hiding her illicit sexual bond with Richard from her mother.

Memories of her mother interfere and prevent her from loving her partner fully. Of course, there are good memories of her mother taking care of her, "the warm sleepy sun as you sat on the bank eating curried potatoes wrapped in hot *puris*. And further back, her teaching you to write, the soft curve of her hand over yours, helping you hold the chalk, the smell of her newly washed hair curling about our face." (37) But the mind predominantly recollects the sad episodes which she has to deliberately push out of her reminiscence. For instance, when she had disobeyed her mother by watching a popular Hindi movie with her friends and her mother had packed her suitcase full of clothes and thrown her out of the house with a note saying, "Better no daughter than a disobedient one." (37) There is another tale her mother used to narrate to her, of a defiant 'spoiled' motherless daughter brought up by the father who was warned by the villagers that "an unmarried girl is like a firebrand in a field of ripe grain." (38) The father did find her a match, but before the day of the wedding, her body was discovered in the lake, perhaps pregnant, seen once or twice with a man. The overpowering recollections are cautionary enough not to let her love Richard as well filling her with a sense of disgrace and guilt "and suddenly his arm feels terribly heavy. You are suffocating beneath its weight, its muscular, hairy, maleness." In one way, love liberates her soul and identity, lending her a sense of fullness, the transience from girlhood into womanhood. Yet, ironically, it is this 'love' only that makes her cognize that she is inevitably being moulded into the conformist role of the woman—where Richard becomes the patriarchal dominant, while she becomes the passive dominated recipient of his love.

Chitra Banerjee dexterously plays with words and their impact. After all, as Margaret Atwood writes in her poem "Spelling," "a word after a word after a word is power."[3] The story begins with the protagonist practising 'words' in front of the bathroom mirror every day, reluctant to confess to her mother that she has been living with a man outside matrimony. It is 'words' that 'melt' and fail to express the love that she feels for her boyfriend Richard. Gradually 'words' make her realize how Richard turns into a patriarchal figure, with an unhappy childhood and finally separated from his divorced parents and is unable to understand the mother-daughter bond. His 'words' are "biting off the ends of words and spitting them out" to hurt her and to show how jealous he is of the love, she has for her mother. It is the mother's words that reverberate in the background reminding her of the 'Mistake' that she has committed, of the 'mess' she has put herself into by falling in 'love' and that "deep down, that words solve nothing." 'Words' don't get right when the mother calls to inform that her cousin Leela is marrying a good Brahmin boy and the protagonist is unsuccessful in either confessing or being apologetic or pleading forgiveness for being the Maggie Tulliver of the family.

> *But now of course need you not come.* Her voice had been a spear of ice. Did you cry out, *Don't be angry, Mother, please?* Did you beg forgiveness? Did you whisper (again that word) *love*? You do know this: you kept talking, even after the phone went dead. (38-39)

'Mother.' The word haunts for days to come. Words are poured in the form of a letter to Aunt Arati, since the phone calls are unanswered and the number has changed. 'Words' are used to plead guilty and apologize but efforts fail, bringing no reply. A registered letter is sent which comes back, "Not accepted. Return to sender." "A word after a word after a word is power." So 'words' eventually bring the power of assertion, the power to assert one's being, the power to love oneself.

Love forms and breaks ties eventually. Familial ties and love are incomprehensible to Richard, who has lived away from his family since childhood and calls his mother only on Mother's Day. For Richard, love exists only in the patriarchal sexual bond that exists between a man and a woman which is not even permanent and hence, when the bond between the mother-daughter breaks, it affects their relationship as well. The love for the man which had led to the cutting of the umbilical cord also changes as she notices Richard flirting and receiving more late night calls from other girlfriends. Love teaches new lessons and new meanings to the protagonist. 'Love' that had so far fettered her in customary and compliant chains leaves her with an option—like the Lady of Shallot, to end her life, to take the sleeping pills and leave a note—making both Richard and the mother regretful, "Will he press repentant kisses on your pale palm? Will she fly across the ocean to wash your stiff eyelids with her tears?" (42) However, the protagonist chooses otherwise—breaking free from the clutches of traditions and heteronormative relations, she decides to move out—out of the boyfriend's apartment, out of the socially expected role of a daughter and a woman, to unfetter the chains of the word 'love' and to find love—love for the self. The conflicting emotions that love brings result in the discovering of a new found love and the final stage of self-discovery, through the power of 'the word love.' Language is the primal mode of power and expression, as explained by Barbara Blakely: "Language ultimately creates significance in a world which exists before and around us, yet is not ours until I is articulated. Through these operations of the body (touch, gesture, posture), of the eye (image and reflection), and speech, human existence is constituted and given meaning."[4]

The heroine does not choose to die but to live a new life. She picks a few clothes, a favourite book, some music but leaves 'the hanging,' the good luck talisman gifted to her by her mother while leaving India, for she will not require it in the new life that she is going to lead for herself. "And a word comes to you out of the opening sky. The word *love.* You see that you had never understood it before. It is like rain, and when you lift your face to it, like rain it washes away inessentials, leaving you hollow, clean, ready to begin." (42)

"Clothes" takes us into a patriarchal heterosexual order where women are treated as 'goods' or 'commodities' traded and exchanged—where one man buys and another man pays for the transaction of marriage to take place. So, it is a transaction of money and phallic power between two men and never between women. Women are objects of male desire that pass from one man to another. So, women as commodities have two things: utilitarian value and reproductive value. In this context, the noted French feminist theorist Luce Irigaray writes in her essay "When the Goods get Together": "The trade that organizes patriarchal societies takes place exclusively among men. Women, Signs, goods, currency, all pass from one man to another or—so it is said—suffer the penalty of relapsing into the incestuous and exclusively endogamous ties that would paralyze all commerce. The work force, products, even those of mother-earth, would thus be the object of transactions among men only."[5]

The narrative picks 'clothes' as a metaphor for the commodification of women, for enwrapping them in traditions and rituals, for enabling them to adapt to cultural variance and their final empowerment. The conservative 'sari' to 'a blouse and a skirt' marks the emancipatory passage of the protagonist Sumita from convention to modernity. The story begins with an acceptance of heteronormativity, of marriage and sex between man and woman as the social norm. The young bride-to-be is teased by her female friends Deepali and Radha who bathe and adorn her to prepare her for the 'bride-viewing' ceremony, a custom to be performed before an 'arranged marriage' has to take place. Sumita is fortunate, for if the groom and his parents like her, "if I'm lucky enough to be chosen," (14) she will cross the seven seas and leave the homeland behind to lead a new life. The ceremony is to be enhanced by the traditional marker—the sari, for "a sari could change one's life." (15) The parents debate, at length, and choose a Kanjeepuram, with *zari* work, to beautify the prospective bride and to prepare her to enter the transaction—the exchange of goods in patriarchy.

Since women cannot escape patriarchy, they do not occupy the subject position—neither in language nor in the household. As tokens of exchange within this masculine economy, Sumita does not even cry, lest she is labelled an ungrateful daughter by her parents, even though she understands the politics of gender inequity. Patriarchy demands this transaction of money and women as 'goods' as tutored by the mother, "Father had worked so hard to find this match for me. Besides, wasn't it every woman's destiny, as Mother was always telling me, to leave the known for the unknown? She had done it, and her mother before her. *A married woman belongs to her husband, her in-laws.*" (14) The word 'belongs' sums it up all. This objectification of women, constructed as the man's 'Other' has been argued by Simone de Beauvoir in *The Second Sex* and by Helene Cixous, that in all binary oppositions in patriarchal ideology, Activity/ Passivity, Father/Mother, Head/Emotions, Intelligible/ Sensitive, the underlying opposition is of Man/Woman.[6]

In this socio-cultural order, Sumita wears the special sari, with real gold *zari*, "its body was a pale pink, like the dawn sky over the women's lake. The color of transition." (15) The piece of cloth becomes symbolic not only of the transition to be in the life of the woman but also carries customary significance, as it would dazzle Somesh and his parents and 'choose' her.

Patriarchy has been a mode of sexual politics and domination making women subservient to men. Kate Millett reveals that 'sexual politics' is "the process whereby the ruling sex seeks to maintain and extend its power over the subordinate sex."[7] As Mrs. Sumita Sen reaches United States of America, she oscillates between performing her 'wifely duty' of gratifying her husband's sexual needs and his demand to learn to blend in the new culture. The 'patient' husband gives time to the new bride to open up, sexually and culturally, and the wife succumbs to his wishes. Submission is further pronounced as the 'thick Kanjeepuram silks in solid purples and golden yellows' give way to western outfits Somesh had bought for her and she is made to model each one for him in the bedroom. Sumita tries to fit in, in new clothes, in a new role and in a new culture. Like the roller coaster ride in the amusement park *Great America,* letters printed on her T-shirt, Sumita's life takes a sweeping turn. The change in attire perplexes her, wavering between the clichéd role of the 'bahu' who "must cover my head with the edge of the Japan nylon sari . . . serve tea to the old women that come to visit Mother Sen, where like a good Indian wife I must never address my husband by his name" and the new emerging identity which is:

> caught in a world where everything is frozen in place, like a scene in a glass paper-weight. It is a world so small that if I were to stretch out my arms, I would touch its cold unyielding edges. I stand inside this glass world, watching helplessly as America rushes by, wanting to scream. Then I'm ashamed. Mita, I tell myself, you're growing westernized. Back home you'd never have felt this way. (18)

Clothes not only give the power of expression but also the power of assertion to the protagonist. Somesh buys 'a cream blouse with a long brown skirt' for Sumita and lays down his next demand—for her to get a degree in teaching and work, as the Indian store that he runs with his partner has not been doing well financially. Sumita, however, furtively desires to work in the store. She plans to wear the western attire and 'charm' the customers with her smile as she would stand behind the cash counter. Her confidence is boosted with a desire to make the business successful and gain financial security to run two households—one where she would live with Somesh and the other where her in-laws would stay. As Sumita tries newer 'clothes,' 'jeans,' 'skirts,' and 'nighties,' the transformation becomes palpable. If words made the protagonist of 'The Word Love' potent, clothes give confidence and courage to Sumita.

The deconstruction of the stereotyped image and the reconstruction of the new identity become finally evident as Sumita's life takes a tragic turn. In order to compensate for the financial loss, Somesh is made to do the 'graveyard shift' as the store is open twenty four hours. The store is looted and Somesh is murdered leaving Sumita back in the traditional white sari, performing the ritualistic 'purification bath,' rubbing the red mark off her forehead and breaking her multicolored glass bangles. Draping the sari now becomes a cumbersome ordeal, literally and metaphorically. She remarks:

> The sari, a thick voile, that will bunch around the waist when worn, is borrowed. White. Widow's color, color of endings. I try to tuck the petticoat, but my fingers are numb, disobedient. It spills through them and there are waves and waves of white around my feet. I kick out in sudden rage, but the sari is too soft, it gives too easily. I grab up an edge, clamp down with my teeth and pull, feeling a fierce, bitter satisfaction when I hear it rip. (37)

The story begins with a traditional sari which the protagonist yearns and longs to clothe herself in. The Indian dress with colours of blue and red marks her rooted in convention when she had boarded the flight to America. The story also ends with a traditional sari—this time white, the widow's color which Sumita decides resolutely not to wear. In the white sari, Sumita reminisces the past, bathing freely in the lake with her friends, attempting to move away from them and trying to curl the body inward. She recollects the memory of swimming and "the desperate flailing of arms and legs as I fought my way upward; the press of the water on me, heavy as terror; the wild animal trapped inside my chest, clawing at my lungs." (22) The recollection lends the protagonist the power to draw strength from within, to assert her choices and clothe herself in a new identity. Not wearing this white sari is the final transition from submission to assertion, the politics of resistance and defiance and the final empowerment of the self:

> I straighten my shoulders and stand taller, take a deep breath. Air fills me—the same air that travelled through Somesh's lungs a while ago. The thought is like an unexpected, intimate gift. I tilt my chin, readying myself for the arguments of the coming weeks, the remonstrations. In the mirror a woman holds my gaze, her eyes apprehensive yet steady. She wears a blouse and skirt the colour of almonds. (22)

Sumita resolves to run the store and face the repercussions of defying the social norms—by not wearing the white sari and not subscribing to the conventional role of a widow. In *The Feminine Mystique*, Betty Friedan emphasizes that "women are people in the fullest sense of the word, who must be free to move in society with all the privileges and opportunities and responsibilities that are their human right."[8]

The two short stories portray the transformation of women from a stage of 'internalization of dominant tradition,' to 'a stage of protest' and finally to a stage of 'becoming a woman' to borrow terms from Elaine Showalter and Simone de Beauvoir respectively. This new-found self that denies tradition and even heteronormativity, as seen in the two stories, enables women to express themselves freely, in language, gender roles and sexuality.

In the words of Bell Hooks: "We will never know how many millions of women stay in relationships with dominating sexist males simply because they cannot imagine a life where they can be happy without men, whether they are satisfied sexually and emotionally with the men in their life or not. If any female feels she needs anything beyond herself to legitimate and validate existence, she is already giving away her power to be self-defining, her agency."[9]

Thus, Chitra Banerjee Divakaruni's feminist agenda becomes clear—to investigate modes of dominance—of gender and nationality and transgress them thereafter. She belongs to the race of contemporary women writers who utilize their writing as a tool to express their long-suppressed anger and protest against oppressive power structures and to write stories where women seek their individuality and identity. This transgression becomes the key concern and the writer offers the readers a non-conformist and deviant world through the stories of *Arranged Marriage*. By rewriting stories from a feminist angle, the politics of resistance is manifested enabling women to rise out of their slumber. To conclude, one is tempted to quote Kaarina Kailo: "By rewriting the very stories that controlled us in so many ways, we can finally have our cake and eat it too. We can kiss ourselves awake from the hundreds of years of fruitless waiting, the miracles that don't happen, the rescuers that more often leave women in the lurch. Stories have the power to reawaken our senses, in all the senses of the word. Stories are . . . our gynocentric wonderlands. They promise hope and healing if we take the time to reconsider the values we transmit through them . . . if we take the time to UN-think."[10]

NOTES

1. Mary Wollstonecraft, 'Introduction,' *A Vindication of the Rights of Women* (London: Walter Scott, 1792), p. xxxiv.

2. Chitra Banerjee Divakaruni, "The Word Love," *Arranged Marriage* (New York: Anchor Books, 1995), p. 35.
3. Margaret Atwood, "Spelling," *Neruda, Walcott and Atwood: Poets of the Americas,* ed. Ajanta Dutt (New Delhi: Worldview, 2002), p. 265.
4. Barbara Blakely, "The Pronunciation of Flesh: A Feminist Reading of Margaret Atwood's Poetry," *Neruda, Walcott and Atwood: Poets of the Americas*, ed. Ajanta Dutt, p. 321.
5. Luce Irigaray, "When the Goods Get Together," *Theoryisms: An Introduction*, ed. Bodhisattva Chattopadhyay (Delhi: Worldview, 2015), p. 119.
6. For details, refer to Toril Moi, *Sexual/Textual Politics: Feminist Literary Theory* (London and New York: Routledge, 1985).
7. Qtd. Toril Moi, p. 26.
8. Qtd. Sandra Burt, Loraine Code, Lindsay Dorney, ed., *Changing Patterns: Women in Canada* (Toronto: The Canadian Publishers, 1993), p. 37.
9. Bell Hooks, https://elisabethlmurray.wordpress.com/tag/bell-hooks
10. Kaarina Kailo, "Refusing to Hold Our Tongues: Women's Folklore, Women's Orality as Self-Recovery, "*Room of One's Own: A Space for Women's Writing*, 17:1 (March 1994), p. 92.

Spaces and Passages: Divakaruni's 'Doors'

MADHURI CHAWLA
Dyal Singh Evening College, University of Delhi

Chitra Banerjee Divakaruni is a potent voice of Indian origin who has influenced the realm of Diasporic literature by expressing the myriad colours of immigrant experiences and has secured a credible place in the genre of South Asian Diasporic Literature. Both her works of fiction as well as her poetry affirm that Diaspora is not merely scattering or dispersion but a prototype of consciousness that encompasses various conflicting characteristics. Divakaruni belongs to the first generation of Indian immigrants in the United States who has spent a part of her life in India and has carried the baggage of her native land offshore. Through her works, she captures the experiences of the Indian immigrants with all its colours. Having keenly observed both the postcolonial society of India as well as the challenges of Diaspora abroad, she has very authentically portrayed the fear of adjustment, struggles and sufferings of her characters.

Divakaruni's initiative and her experience as a co-founder and as a former President of 'Maitri,' a helpline founded in 1991 to deal with domestic abuse of South Asian women, discrimination and cruelty suffered by these women, finds expression in her very first collection of short stories *Arranged Marriage*.[1] This collection of eleven short stories portrays vivid pictures of women caught between two worlds, their dejection, and disillusionment and struggle to adapt to such conditions, evaluates their attitude and approach towards life and abandonment or preservation of their cultural values. She very skilfully narrates the stories of Indian women immigrants caught in a perpetual socio-psychological conflict.

Rudyard Kipling in *The Ballad of East and West* says: "East is East, and West is West; and never the twain shall meet." Kipling's perception was coloured by the reality of the Empire's domination over the eastern world and he had perhaps not envisaged the age of globalization with transnational movement of people and large number of second and third generation of settlers no longer confined to subordinate positions and manual labour. In the brave new world, East and West have indeed met due to migrations that have resulted in cultural fusion, sharing of spaces, etc. and have created diverse Diaspora populations. This Diaspora populace is however engaged in complex interpersonal and intercultural relationships with both their society of origin and that of their adopted homeland.

This Diaspora with different cultural beliefs, values, attitudes, customs, and material aspects, nevertheless does encounter difficulties, breakdowns, misunderstandings, conflicts and confrontations. People in Diaspora are caught between the two worlds, which negates their belonging to either the native land or their country of adoption. The effort to keep hold of the values of the homeland in the new atmosphere of the adopted land, often leads to mental conflict, dilemma, and unanswered questions, which ultimately leads to identity crisis. Displacement or dislocation creates a position of 'live in between' or 'living on the border' as discussed by Bhabha in his *The Location of Culture*.[2] Their powerful and poignant experiences from their original culture remain with them which does not allow total amalgamation in their adopted homeland; and then they can't really go back and be quite at home in their original homeland either. (Divakaruni Profile by Arthur J. Pais). In Salman Rushdie's words:

> Exiles or immigrants or expatriates are haunted by some sense of loss, some urge to reclaim, to look back, even at the risk of being mutated in the pillars of salt. But if we look back, we must also do in the knowledge—that our physical alienation from India inevitably means that we will not be capable of reclaiming precisely the thing that was lost: that we will, in short, create fictions, not actual cities or villages, but invisible ones, imaginary homelands, Indias of the mind.[3]

The word Diaspora, though initially used to refer to the dispersal of Jews in terms of exile (galut) from Babylonia who longed for their return to the homeland, today signifies any community of a nation or region living outside its own country and sharing some common bonds that give them an ethnic identity and bonding. For the first generation it means a strong bond with the country of origin. The second generation onwards the bonds begin to erode with the country of origin and are replaced by those with the adopted country. Cultural differences with the adopted country remain, but become wider from the homeland.

Because of its inability to completely integrate into the society of its adopted land and its clinging to its cultural and religious tradition, the nature of this *diasporic self* is fragmented. The fragmented self or the conflict of the displaced populace, the rupture of their binary self is vividly expressed by almost all Diasporic writers.

In recent years, a new generation of South Asian women writers has particularly begun to make their unique mark upon the world of Diasporic literature. Their works abound with the Diasporic consciousness of isolation, mental trauma, dispersion, quest for identity, unresolved dilemmas, conflicts, and complexities.

The present paper delves into the conflict faced by Preeti, the protagonist of the story 'Doors' in the collection of short stories, *Arranged Marriage* by Chitra Banerjee Divakaruni. 'Doors,' perhaps most poignantly, conveys the conflict faced by the Diaspora caught between two opposing worlds—the Eastern and the Western, and expresses the destructive influences of being from one culture and living in another. Preeti, an Indian girl in the United States since the age of twelve, is warned against marrying Deepak, who is "straight out of India" (101) where "men have a set of prehistoric values" (101) according to Preeti's mother. She knows that marriage, in South Asia, is a relationship between families wherein the duty to the family outweighs individual desires. Marriage in South Asia is seen as an essential institution and defines a woman's social status. This cultural and social pressure applies to first generation immigrants as well as to second or third generation Indian-American women. For several immigrant Indian women, regardless of class, arranged introductions are the primary means through which men and women meet and marry. The observance of Indian family values and cultural norms is also often expressed through marriage. Guided by the same principles, Preeti's mother too had been introducing her to several of her friend's sons for the purpose, as she wishes her daughter to marry a 'nice Indian boy.'

Preeti insists that Deepak, the boy she wishes to marry, is different and that they will be fine. The mother who had migrated to US after her marriage when Preeti was twelve years old is well aware that Indian men expect their women to be "obedient and adjusting and forgiving" (101). She knows that though conditioned by the Indian upbringing, Preeti has moved beyond the traditional constraints. She is apprehensive right from the beginning about the success of the marriage. Preeti brushes aside her mother's caution believing that she understands her Indian roots well enough and that Deepak too is unlike other men. The couple lives in perfect harmony for a few years. Both adjust to each other's needs and are accommodating. Deepak openly asserts that he is proud of Preeti's independent spirit and her decision-making power and disapproves of his friend's suggestion that it is preferable to marry a home-bred girl, for according to popular notion, women brought up in USA are bossy and dominating and are referred to as "ABCD," i.e., 'American Born Confused Desi.' To this Deepak retorts "Women aren't dolls or slaves" (102) and that he strongly believes in a marriage based on mutual respect. He even gives Preeti a free hand in decorating the house because he thinks the house is her domain and she has been considerate and understanding in moving to a house closer to his place of work while she herself commutes a longer distance. At the party they host for their friends in the new home Preeti like the traditional Indian wife makes 'Gulab-Jamuns' while Deepak 'refills her plate' for her. The fears of the family and friends are allayed and Preeti and Deepak are seen as a 'perfectly matched couple.'

The only disagreement between the two is apparently an unimportant one about the 'doors.' "Deepak liked to leave them open, and Preeti liked them closed" (104). She is used to closing doors behind her, in her study, in her bedroom, in the bathroom symbolizing perhaps her 'stubborn and close mouthed' nature as her friend Cathy understands her. Deepak mocks at her saying there isn't anyone else in the house, 'the pots and the pans' are not going to peep in. Preeti defends herself, "I guess I'm just a private person. It's not like I'm shutting you out. I've just always done it this way. Maybe it has something to do with being an only child." (104) Deepak has grown up in a more open and doorless environment: doors were interpreted more as a formality or even a hostility in India. So though Deepak is bothered by her closing of doors but the initial ecstasy of love helps him overlook and tide over the irritant.

Cultural differences come to the fore in a more pronounced way with the arrival of Deepak's friend Raj and are highlighted through the lens of relational interactions and their complexity. Raj's arrival and his extended stay leads to situations which give an excellent perspective of life torn by conflict between two cultures.

The mother's fears, expressed in the first sentence of the story, about there being signs of trouble reverberate in our mind as Deepak ecstatically announces the arrival of his close childhood friend Raj the very next day. An aghast Preeti for the first time actually finds herself torn between traditional ethos and modern culture as she tries to hide her distress. Now begins Preeti's struggle to adjust to the demands of the two conflicting value systems, between the selflessness required of women in India and the freedom they get in their adopted land. Though completely distraught, yet conditioned by her Indian upbringing she perceives that 'it's a cultural thing' and her mind immediately "raced over the list of things to be done—the guest bedroom dusted, the sheets washed, a special welcome dinner cooked (that would require a trip to the grocery and the Indian store), perhaps some flowers." (104)

She tries to be the perfect host, struggles to live up to the expectations of her husband and the Indian philosophy of 'atithi devo bhava,' and despite the fact that her advisor was pressurizing her to turn in the second chapter of her dissertation, which wasn't going well, she does not voice her disapproval at being totally kept in the dark regarding the invitation to Raj and his extended stay. Though she objects to Raj's sleeping in the living room, she tries to overlook Raj's belching and loud snoring but her western sensibility is shocked by such uncouth behaviour. She struggles to balance the pulls and pressures of the two worlds and tries to assure herself that she will survive the year and a half.

However once the 'doors' of the house and the country open to Raj, he begins to encroach in her space. The guest assumes unlimited access to most spaces and the level of access and informality make Preeti uncomfortable. The crisis escalates when, with total disregard to the value of privacy and closed doors, Deepak totally neglects his wife, takes leave from work to take Raj around, enjoys Indian snacks and movies with his friend.

There is total bonhomie between the two friends as Deepak relapses into the patriarchal Indian male, spending minimal time with his wife. The time that Deepak shares with his friend, reaffirms his shared values and isolates Preeti. There are hints of homo-eroticism as Preeti finds Raj and Deepak sitting together on the couch watching a movie, and as Deepak casually lets an arm fall over Raj's shoulder as he shifts closer to him making space for Preeti. Though Divakaruni leaves it open, suggesting that it might just be male-bonding, Raj definitely takes away from Preeti's space, spatially and symbolically.

Deepak by and by proves Preeti's mother's warnings true. Her mother had warned Preeti "It'll never work, I tell you, she had declared gloomily, . . . What do you really know about how Indian men think and what they expect from their women? You are making a joke of everything, thinking the world will always let you have your own way. I wish I had trained you better, like my mother did me" (101). Deepak's friends from India too had warned him of the Westernized values of Preeti saying that a love match between an Indian and an American does not work because of the inequitable values. Preeti and Deepak soon learn the truth of the views of the mother and the friends.

In *Communication Ethics: Between Cosmopolitan and Provinciality*, Kathleen Glenister Roberts and Ronald C. Arnett say that the arranged marriage structure is embedded in an ideology of familial obligation. It is an alliance between two families rather than a mere union of two individuals.[4] Through the marital discord of Preeti and Deepak the present story brings forth the notions of individualism and collectivism as it defines the Western and Eastern ideology and in this process, the doors become the symbol of their conflicting approaches.

Preeti has grown up in an individualistic society. In such societies according to Hofstede the ties between individuals are loose: everyone is expected to look after himself or herself and his or her immediate family and individualistic societies emphasize "I" consciousness, autonomy, emotional independence, individual initiative, right to privacy, autonomy, pleasure-seeking, financial security, need for specific friendship and Universalism.[5] Preeti's inability to adapt and obsession with privacy is the result of her being a part of the western social ethos since the age of twelve.

Deepak on the other hand carries the baggage of collectivism from his native land where people from birth onwards are integrated into strong, cohesive in-groups, which throughout people's lifetime continue to protect them in exchange for unquestioning loyalty. Collectivistic societies stress "we" consciousness, collective identity, emotional dependence, group solidarity, sharing duties and obligations, need for stable and predetermined friendship, group decision etc.[6] Also as Roberts & Arnett assert: "marriage is an ideal, a duty, and a social responsibility. . . . Interdependence is an important value taught early in life that promotes integration with and emotional investment in the family. Arranged marriage is a central means of maintaining the integrity of the immediate and extended family."[7] Preeti conditioned by the Indian value system of her family realizes the importance of being integrated and therefore does try to adjust even though she confides in Cathy, that Raj is driving her up the wall. Cathy notices Preeti has dark circles, has lost weight, Deepak on the other hand does not seem to notice her discomfort at all. Caught between the two worlds she consoles herself saying that it wouldn't last forever, and that she would be able to swim across. The conflict is rendered very sensitively through the idea of doors which in the story symbolizes the concept of space both in literal and metaphorical terms—the door of mind and of physical space; Doors which can both shut in and shut out. The whole idea of 'I' and 'We' as it exists in the two conflicting ideologies of the East and the West is explored and used to connote the collision of space in terms of gender, class and the concept of family.

Preeti's trials and tribulations and her struggle to maintain the old values and yet carve out an identity of her own in the new world is rendered most vividly. With the quest for happiness and harmony at the heart of her struggle Preeti seeks to synthesize traditions with the modern values even though she knows how difficult it is to bring in new ideas in the patriarchal set up that Deepak belongs to. She feels that she needs to make more effort to communicate with Deepak and decides to make his favourite dish and later asks him to come to the room early. Deepak's short stint in US as a grownup immigrant has not prepared him to understand her needs. He is not able to understand the meaning of privacy that Preeti desires in their marriage as he has never seen any 'door' being shut in a traditional Indian family. He seems totally oblivious of her drifting away, of her alienation and even supports Raj when Preeti voices that she can't tolerate him any longer.

Doors if they open are passageways. Preeti does try to open the door metaphorically even though she was literally closing the doors all the time. Deepak has grown up in the Indian culture known for its inclusiveness and hence for him the doors are redundant. He had earlier accepted the closing of doors but on Raj's arrival he too is caught between the two worlds. He did seem to have assimilated the values of the West but now he slips back to his roots paradoxically closing the doors to an understanding of Preeti's cultural assimilation. It is also accompanied by a desire to prove to his friend that he has not become an 'amreekan.' He instantly becomes the chauvinist. Preeti discerns a coldness in his eyes, the adamant dominating patriarch immediately surfaces . . . and it is Preeti who puts on her smile to smoothen the relationship. Deepak seems to belong to a different world altogether. Preeti is neither a part of that world nor can she, despite her Indian upbringing, appreciate it much. Deepak is no longer the man she had married. Brought up in an unfettered environment, trained to pursue and achieve her choice in the world Preeti suddenly finds herself losing control over her life, her relationship and even her grades. Her teacher says her work lacks originality now, while Raj comes back flashing his ace in Maths. This perhaps is the last straw and her perseverance gives in. It seems to her as if her work, her grades, her identity have been filched away by Raj. Try as she does she can no longer play the accommodating host and the submissive wife. She packs up her bags and decides to stay with Cathy for a while. Deepak's reaction is not surprising as he says, "You can't go. What will people say? You are my wife. You belong in my house." (110) His reaction reeks of feudalism and patriarchy. It is 'my house,' and the public opinion is what matters and is the driving force behind his response and one discerns no trace of concern for Preeti.

Torn between old and new world values Preeti questions the nature of her life, and her role as a wife and a professional, re-thinks about her own life as a woman, and finally decides to forge ahead. "I won't let him ruin my life, she said. For a moment it wasn't clear to her if it was Raj or Deepak." (108) But the reader knows it is not Raj's invasion but Deepak's inability to understand her that leads to conflict. Preeti chooses her social and economic growth and decides to leave her futile relationship. Though she craves for the love of her husband as, "A part of her cried out to go to him" (110) yet there is a finality "when the door finally clicked shut, she did not know whether it was in the guest room or deep inside her own being" (111). But a closure there is.

The title of the story aptly conveys how doors, a simple part of our everyday life, come to represent the unconscious values that we associate with ostensibly insignificant actions. In a marriage across countries when values change, adaption is necessary. Preeti and Deepak fail to recognize this fact of life and close their doors. Their perspective is different but neither can be said to be wrong. While for Deepak Doors symbolize barriers and mistrust, Frost's "good fences make good neighbours," seems to be Preeti's mantra in life. A superficial distinction initially that becomes the catalyst for discord. A little more consideration of each other's values would have ensured better appreciation, regard and admiration.

Thus, we see that in the story, Chitra Banerjee Divakaruni brilliantly depicts the cultural dialect of immigrant experience. She accurately fuses eastern values with western ethos as she depicts Preeti struggling in her bicultural life, grappling with two identities, her psychological claustrophobia trapped as she is in a dilemma of tensions between Western unfettered nurture and the traditional constraints surrounding an Indian wife, between a feminist's desire to be assertive and the patriarchal demand for submission.

NOTES

1. Chitra Banerjee Divakaruni, *Arranged Marriage* (New York: Anchor, 1995).
2. Homi K. Bhabha, *Location of Culture* (New York: Routledge Classics, 2004).
3. Qtd. Satendra Nandan, "The Diasporic Consciousness," *Interrogating Post-Colonialism: Theory, Text and Context,* ed. Harish Trivedi and Meenakshi Mukherjee (Shimla: IIAS, 1996), p. 52.
4. Kathleen Glenister Roberts & Ronald C. Arnett, ed., *Communication Ethics: Between Cosmopolitanism and Provinciality* (New York: Lang, 2008), p. 35.
5. G. Hofstede, *Culture's consequences: International differences in work-related values* (CA: Sage, 1980), p. 84.
6. Kumari, Archana. "The Matrix of Diasporic Consciousness in Chitra Banerjee Divakaruni's *Arranged Marriage*." *International Journal on Studies in English Language and Literature*, Vol. 2, No. 11, November 2014, pp. 59-64.

Gendered Violence in Chitra Divakaruni's *Arranged Marriage*

BRATI BISWAS
Dyal Singh Evening College, University of Delhi

The paper is an attempt to locate the nuances of gendered violence as it manifests in the stories collected in the volume *Arranged Marriage*. Divakaruni writes of South Asian women located in their homeland and also those who are part of the Asian Diaspora settled in the United States of America. This population is both rooted to their Asian cultural base and also negotiating a space for themselves with in the American cultural space. Divakaruni herself straddles both these worlds and is well aware of the complex nuances of such transactions. Her narratives locate women at various junctures of their lives negotiating a tenuous space for themselves within the locale of patriarchy. The stories look at women's struggle to create a sense of independent self and the resistance they face in their endeavours. The women in their efforts to speak up for themselves or their sisters face different forms of violence.

Violence is endemic to their life and sometimes they get so accustomed to it that they are at a loss to resist it or rebel against it. Part of the problem lies in the fact that women are socialized to accept violence as a legitimate tool of censure. Violence toward women has a legitimate space within patriarchy. In India people quote Manu to support use of violence against women to keep them in control. Patriarchy treats women as dispensable commodities which exist in the market to gratify its demand for sexual pleasure or it is the vessel that delivers the all-important male heir. The failure to do so or a reluctance to conform to the dictates of patriarchy expose them to different methods of coercion that are both physical and mental. Women have no separate space within the limits of its domain.

In the story 'Bats,' the lower middle class woman is imprisoned within an abusive marriage where she suffers physical battering almost every night. The violence and its debilitating impact on her are witnessed by her young daughter. The child is both a witness and a fellow sufferer. She observes her mother crying every night and understands her need to be comforted. However, she is unable to extend that solace to her. The narrative opens with the daughter's account of her mother weeping and her attempts to understand it.

> That year Mother cried a lot, nights. Or maybe she had always cried, and that was the first year I was old enough to notice. I would wake up in the hot Calcutta dark and the sound of her weeping would be all around me, pressing in, wave upon wave, until I could no longer tell where it was coming from. The first few times it happened, I would sit up in the narrow child's bed that she had recently taken to sharing with me and whisper her name. But that would make her pull me close and hold me tight against her shaking body, where the damp smell of talcum powder and sari starch would choke me.[1]

If the mother is portrayed as a victim the child is doubly oppressed due to her gender and age. She feels suffocated and smothered within the small cramped space of their city house and the demands of her mother for love, understanding and comfort. The father beats and scares her into silence. The house symbolises the limitations these women face within patriarchy. These impact the interpersonal relations between men and women and among the women too. The daughter does not connect with the mother, she feels betrayed by her adult world. The only person she connects with is the grandfather who has a caring, sharing attitude with the child and treats her as a companion without being gender biased. He teaches her fishing and tells her about the countryside. The fond memories she narrates are of this man, her mother's uncle who gives them shelter when the mother runs away from the city and seeks refuge in the countryside.

On the other side of the spectrum is the father. The girl has no attachment toward her father; she is relieved when the mother runs away from him. The man is himself depicted as a victim of the city; he has a low paying job as a foreman in a printing press and finds it difficult to make both ends meet. The man is frustrated and drinks to alleviate the pain and probably a sense of failure. He comes home drunk and vents his anger on the hapless wife and child every night. There is no break in the pattern of repeated violence and abuse the woman suffers. It is a vicious cycle.

The story explores the potential damage skewered gender dynamics have on inter-personal relations and ultimately the family. The violence-ridden unequal marriage creates a dysfunctional family. The man communicates with the wife and daughter through violence. The earliest memory of the young girl is of being thrown up and down by the father and being scared. She does not share a very warm bond with the mother who remains trapped in her own world of pain and fear to share a happy space with the girl child.

The ideal notion of a father is presented in the figure of the grandfather who is gentle, supportive and protective toward the mother and daughter. The complexities of the man-woman relationship are explored within the matrix of patriarchal assumptions and demands through the image of the woman who runs away from an abusive husband only to return to him. It is not that she has no other option, the uncle had given her unconditional shelter and there was no pressure on her to leave him. The young daughter too does not want to go back to the father. Nevertheless the woman chooses to return to her abusive husband. The woman is like the Bats in the story:

> You would have thought that after the first week the bats would have figured it out and found another place to live. But no. Every morning there were just as many dead bodies. I asked Grandpa-uncle about this. He shook his head and said he didn't understand either. "I guess they just don't realize what's happening. They don't realize that by flying somewhere else they'll be safe. Or maybe they do, but there's something that keeps pulling them back here." (9)

The bats it is hoped will not come back to the mango orchard once they realize it is dangerous to do so. They do not seem to learn from the casualties they suffer due to the poison. They, like the woman, return to a hopeless deadly trap. They are like the moth that is drawn to the taper that burns it. After some time they do seem to figure out the danger and stop coming to the orchard.

The woman tells her uncle that she needs to go back because she misses her husband and other women whisper about her. Her need is both sexual and social. She keeps shifting between conformity and rebellion; the need for social acceptance and the desire for an individual space. Her need cannot be understood by the young daughter who feels betrayed by the mother and the adult world. The complex web of adult emotions is not decipherable by the young girl. Her narration has gaps that suggest not just her inadequacy but her lack of vocabulary to express the violence that pervades her life. This violence is both physical and mental. Her young world is ruptured by both the father and the mother in their respective ways. She epitomizes the loss faced by the marginal in any given power play.

The place of women within patriarchy is always a fraught and contested space. 'The Maid Servant's Story' explores this through the prism of class. The worlds of the upper caste and upper class women are apparently different from those of their less privileged underclass sisters. Manisha, the bright young scholar returns to India for a break after a teaching assignment at the University of California. She is confronted with questions of marriage by her aunt and feels irritated and hemmed in by the need to maintain a conservative facade for the genteel folk. She understands that back home things are in a time warp and the two women in her life would strongly object to her relationship without marriage with the young Bengali professor in the United States of America. Manisha feels she is liberated from the protocols of womanly behaviour deemed fit for young Indian women after her western sojourn and exposure. She nevertheless maintains her silence on her love life and participates in the discussions surrounding her marriage. Thinking about her relationship she realizes that she too was initially burdened with a sense of guilt and shame for having given in to the demands of Bijoy who wanted a relationship with no strings attached. She convinces herself that she too wants to be sexually liberated like the Americanized Bijoy and be free from prudish notions inculcated into her in India. She suppresses her feeling of insult when Bijoy wants her without the promise of marriage. The nagging doubt that you do not treat a woman you respect as a mere body remains in the background of her mind and the text despite the trope of sexual liberation and a woman's control over her body.

Manisha's relationship with her mother is a strained one; there is an invisible wall that distances them. She feels there is a lack of parental warmth in her bond with her mother. The distance between her mother and Manisha makes her rebel in order to get her attention. The reason behind the mother's aloof behaviour remains a mystery to the girl.

> She watched over my life carefully, vigilantly, if from afar. All through my childhood, everything I wanted—everything material, that is—was provided for me, often before I needed to ask. But what *she* thought, what *she* longed for, what made her cry out in her dreams (for I'd heard her, once or twice), I never knew. It was as though she'd built a wall of ice around her, thin and invisible and unbreakable. No matter how often I flung myself against it, I

> was refused entry. Maybe she no longer knew how to let me. Maybe people were right when they said that the death of her husband and baby in a cholera epidemic that had struck Calcutta overnight when I was about five had killed a part of her too. (Why had that explanation always seemed too facile for me?) At any rate, she'd relinquished me to Deepa Mashi who, herself childless, enthusiastically took on the role of second mother. (64)

The aunt narrates a story of two sisters and a maidservant which remind the girl of her long forgotten childhood. The narrative of the maidservant is embedded within the narrative of the successful young upper class girl who can make her choices without being fettered by economic constraints. Her life choices are facilitated by her mother who helps her achieve her dreams. The girl remembers vaguely her father and brother who died when she was young.

The story of the maidservant brings the issue of sexual violence and agency within patriarchy that women of the different classes face daily. The young maid seeks refuge in the rich household of the upper class woman who is expecting her second child. Since the first child is a girl the husband and his aunt hope the second one would be a boy. The preference for a son is seen as a natural desire for a male heir and the woman is shown as a docile wife who humours her husband. The pregnancy makes her feel unwell and not in control of herself and that is why she requests her young sister to come over and stay with her to see her through the pregnancy. The husband and his aunt are not able to fill the need for a soul and helpmate that the sister would probably be. They humour her because they do not want to upset her and harm the baby.

The young sister of the wife feels uncomfortable in the husband's presence. The sexual gaze of the husband is instinctively felt as a hidden threat by the girl who avoids being alone with him. The girl is a visitor to her sister's marital home to help her with her confinement. She is dependant on her brother-in-law and hence vulnerable. The suave upper class man is a sexual predator who camouflages it well and his wife remains unaware of the discomfort her sister feels in his presence.

The young maid instinctively avoids the husband and deliberately dresses in an austere manner to deflect any probable misreading of her as sexually attractive or available. The class she comes from renders her doubly vulnerable to the sexual overtures of men of the upper class who perceive lower class women as easy prey. The fact that she has most probably run away from her home and has no guardian renders her position in the upper class household to be very precarious and solely dependent on the benevolence of the woman who has taken her in.

The husband and his aunt are hostile toward the maid as they perceive her to be of questionable character and morals. The other servants too are wary of her as she is bright and a fast learner. The maid soon becomes indispensible for the wife and gradually a bond of love and trust develops between the two women. The young wife takes the maid under her wing and begins to teach her to read and write. She takes the role of being the maid's benefactress seriously but the rest of the household does not approve of her initiative to educate and groom the maid. The maid reciprocates the wife's love and affection for her and a bond of trust develops between these two women from very disparate backgrounds.

The maid and the wife create a space through their mutual trust which subtly challenges the patriarchal hold of the husband and his aunt on the household and the woman. The woman does not heed her husband's advice and takes the girl in without any references and only on instinct; that in itself is a silent challenge to his authority. The man treats the wife like a fragile piece that needs protection. His concern for her is an extension of him, the mother of his child and not as an independent self. The moment she asserts herself with regard to the maid servant he feels threatened and becomes angry. The moment the woman wants some agency to decide her domestic affairs she faces resistance from both the patriarch and the surrogate patriarch the aunt. For both these figures the woman's prime importance is due to her unborn child, a probable male heir for the family. They pamper her and give in to her wishes in order not to harm the unborn child. She matters not as an individual but as a vessel/body that will deliver the male child. Her importance in the household is not for what she is but for what she gives of herself to the man of the house. Her pregnant body constrains her in giving him sexual pleasure and he feels it legitimate to look for it elsewhere.

The sister witnesses episodes of sexual indiscretion by the husband; he embraces the maid from behind and pretends that it was a mistake as she was wearing the wife's saree, he also attempts to forcibly enter the maid's room at night. He feels the maid would willingly surrender to him because she has nowhere to go. On being rebuffed he threatens to send her back to her mother. The girl had run away from home to escape being sexually exploited by the mother who wanted to push her into prostitution. Her so-called husband is in connivance with her mother to commercially exploit her body. The girl's body is a commodity that each one of her guardians wants to use for their profit. Violence is used to force her to put her body for sale in the market. The only one who appreciates her potential is the young wife who wants to hone her skills. Ironically she too notices her beauty and gives her own saree to her to wear which attracts the gaze of the husband and other men toward her body. Till that moment the girl had successfully deflected people's gaze from her body by dressing unattractively. Her instinct for self preservation makes her choose to stay in the store room, the most unattractive and poorly ventilated room in the house that can be bolted from inside. She hopes to find a safe space within the cloistered seclusion of this room but the penetrating gaze of the patriarch finds her and wants entry. The barter or exchange offered to her by him for not throwing her to the wolves who are waiting outside the boundaries of the house is her body. His argument is simple and flawless; she has to barter her body for money or safety because that is the only currency she has. In that case it is better to be a rich man's mistress, in secret, than be up for sale to many in the open market.

The girl's refusal to bow down to the patriarch is based on her belief that the young wife would stand by her and protect her. The circumstances prove contrary to her expectation as the wife becomes critical and is hospitalized till the delivery and the young sister is not match enough to counter the machinations of the man and his aunt to ouster the maid servant. The maid has to pay the price of saying 'no' to him.

The maid servant's story raises some critical issues regarding gender and violence. The upper class women apparently seem safe within their well provided homes but this turns out to be a false premise. The wife has to go through a very difficult pregnancy in order to give the family a male heir. The space given to her in the marital home is dependent on how well she performs the role of the dutiful wife. Initially the wife conforms to the roles ascribed to her by patriarchy; she is a good wife, mother and a dependable daughter-in-law. She allows the aunt to boss over the house and herself. The fissures appear when the maid comes into the family and the wife begins to assert herself in order to protect her. The maid gives the wife a sense of purpose and agency. The woman treats her like a younger sister and suffers a lot of mental agony and verbal violence on her account from the husband.

The wife is sent to hospital and in the gap the maid is thrown out of the house on the pretext of the security of its inmates. The mother of the maid comes and creates a scene in the house and this opportunity is seized by the husband to chuck her out. He is fully aware of what awaits her outside yet he is remorseless in his vengeance toward the maid. The narrative then moves on to talk about the pampering the wife gets after she delivers a boy, the young sister's marriage is fixed and everybody seems to have conveniently forgotten the maid. The wife's questions about her remain unanswered and she too gradually stops asking about her. It is a coincidence that the paths of the two women cross again. The woman and the children get caught in a traffic jam and the husband orders the driver to take a route that passes through the red light area. She observes the young maid garishly made up soliciting customers on the road. The woman rolls down the car window, calls out to the girl and extends her arm out of the car. The girl spits on her extended palm with a look of hatred. The woman's hand becomes stained with the blood red paan juice which she tries to erase. The husband scolds her but from that day a part of her dies.

Violence perpetrated by patriarchy on these women scars them and mars the psychological growth of those around them. The mothers in both the stories are so traumatized and scarred by the violence that they fail to perceive its impact on their daughters. In 'Bats' the daughter has no connect with the mother, similarly in 'The Maidservant's Story' Manisha is not able to penetrate the wall of ice the mother has built around her. The violence thus creates a ripple effect. It cascades from one generation of women to another and also impacts man-woman relationship. The narratives are also stories of betrayal wherein the men betray the wives and the women as victims are so benumbed by the violence that they are unable to give emotional solace and sustenance to their daughters. The violence thus creates a vicious cycle which is difficult to break.

NOTE

1. Chitra Banerjee Divakaruni, "Bats," *Arranged Marriage* (New York: Anchor Books, 1995).

The Letters and Letter-Writing in Chitra Divakaruni's "Mrs. Dutta Writes a Letter"

E. ANITA
Res. Sch., Mother Teresa Women's Univ., Kodaikanal

Letter-writing is a central device of character construction in "Mrs. Dutta Writes a Letter." It explains the function of letters in the process of female immigrant self-discovery. The process of writing a letter underlies Mrs. Dutta's experiences in her son's family. Actually, the impulse of writing is caused by the fact that Mrs. Dutta receives one letter from her friend in India. Mrs. Roma Basu, the sender, wants to know whether Sagar's mother is happy in America. In the beginning, the answer seems very simple to Mrs. Dutta, but she gradually changes her ideas about happiness. The writing of the letter becomes more difficult than imagined, as it forces the woman to disentangle the confusing new experiences: "Oh, this new country, where all the rules are upside down, it's confusing her" (28). The short story describes the difficult process of writing a real letter that can faithfully render Mrs. Dutta's life abroad. Overwhelmed by new impressions, the character needs a preparatory stage of letter-writing in order to make sense of what goes on around her. Soon after receiving news from Mrs. Basu, Mrs. Dutta writes a first letter that contains her fresh impressions after arrival. The author inserts this letter towards the end of the short story. This strategy is meant to offer a contrast between the character's different dispositions in the beginning and at the end of her stay in America. The initial letter expresses an unambiguously optimistic attitude. Sagar's mother is happy to be with her family. She counts on old women's ability to adjust as a means to get accustomed with the American life-style: "Dear Roma, although I miss you, I know you will be pleased to hear how happy I am in America. There is much here that needs getting used to, but we are no strangers to adjusting, we old women. After all, haven't we been doing it all our lives?" (32). Other sources of happiness are cooking Indian food to the family, getting to know her grandchildren, spending time with Sagar and secretly admiring her daughter-in-law's emancipation. This serene attitude expresses Mrs. Dutta's feelings at the beginning of her stay in America. Gradually, her disposition changes as she encounters American practices that contradict inherited beliefs.

It focuses how letter-writing functions as a means of self-analysis; this aspect is proven by the fact that Mrs. Dutta hesitates to write the final letter. The reason she postpones and reformulates her impressions is because she is confused by her experiences in America. The letter-writing process expresses her doubts about the new values encountered. Consequently, the story contains several "mental letters," i.e. thoughts rendered in the form of imaginary letters. Campbell analyses the role of letters in women's epistolary fiction. She considers that letters that are written, but not sent stand for a process of self-discovery: "Once the letters are begun, the writers seem to be speaking to themselves, and, though the reader is ever-present, the writer becomes immersed in a discovery of herself." (Campbell). The fact that these thoughts are never given the shape of a concrete letter illustrates their self-examination function. Before writing the final letter, Mrs. Dutta talks to herself about life in the new country. She tries to make sense of everything, before communicating a final judgment to Roma Basu. In the first letter of the mind, Mrs. Dutta expresses her nostalgia for home: "Oh, Roma, I miss it all so much, sometimes I feel that someone has reached in and torn out a handful of my chest" (8). Still, the old woman tries to focus on positive aspects. Therefore, the tonality of her next imaginary letter changes as she speaks about the satisfaction of cooking Indian food for her loved ones: At least the family's eating well since I arrived, she writes in her mind, proper Indian food, fruits that puff up the way they should, fish curry in mustard sauce, and real pulao with raisins and cashews and ghee-the way you taught me, Roma, instead of Rice-a-roni" (9). The next event that makes Mrs. Dutta add a new section to her imaginary letters is her successful subversion of her-daughter-in-law's rules. The old woman tries to use the washing machine, but she is too scared by technology and cannot turn on the device. Thus, she washes her clothes by hand and then she secretly dries them on a clothesline in the garden. She does that because she cannot stand keeping the laundry in "the same room where she kept the pictures of her gods. That brought bad luck" (14). This small "victory" makes the old woman feel enthusiastic and gives her the feeling she can adjust to the new realities: In her mind she writes to Mrs. Basu, "I'm fitting so well here, you'd never guess I came only two months back. I've found new ways of doing things, of solving problems creatively. You would be most proud if you saw me" (17).

One of the scenes that best illustrates Mrs. Dutta's different cultural assumptions is her encounter with the American female neighbour. When Mrs. Dutta hangs her clothes, she sees the neighbour across the fence. The Indian woman's impulse is to communicate with her. But her attempts to make contact are impeded by the American's indifference. Interestingly, Mrs. Dutta cannot conceive that the woman does not want to talk to her. She tries to account for the neighbour's silence by invoking a presumable inability to move that keeps her inside the house. At the same time, Mrs. Dutta is aware of certain cultural assumptions that clash with her attempts to initiate conversation: "Perhaps she is not well?" Mrs. Dutta feels sorry for her, alone in her illness in a silent house with only cigarette for solace and she wishes that the etiquette of America had not prevented her from walking over with a word of cheer and a bowl of her fresh-cooked alu dum (23). Later on, she realizes that the neighbour is not ill, but annoyed at Mrs. Dutta's hanging the clothes over the fence. Shyamoli is the one who receives the complaint. This event acts as a trigger of Shyamoli's frustrations. The young woman has the impression that Mrs. Dutta has taken over the authority in the family. She feels excluded and talks to Sagar about her feelings. Mrs. Dutta is outraged by the young woman's sense of revolt. She writes another fragment in her imaginary letter, expressing adherence to a more obedient ideal of femininity: "Women need to be strong, not react to every little thing like this. You and I, Roma we had far worse to cry about, but we shed our tears invisibly. We were good wives and daughters-in-law, good mothers. Dutiful, uncomplaining, never putting ourselves first." (27).

The act of postponing the writing of a final letter is related to the character's hesitation and need to process the phenomena encountered. Another significance of the imaginary confessions is that they enable Mrs. Dutta to select the content of what she chooses to communicate. Letter-writing becomes a channel of meditating upon disturbing aspects, while concealing them from a potential letter-reader: "Women as writers in epistolary fiction open up their consciousness in letters because the form, with its distancing yet mediatory nature, frees the writer to say what she cannot say in the presence of the addressee" (Campbell).

In one of the imaginary letters, Sagar's mother criticizes the excessive TV watching in her son's family: "*Really, Roma*, she writes in her head as she feels her way along the unlighted corridor, *the amount of TV they watch here is scandalous. The children, too, sitting for hours in front of that box . . . and then talking back when I tell them to turn it off*' (28, original emphasis). Mrs. Dutta is divided between loyalty to her family and her own dissatisfaction with their American life-style. Although she wants to share her feelings with Mrs. Basu, Mrs. Dutta cannot openly admit her disappointment. In the beginning of her stay, the woman is reluctant to face her own feelings: "And so, she has been putting off her reply while in her heart family loyalties battle with insidious feelings of—but she turns from them quickly and will not name them even to herself" (5). Torn between these different attitudes, she gradually finds a certain comfort by way of writing letters in her mind. This is why, after criticizing her grandchildren, she realizes there are certain things she cannot write about, but which she has to say in order to feel better: "Of course, she will never put such blasphemy into a real letter. Still, it makes her feel better to say it, if only to herself" (29).

On the other hand, despite her criticism of American ways, the old woman modifies some of her beliefs while staying there. The most important aspect of her change refers to the inherited model of womanhood. Before coming to America, Mrs. Dutta lived on her own, as a widow, enjoying the benefits of solitude. Her experiences in Sagar's house contribute to a further change of her perspective with respect to women's roles. Through Shyamoli, the old woman is faced with a different model of womanhood that impresses her. Although Mrs. Dutta believes that a woman is defined mostly in relation to others (as a mother, daughter-in-law and wife), there are instances when her behaviour illustrates a more individualistic conception of identity. While looking at herself in the mirror, Mrs. Dutta is proud that her hair is more beautiful than "her daughter-in-law's permed curls" (6). Even though she considers this an act of vanity, Sagar's mother cannot help indulging in self-admiration. During Sagar and Shyamoli's fight, Mrs. Dutta decides to ignore the conflict and write her letter.

Finally, Mrs. Dutta realizes she does not belong to her son and his family. I interpret her decision of going back to India as the ultimate gesture of self-assertion. During the couple's argument over the clothes incident, the old woman realizes she feels "alone and unnecessary" in "this land of young people" (33). Ironically, while her decision to come to America is dictated by an Indian norm—a widow's place is with her son's family—her decision to go back to India seems to be motivated by a sense of personal desire. Mrs. Dutta is afraid of the community reaction to her return; once again, she judges the consequences of her acts through the eyes of others. She knows that her relatives will interpret her return as a failure to find her place in Sagar's family. She also thinks of "what she owes to Sagar" (33). While assessing the consequence of her acts through the perspective of others, Mrs. Dutta wonders about what "she owes to herself" (33). This fact proves that her experience in America awakened a latent sense of individuality. Despite the fact that "all the certainties she trusted in collapsed upon themselves like imploded stars" (33), the old woman has come to understand where she truly belongs. Contrary to her initial belief that placed a widow in a position of dependence, Mrs. Dutta realizes that she wants to live in India on her own. The story significantly ends with Mrs. Dutta's actual letter that registers her change and the beginning of a new learning process. The next section will analyze the character's actual letter that sums up her experiences. Mrs. Dutta's letters of the mind are intermediate stages in the process of understanding her reactions to a new experience. They involve a sense of confusion and reluctance to accept unpleasant truths. They are acts of censoring inconvenient aspects from a potential addressee. These mental epistolary forms express the character's struggle to define herself in a new context. Mrs. Dutta's actual letter sums up the results of her attempts to find happiness. Her confessions formulate an ironical definition of certainty, i.e. she only knows that everything she believed in is no longer valid: "Dear Roma, Mrs. Dutta writes, I cannot answer your question about whether I am happy for I am no longer sure I know what happiness is. All I know is that it isn't what I thought it would be" (33). The fact that the old woman can only provide negative definitions for what she seems to have discovered illustrates the need to reconstruct her system of values. She is still placed in an intermediary phase: between giving up old notions and trying to find new equivalents. Her short cultural transplantation has cast doubts on familiar ways and cultural assumptions. She now conceives happiness in different terms: a denial of familiar ideas of dependence and a distinct, yet unspecified conception of love: Happiness "is not about being needed. It isn't about being with family either. It has something to do with love, I still think that, but in a different way than I believed earlier, a way I don't have words to explain" (33). The woman is aware of the change within herself, but she cannot account for it completely. She realizes she is about to start a new journey of self-discovery back home. Happiness itself becomes less important than the process of shaping one's beliefs and understanding where one belongs. This is what Mrs. Dutta attempts to do after her homecoming: "Perhaps we can figure it out together, two old women drinking cha in your downstairs flat. . . . If I'm lucky—and perhaps, in spite of all that has happened, I am—the happiness will be in the figuring out" (34).

Thus, by writing a final letter Mrs. Dutta clarifies one aspect: the feelings of belonging. With all its intricacies, the experience in America has made her realize that she feels happy on her own in India, rather than with Sagar in America. The next section of the paper focuses on letter-writing and the condition of isolation implied by migration. Letter-writing may assuage the feelings of alienation and provide a sense of comfort to dependant female immigrants. According to Campbell, the process of writing in order to better understand oneself is also a consequence of feeling isolated: The letter writer in epistolary fashion is usually isolated, especially in novels in which there is no exchange of letters, and very often when there is an exchange. In fact, the isolation of the writer is essential to the epistolary urge (Campbell). The experience of immigration involves a degree of alienation that all the characters analyzed have to face. There are several instances when the character alludes to the isolation she feels in the new country that seems deserted when compared to the Indian cityscape: "It's been a good day, as good as it can be in a country where you might stare out the window for hours and not see one living soul. No vegetable vendors with wicker baskets on their heads, no knife-sharpeners calling scissors-knives-choppers, scissors-knives-choppers to bring the children running" (20). She tries to find comfort in cooking and through (failed) attempts to communicate with her neighbour. The short time she can spend with her son talking about his childhood is also a way of finding solace. Her inner epistolary meditations can be also interpreted as ways of dealing with loneliness.

Letter-writing performs several roles in the story "Mrs. Dutta Writes a Letter." In Mrs. Dutta's case, letters function mainly as means of reflecting upon and clarifying a confusing experience. The character writes two actual letters, while the rest are personal meditations in the shape of mental letters. This suggests that the letters' role as connectors to India is a pretext for allowing the female immigrant to confront her doubts regarding life in America. While writing to herself, Mrs. Dutta is able to both criticize and take over aspects from the new culture. The selective content of the imaginary letters and the character's hesitation to write a real one illustrate the impossibility to fully comprehend an alien culture. Letters function ambiguously: they are both connectors and marks of separation, illustrating the layered construction of immigrant identities.

Works Cited

Banerjee Divakaruni, Chitra. "Mrs. Dutta Writes a Letter." Cengage Learning. The Gale Group, 2003.

Grewal, Gurleen. "Indian-American Literature." *New Immigrant Literatures in the United States. A Sourcebook to Our Multicultural*

Heritage, Ed. Alpana Sharma Knippling. Westport, Connecticut, London: Greenwood Press, 1996.

Pandurang, Mala. "Conceptualizing Emigrant Indian Female Subjectivity: Possible Entry Points." *South Asian Women in the Diaspora*. Ed. Puwar Nirmal. Berg Publishers, 2003.

Campbell, Elizabeth. "Re-visions, Re-flections, Re-creations: Epistolarity in Novels by Contemporary Women." *Twentieth Century Literature*, Vol. 41, 1995. Questia Online Library.

9/11 and the Terror Fear in the Diasporic Community: The Recent Fiction of Chitra Divakaruni

BANANI CHAKRABORTY
Assam University, Silchar

Since the beginning of society, human beings have been on the move. So migration in small and large groups, formation of new homes in new territories and settlement in the new land constitute an integral part of human history. This movement or dispersion and settlement are embedded with myriad experiences of cultural, religious, racial and ethnic conflicts, adjustment, adaptation, assimilation etc. Diaspora Studies aim to study the experiences that construe the journey and dispersion of people from one land to the other for varied reasons. There are few locations that attract and give shelter to immigrants more than those of the other places in the world. The United States of America seems to be one such location that has embraced people from different origins with surging enthusiasm and boasts of having a melting pot culture initially and salad bowl culture subsequently. Whereas the early diasporic experiences tell mostly the tales of forceful migration due to political or imperial pressure—indentured labour, slavery, etc.—the 19th and 20th centuries have witnessed voluntary migration of people from different nations of the world with the pursuit of better economic gain in the wake of globalization and transnationalism. But the solidarity long enjoyed by the diasporic community suffered the most after the terrorist attacks on the

World Trade Centre in New York and the Pentagon in Virginia on September 11, 2001. This article attempts to throw light on the calamities faced by the South Asian diasporic community with special reference to three novels, namely, *Queen of Dreams* (2005), *One Amazing Thing* (2010) and *Oleander Girl* (2013) by Chitra Banerjee Divakaruni.

The horrific incident of 9/11/2001 not only jolted the United States of America with irreconcilable wounds, but shocked the whole world, irrespective of its East and West binaries. 9/11 became synonymous with terror, destruction, loss, suffering and hatred. Litterateurs, sociologists, activists and politicians across the world condemned and became vocal to the manslaughter and destruction carried out by the terrorists in such a gruesome way. The violence was not only confined to the territory it directly hit but the violence, as Jana Evans Braziel notes it, reached beyond those whose lives were directly impacted through death and injury. This attack, on the other hand, had affected international migration to a great extent and diasporic community, especially the South Asians suffered from immense discriminations by the military and security forces as well as the citizens of America. Chitra Banerjee Divakaruni as a South Asian immigrant in America had herself experienced the terror spread by the massive attack of 9/11. Through insightful reference to the events of 9/11 and its subsequent effect on the lives of the South Asian diasporic community in America, Divakaruni's novels make the readers brood over the tough situation of discrimination and segregation faced by the immigrants who, at that time, were viewed through the lens of suspicion and "otherness."

The attack shattered the equation of power as well by posing question to the supremacy and security of the United States of America which boasts of the victories it achieved in so many wars fought against the opposite forces. This testifies to the fact that any nation, even a developed First world nation can be vulnerable to the hand of hatred and terrorism as Seamus Heaney in his poem "Anything can Happen" written in the aftermath of 9/11 had metaphorically said,

> Anything can happen, the tallest towers
> Be overturned, those in high places daunted,
> Those overlooked regarded. Stropped-beak Fortune
> Swoops, making the air gasp, tearing the crest off one
> Setting it down bleeding on the next.
> Ground gives. The heaven's weight
> Lifts up off Atlas like a kettle-lid.
> Capstones shift, nothing restless right.
> Telluric ash and fire-spores boil away.

The poem symbolically projects the scenario of the fatal loss and destruction that the US experienced. Jana Evans Braziel in the book *Diaspora*: *An Introduction* points out that "September 11, 2001 marked a significant turning point in global geopolitical restructuring."

9/11 refers to the attacks launched by the Islamic terrorist group Al-Qaeda on United States of America in the year 2001. It is recorded that the attacks killed over 3000 U.S. citizens, permanent residents, immigrants and foreign visitors in New York, Pennsylvania and Washington, D.C. (196) and caused damage of property and infrastructure amounting to $10 billion (Wikipedia). Identification of the mastermind behind this massive attack brought in more chaotic situation resulting into protest and discrimination against diasporic community who bore allegiance with the terrorists through national, cultural, ethnic or religious background. In a taped statement released shortly before the U.S. Presidential election in 2004, Osama bin Laden acknowledged his direct involvement in the attacks blaming the U.S.A. for curbing their freedom. Arjun Appadurai, in analyzing the attacks of 9/11, points out: "Its newness was its efforts to inaugurate war defined only by an enemy, the enemy being the United States" (16). The attackers showed and justified their own reasons behind the attack whereas, the United States, being a First World Nation had its own justifiable reasons to hunt the perpetrators, punish them and ostracize the root cause of such hatred right from the root. However, it can in no way be ignored that the attacks and counter-attacks or "terror" and "war on terror" had made the lives of innumerable innocent people living both in the Muslim regions and United States of America and Britain full of threats and terror.

To tighten the security of the homeland and tackle further casualties, the U.S. initiated its "War on Terror." In the context of the situation aroused post-9/11 in America, it can be observed that "Diasporic communities have been (and continue to be) vital sites for . . . the War on Terror" (Braziel, 158). Immigration laws had been increasingly restrictive not only in the United States but other historically immigrant receiving countries like Canada, Britain, Australia, New Zealand, etc. Under the Presidentship of George W. Bush, the U.S. Senate on October, 2001, passed the U.S.A. Patriot Act. This particular law that stands for United and Strengthening America by Providing Appropriate Tools Required to Intercept and Obstruct Terrorism (USA PATRIOT) adheres to no compromise and imposes draconian measures for surveying, tracking, and regulating citizens and their financial transactions, internet searches, international telephone calls, purchases and even library records and authorizing arrest, search, interrogation and detention of immigrants (Braziel, 198). Post-9/11 was the time when civil rights of the immigrants were snatched away on the basis of mere suspicion as Jana Evans Braziel points out in his book *Diaspora: An Introduction*: "The U.S.A Patriot Act has indeed had deleterious effects not only on U.S foreign policy, but also on the nation's domestic policy, allowing for unprecedented and modes of surveillance as well, as well as broadly and loosely defined latitude with respect to detention, interrogation and prosecution of U.S citizens and immigrants within the U.S." (201) The above quotation perhaps explains the events that we encounter in the selected novels for study.

It became mandatory for the immigrants to show their respect and allegiance to America. Chitra Banerjee Divakaruni, in her essay "The Reluctant Patriot" written after the massacre of 9/11, expresses her grief about the traumatized condition of the immigrants:

> I've been aware, since Sept. 11, of the backlash in this country against people who are or, to the uninitiated eye, look Islamic or Middle Eastern. My own South Asian community has suffered from hate crimes and racial profiling. Sikhs in turbans and beards have been beaten and even shot to death; women in veils have been called terrorist bitches; businessmen in suits and ties have been asked to get off airplanes because their skin color made the crew nervous. The other day, outside our local grocery, a man shouted at my children and me, using an obscenity I won't repeat, "Ay-rabs, go home!" (*Los Angeles Times*, October 21, 2007, 2)

The personal experiences of the author in collaboration with the average experience of all immigrants belonging to her background, find expression in her literary projection. *Queen of Dreams* (2005), written four years after the tragedy of 9/11, shows how the lives of the second generation immigrants who have been brought up in America and therefore have started to consider this land as the homeland, can suffer from identity as well as existential crisis in the United States of America with the rise of indiscriminate hate crimes after September, 11 terrorist attack. In an interview given to Terry Hong and published in *The Bloomsbury Review,* Vol. 24 (2004), Divakaruni opens her heart saying:

> I want to touch people, to have them think about issues they haven't considered before, to make them more compassionate towards other people, . . . That was my major intention with writing this book after 9/11. If I could make the pain and the hope powerful enough in the book, then maybe I might stop some of the

> prejudice out there, and have some sort of counter effect to what followed 9/11.

Queen of Dreams, a novel apparently falling into the genre of magic realism, tends to realistically represent the turmoil of the diasporic community in post-9/11 America. The protagonist Rakhi being inspired by her father intended to explore the authenticity of her origin in the Kurma House. Soon the Kurma House emerged out to be the meeting place of many Indian origin immigrants and served as the emblem of her ethnic identity where the young and the octogenarians alike felt an emotional connection with the Kurma House. However, that was only a short-lived experience. The unexpected calamity carried out by the terrorists changed it all. Although she craved for the recognition of her ethnic identity, she perceived America as her home as she said in the novel while scattering the ashes of her dead mother: "If I died, I too would want my remains to become part of this land, this water, because there's a way in which the geography of one's childhood makes its way into one's bones" (134). But, 9/11 made it difficult and even punishable for the immigrants, had they asserted their ethnic identity publicly. The immigrants, who wanted to sympathize with the condition and express grief at the outburst of the incurable injuries, were sidelined.

The incident of 9/11 was undoubtedly brutal, cruel and horrific, but the events that followed that terrible attack were no less torturous than that: "A stern newscaster announces that a certain Osama bin Laden is the mastermind behind this plot. A picture of him in white robes, with a turban and beard and black fanatic's eyes, flashes on the screen" (265).

Any resemblance with the appearance of the terrorist was strictly abused. Suspicion, rather than evidence ruled the context. The characteristic "otherness" of the mastermind behind the attack came to be considered as the yardstick for discrimination and exclusion of the immigrants, especially the South-Asians whose appearance and attire were somewhat similar like the terrorist. Rakhi, in her agony, says, "Is this California, year 2001 . . . or is this Nazi Germany?' (264). The second generation immigrants suffered the worst due to the unleashing of strict laws. Growing up in America imagining the land to be their own homeland, the Second generation immigrants like Rakhi, failed to come to terms with the segregation. Referring to Anastasia Christou and Russell King, it can be said here that the second generation immigrants are 'not fully understood, especially in relation to such fluid notions as 'belonging' and 'identity,' which appear suddenly volatile' (2).

In *Queen of Dreams*, the writer also shows how important it had become for the immigrants not to insist on wearing their typical community costumes or performing typical gestures representing their ethnicity as that may generate suspicion in the U.S. authority. It was necessary to put up a banner that announced PROUD TO BE AMERICAN or GOD BLESS AMERICA. This, at times, destabilized the intellection of the diasporic people. Rakhi, a second generation migrant, aspires to share the cultural root of her parents but at the same time, she has accepted the lifestyle and livelihood in America and so she says: "I don't have to put up a flag to prove that I'm American! I'm American already. I love this country—hell, it's the only country I know. But I am not going to be pressured into putting up a sign of her to announce that love to every passerby" (264).

These situations, as it were, hit the immigrants with permanent scars. Their familiar selves seemed to be alien suddenly. With reference to her identity crisis, Rakhi articulates some sensitive words which tend to be the voice of all immigrants facing the toughest times:

> You ain't American, one of the men said.
> He is a racist idiot, I tell myself.
> Is that so? my whisper voice gibes. And how many others in this country would have agreed with him today?

But if I wasn't American, then what was I? (271)

Although *Oleander Girl* predominantly emphasizes on the protagonist Korobi's quest for her parental identity, it throws some light on the conditions of the traumatized immigrants in America terrorized both by 9/11 and by the backlash of 9/11. Seema and Mr. Mitra become exemplary in this case. Mr. Mitra became a transmigrant being allured by the glittering success in America through a job offered by Mrs. Bose, the would-be mother in-law of Korobi. It is then that he proposed to Seema, his co-worker in the call-centre in India. A thrilled and relieved Seema readily accepted the proposal being delighted "at the prospect of living in America, of having the chance to walk the magical streets that had popped so many times in her screen in the call centre" (96). The grand opening of the Mumtaz, the Art Gallery owned by the Boses, enjoyed exciting sales and write-up in dailies too. Both Mr. Mitra and Seema swayed themselves with the "heady life of New York—restaurants, plays, museums, shopping" (96). Despite having occasional pangs of home-sickness, Seema had to adjust with the newly adopted American lifestyle as "They had not come to America . . . to stay closeted with their own kind" (96). Pampered by the glitters of America, they could not even imagine the dangers that America may trap them into. In fact, they often exclaimed 'how much safer it was than India—no pocketmaars snatching your wallet, no burglars breaking into your apartment, no corrupt police who showed up at your store for "tea-money" ' (96-97).

Like most of the immigrants who come to America with the prospect of achieving something bigger and get overwhelmed when things are underway, the Mitras also got stuck by the rosy picture in the United States of America until the 9/11 event turned everything topsy-turvy. Seema and Mr. Mitra were having a promising life, full of positive impulses. "Then the Towers fell, and everything changed" (97). The change engulfed with sorrow and destruction not only touched the lives of the Americans but hundreds of thousands of immigrants who lived in the U.S.A, in many ways. The hunt for the perpetrators made the authority impel strict measurement on the immigrants. 9/11 and its aftermath destroyed the peace, happiness and economic prospects of the Mitras. Bad financial condition forced the Mitras to reduce themselves to a dingy rented house, plunging pregnant Seema to depression and deviating Mr. Mitra from honest path to the territory of the burglars so that he could manage enough money to sail Seema back to India.

As a result of the widespread effect of hatred and discrimination, the economic condition of the immigrants was in a miserable state. Flourishing business stopped to make even a grain of profit. The Mitras in *Oleander Girl* and Tariq and his family in *One Amazing Thing* like the Guptas in *Queen of Dreams* faced this gloomy lot in business. Seema in *Oleander Girl* asserts in exasperation that "South Asian businesses were boycotted, especially those with Muslim names" (101). The Art Gallery Mumtaz, thus was aimed with attacks by the patriots causing damage and destruction. "The Mitras had arrived at the Mumtaz one morning to find the plate glass cracked, paintings slashed, the floor filthy with urines and feces, threats scrawled over the walls in terrifying red letters" (101). Again, Chitra Banerjee Divakaruni makes it clear through the characters of Tariq and his family in *One Amazing Thing* that their financial condition suffered from the hardest ever blow since their settlement in America. His father's 'Jalal's Janitorial Services' built from a scrap to a flourishing enterprise could not persuade the clients to change their minds and accept their service. In *Queen of Dreams*, we find Divakaruni representing the disappointment of the diasporic people in business dealing in a different way. The brisk business in Kurma House declined and experienced vandalism and abandonment: "For a long time after we open, no one comes into the shop. Most of the businesses around us are closed, and the street appears abandoned. Even the homeless people have disappeared, leaving the street lamps to throw shivery pools of light on empty pavements" (263).

That the Muslim diasporic community had to suffer the worst due to their religious identity is beyond argument but there had been cases of unleashing physical and mental torture on Sikhs and other communities also due to the mistaken identity. The Sikhs had to bear the pangs of discrimination due to their appearance and attire—long beard, turban, etc. which were identical with Osama bin Laden, the mastermind behind the attack. Jespal, the fiancé of Rakhi's best friend Belle and a stern follower of his own ethnic identity, became victim of such mistaken identity as it is exposed by the author in the novel *Queen of Dreams*. A group of Americans claiming themselves to be "patriots" broke into the Kurma House stigmatizing Rakhi and her partners as "terrorists" and accusing them of bringing about the calamities of the Americans. As Jespal tried to stop them from making further damages saying, 'We haven't done anything wrong. Those men in here—were mourning. We're Americans, just the way you are. We all feel terrible about what happened' (267), the patriots got more infuriated and shouted at him with abusive language and this makes it clear what they thought of Jespal's identity: "Looked in the mirror lately? One of them spits. You ain't an American! Its fuckers like you who planned this attack on the innocent people of this country. Time someone taught you faggots a lesson" (267).

Detention, physical and mental assault, interrogation, search without warrant were some of the common means to tackle any terrorism within the United States. Tariq's father had been abducted and detained by the U.S. officials one fine morning. Just as there was no reason behind the detention, so the reason behind his release could not be properly understood. He had gone into depression and silence seemed to be his only language. The trauma, however, carried no physical mark of torture, but it left too deep an imprint on his psychology that it had culminated into stroke and paralysis subsequently. Whereas Mr. Jalal had the fate of being released, no trace could be found of his companion Hanif who too was detained. Hanif's disappearance tends to throw light on the deportation of the suspects and detainees to a territory beyond the reach of the common citizens as it was reported by the Associated Press that "the US has created a global network of overseas prisons, its islands of high security keeping 14,000 detainees beyond the reach of the established law" (Qtd. Braziel, *Diaspora: An Introduction*).

The detention of Mr. Mitra in *Oleander Girl* was also without any convincing reason. He was detained when he had gone to complain to the police about the ransacking in the Mumtaz. Neither did Mitra say, nor did Seema know, where "they'd taken him, or what they exactly did. When he returned, haggard-eyed, Mitra refused to talk about it. Those two days had changed him, made him bitter silent the way he had never been" (100). Divakaruni's details of the detentions faced by the immigrant characters bear testimony to The Anti Terror Crime and Security Act (ATCSA, 2001) and Prevention of Terrorism Act (PTA, 2005) passed after the incidents of 9/11. The laws were designed to prevent terrorist suspects from using the immigration system to prevent detention. The law meant to deliver justice was often implemented wrongly on the innocent immigrants. Divakaruni makes an attempt to portray such injustices through the characters drawn in her novels.

After a long stay for generations in the host land, the diasporic communities acculturate the habits of the host land and tend to think of that land as their native land when they are accepted by the host society by and large. This notion, however, becomes problematic when nativism rather than nationalism comes to appear to be the main issue with the native people of the host land when the land is under the threat of invasion and destruction by outsiders, terrorists and other alien organizations.

So, the long-sustained security and safety no longer prevail to give comfort to the people of diaspora. Walker Conner's insightful words can be cited in this connection: "History is liberally sprinkled with cases in which diasporas have appeared relatively secure only to be faced with an unexpected outbreak of xenophobia and nativism. The pattern of such outbreaks appears too complex to lend itself to predictability." (19)

"Terrorism" and "war on terror" are thus inexorably defined differently and through alternate terms depending on one's location (ideological as much as geopolitical, and perhaps more)—for others, these terms (terrorism and war on terror) may be defined alternately as revolutionary resistance fighters and global economic imperialists (Braziel, 195). It came as a relief after the "war on terror" finally became successful in slaying the mastermind Osama bin Laden in Pakistan with the help of Pakistani authorities in 2011 under the presidentship of Barak Obama. But the fact still remains a problem as hate crimes keep on making its presence in different walks of life in the European territory. Perhaps, generalization of one's identity by the other and preconceived notion about particular race, culture and nationality generate hate without any convincing reason. It appears that in this era of globalization and transnationalism, if the diasporic community faces unprecedented discrimination, it may affect the world economic relation as a whole.

Works Cited

"Anything can Happen," *Academy of American Poets*. nd. 10 May. 2014. <www.poets.org/. . ./anything-can-happen>

Appadurai, Arjun. *Fear of Small Numbers: An Essay on the Geography of Anger*. Calcutta: Seagull, 2006.

Braziel, Janna Evans. *Diaspora: An Introduction*. Malden: Blackwell, 2008.

Christou, Anastasia. "Narrating the Agonising homecoming: Gender, Place and Identity in Life Stories of Second-Generation Greek-Danes," pp. 1-26.

Divakaruni, Chitra Banerjee. *Queen of Dreams*. London: Abacus, 2005.

____. *One Amazing Thing*. New Delhi: Penguin, 2010.

____. *Oleander Girl*. New York: Simon and Schuster, 2013.

____. "The Reluctant Patriot." *Los Angeles Times.* 21 Oct. 2001. <www.chitradivakaruni.com/personal-essays>

Hong, Terry. "Responding With Hope to 9/11A Talk With Chitra Banerjee Divakaruni about Her Latest Novel. *Queen of Dreams,"* *Bloomsbury Review,* Vol. 24. Issue 6, 2004.

September 9/11 Attacks. <en.wikipedia.org/wiki/September_11_. . .>

Sheffer, Gabriel. *Modern Diasporas in International Politics*. London: Croom Helm, 1993.

Emerging Relationships in Diasporic Locations: An Examination of Chitra Banerjee Divakaruni's Fictions

NANDINI BHADRA
B.K.M. Sc. College, South Gujarat University

Chitra Banerjee Divakaruni is a distinguished Indian American writer of the South Asian diaspora who finds a rich voice through portrayal of human relationships which are made 'new' in the diasporic location the Indian immigrants inhabit. In this chapter I examine Divakaruni's novels, *The Mistress of Spices* and *Sister of My Heart* and some of the short stories in her collection, *Arranged Marriage* where Indian women have been represented as powerful female subjects who seem to ask difficult questions about their identity, selfhood, and familial and social role even as they attempt to re-inscribe their selves in their community, history and society.

Feminism, Divakaruni urges in her life and work, is primarily a philosophy of action and engagement. As a writer and activist, championing South Asian women's causes in the bay area of California, issues of different forms of gender subordination in the lives of diasporic women is something very close to Divakaruni's heart, and in her fiction, she deconstructs the stereotypical representation of Indian women as docile, passive and subordinate objects lacking agency and creates powerful female subjects.

Divakaruni's writing often centres around the lives of immigrant women as she says, "Women in particular respond to my work because I'm writing about them, women in love, in difficulties, women in relationships" (Divakaruni Website). In her novels, *The Mistress of Spices* and *Sister of My Heart*, Divakaruni explores relationships between women as friends and sisters and also between mothers and daughters, both in the Indian context and in the context of diaspora. In an essay in *Bold Type* in 1998, she confesses how she was influenced by the stories from Indian epics narrated to her by her grandfather, and searched in them for that sense of sisterhood she knew must have existed among them ("What Women Share").

After she migrated to America, Divakaruni realized that women from the postcolonial world faced double effacement of race and gender as their lives were shaped not only by Western hegemonic discourse but also by patriarchy. In the Indian context, after independence, gender division became more pronounced in Indian societies. Indians who migrated, continued to practise severe forms of gender oppression even in their diasporic locations. Yet in America in the late 1970s and early 1980s, the feminism that was gaining momentum was dominated by mainstream media and white Women Studies department, ignoring the agenda of women of color and Third World women. Chandra Talpade Mohanty, a third world woman intellectual living in the U S recounts:

> I was for the first time enabled to think through my own gendered, classed, post-colonial history. . . . For me, engagement as a feminist of color in the U.S. made possible an intellectual and political genealogy of being Indian that was radically challenging as well as profoundly activist. Notions of home and community began to be located within a deeply political space where racialization and gender and class relations and histories became the prism through which I understood, however partially, what it could mean to be South Asian in North America. Interestingly, this recognition also forced me to re-examine the meanings attached to home and community in India.

> What I chose to claim, and continue to claim, is a history of anti-colonialist, feminist struggle in India. (Mohanty 353)

Chandra Mohanty's dissatisfaction with the mainstream feminist movement in the United States and her desire to 're-examine' and reclaim South Asian feminism could be Chitra Banerjee Divakaruni's own, as in both her novels, *The Mistress of Spices* and *Sister of My Heart,* she looks back to her own indigenous tradition to write about bonding between women which goes deeper than conventional familial ties despite all patriarchal conditioning. She also, like Shamita Das Gupta, the woman writer-activist in the US, recognizes that the "icon of the strong South Asian woman is lost in the Western stereotype of her," and that in South Asian culture, apart from the oppositional models of good and bad girls, there is also a "well accepted, third ideal of femininity, that of the Virangana or brave mythic warrior woman," which one can find in Indian mythology, history and also among women organizers of South-Asian countries (Dasgupta 11-12).

Of course, literary representation of Indian women during the colonial period had been quite discouraging. In the colonies, European women were valorized and their native counterparts were often perceived as passive, docile and subservient creatures, lacking any separate identity though in England itself, womanhood was devalued. In E.M. Forster's *A Passage to India*, Indian women were shown to be passive, shadowy creatures on the margin of the text. In his novel, *Around the World in Eighty Days (*1873), Jules Verne portrays Indian women as passive objects who can only be rescued from native barbarians by the civilized and masculine Englishmen.

Colonialists constructed Indian women as exotic yet oppressed to justify their civilizing mission. In response to such colonial claims, a patriarchal, anticolonial nationalism supporting women's education and social reforms emerged, yet they restricted the woman to an ideal role in the realm of the spiritual, identified as the home or the inner sphere (*ghar*) as opposed to the material sphere where practical considerations reigned supreme, identified as the world or *bahir (*Chatterjee 119-20).

Thus while the Indian middle or upper class woman was perceived as equal to her western counterpart in terms of education, clothing, food and cultural sophistication, she was considered superior to European or lower class women in the preservation of the traditional domain of her home. She was represented as the virtuous and chaste 'new' woman, an image which though emancipatory to some extent, imposed certain limitations on her freedom.

Women thus found themselves subordinated simultaneously to colonialism as well as to patriarchy, and the resistance to these twin forces of subordination found expression in women's autobiographical writings. Maitrayee Devi's academy award winning autobiographical narrative, *Na Hanyate*, translated as *It does not Die* (1972) written in response to a colonialist work *Bengal Nights* by Mircea Eliade (a European Oriental scholar living in India with Devi's family in the 1930s), explores the Orientalist and liberal reformist dimensions of colonial and national thought and the way such bipolar nexus complicated a woman's life. Eliade's semi-autobiographical novel on the other hand, charts the protagonist Elaine's orientalist fascination with India and in his portrayal of his romantic encounter with the woman protagonist (a fictional representation of Devi), he constructs the Indian woman as a mysterious and exotic creature oppressed by patriarchy.

An examination of Divakaruni's novels will show how writing from the diasporic space, she, like Kingston, Tan or Chang, deconstructs literary representation of ethnic women by Euro-American writers, and empowers the marginalized Asian-American women in the diaspora. It is to be noted here that both Chinese and Indian women or for that matter, all ethnic women were often exoticized in the diasporic space and stereotyped as either demure and delicate creatures needing male protection or sexually licentious *femme fatale;* alluring men with their diabolical charms. In other words, Asian American women were perceived as anything but normal in the American popular imagination. Divakaruni, like Tan or Kingston, in her narratives, portrays real women of flesh and blood, who, with their desires and wants, are also powerful women—agents of their own destiny.

II

In her first novel *The Mistress of Spices*, Divakaruni takes recourse to mythmaking from a woman-centred point of view and creates the powerful and suggestive figure of Tilottama who not only 'writes' her own destiny, but also helps other oppressed women in the diaspora find their voice, mind and selves. Creating a woman-centred myth was only natural for Divakaruni who had been championing women's causes in the Bay area of California through her organization—Maitri. In an essay entitled, "Revisionist Mythmaking as Resistance," which is a part of her book *Writing Resistance: A Comparative Study of the Selected Novels by Women Writers*, Usha Bande points out how contemporary women's discourse employs myths to explore "how women writers, women media persons, and visual and performance artists, subvert and reinvent existing cultural and mythic structures and ideologies oppressive to women, and create an emergent and emancipatory mythology" (171). Elaine Showalter too shows how revisionist mythmaking is the potential of the writer to appropriate the mythic tale or the mythic figure for altered ends, which may ultimately make cultural changes possible (317). Adrienne Rich terms it 're-visioning,' "of looking back, of seeing with fresh eyes" (603), and by looking back, "women's discourse deconstructs the locus of power and reconstructs the past" (Bande 172), and demonstrates the power of mythic images as sources of strength, thereby privileging female agency (172).

Chitra Banerjee Divakaruni in her first novel, *The Mistress of Spices* negotiates new boundaries by remaking herself and re-inventing and re-visioning new forms of writing. In a somewhat similar vein, Amy Tan, in her novel, *The Kitchen God's Wife* deconstructs mythology to tell the tale of the Kitchen God from a contemporary feminist standpoint, and like Divakaruni's *The Mistress of Spices* or *Sister of My Heart*, Tan's *The Joy Luck Club* or *The Kitchen God's Wife* relies to a great extent on non-written, non-western, cultural forms like talk story, myth and legend. Both Tan and Divakaruni, like Kingston, realize the fact that myths have a great potential to be "recontextualized and inscribed with new meanings" (Kingston qtd. Bloom 151).

All Divakaruni's female protagonists (Anju, Sudha and Tilottama) like the principal female characters in Tan's novels (Winnie, her daughter Pearl, or the mothers and daughters of *The Joy Luck Club*), emerge as survivors or winners, who "write" their destinies and their life stories. Like Panchali in Divakaruni's narrative, *The Palace of Illusions*, who narrates her story from the point of view of a female protagonist (thus reversing her object position as portrayed in the epic the *Mahabharata*), Tan decentres the patriarchal world of the myth of the Kitchen God and allows Winnie, the abused wife, to narrate her own tale. And just as Panchali moves from strength to strength, finally achieving the power to rewrite her destiny, Winnie too emerges as a survivor who is able to tell the story of her traumatic past after years of silence. And this "telling," provides her daughter the strength to come to terms with a ghastly disease like multiple schlerosis.

Divakaruni's woman protagonist, Tilo, in her novel, *The Mistress of Spices,* is an emblem of power and gentleness, who, with her concoction of spices, suggests remedies for the various ailments of her customers—both physical and metaphoric, in the American diasporic space they inhabit. Through the sustained metaphor of spices, Divakaruni, in her narrative, looks back to the Indian tradition, and appropriates the form of the fable to solve the problems and complexities in the life of immigrants, and the text owes much to non-written, non-western cultural forms like story-telling, myths and fables.

In this context, it would be quite interesting to note that Divakaruni, like Tan, seems to agree with the simple, matter-of-fact connection that Toni Morrison, the African American novelist makes between novel and story-telling: "We don't live in places where we can hear those stories anymore, parents don't sit around and tell their children those classical, mythological, archetypal stories that we heard years ago. But new information has to get out, and there are several ways to do it. One is the novel" ("Rootedness" 340).

Indeed story-telling can be a therapeutic exercise, both for the teller and the listener, more particularly for a diasporic community, as tales from legends and myths can help people reconnect with their lost culture and tradition. Walter Benjamin very aptly states:

> The storyteller takes what [s/he] tells from experience—[her] own or that reported by others. And [s/he] in turn makes it the experience of those who are listening to [the tale]. . . . In every case the story teller is a [wo]man who has counsel for [his or her reader]. . . is beginning to have an old-fashioned ring . . . because the communicability of experience is decreasing. (Benjamin *The Storyteller* 86-87)

Story-telling perhaps came naturally to Divakaruni who grew up on fables and stories narrated by her grandfather, and in both her novels, *The Mistress of Spices* and *Sister of My Heart*, Divakaruni, like many other Asian American writers of her generation, particularly Tan, Kingston and Chang, finds a rich voice through portrayal of family relationships, often going back to Indian folklores, myths and legends. Thus for her (Divakaruni), the act of writing becomes a way of building bridges that spans the geographical, social and cultural distances she has travelled, and Geoffrey Kain rightly asserts, that by the act of writing, diasporic writers attempt to "re-inscribe themselves within the new world,

. . . creating a fresh mode of relation towards their present" (Kain 11).

Divakaruni, who had migrated to America as a student of English Literature at the age of nineteen, continues to write about India and finds this position of writing from outside quite advantageous, as she confesses in an Interview how expatriates have "powerful and poignant experiences when they live away from their original culture and this becomes home, but never quite, and then you can't go back and be quite at home there either, so you become a kind of outsider to both cultures. Which is hard, but very good for writers, I think, to be in the position of looking in from the outside, observing" (Interview, Smith 1997).

Trinh T. Minha in an article entitled "Not You/like You: Postcolonial Women and the Interlocking of Identity and Difference," acknowledges the double vision entailed in such a positioning as she says "the moment the insider steps from the inside she is no longer a mere insider. She necessarily looks in from the outside while also looking out from the inside" (418). Salman Rushdie, who too, has been writing only about India, feels that any member of the post-diaspora community while looking "in" from the outside, has a right to draw on its roots for its art just as all the "world's community of writers" have done (Rushdie, *IH* 15). Yet there is a difference between Rushdie's position and Divakaruni's. While Divakaruni finds this double-vision a boon for the migrant writer, Rushdie suggests that perhaps the Indian writer looks back at his homeland through "guilt-tinted spectacles" as he says: "We are Hindus who have crossed the black water, we are Muslims who eat pork. And as a result—as my use of the Christian notion of the Fall indicates—we are now partly of the West" (15).

Yet both Divakaruni and Rushdie, in a manner similar to Tan, Kingston, Chang and many other migrant writers, acknowledge that the expatriate writer may reach out towards his/her cultural and ethical mooring in two ways—down memory lane and through a re-vision, re-appropriation of history, epic, legends and myths of the native land. More than nostalgia, is a passionate desire and longing to relocate the vision of the homeland in an alien space, and many Indian expatriate writers live in the greater India of the imagination. The *Mahabharata*, the *Ramayana* and fables like *The Panchatantra* or *The Arabian Nights* have been a decisive force in the formation of the Indian mind, and in some writers, the urge to bring in characters and contents from epic sources is a compelling force, as Raja Rao says, "I carry India with me wherever I go." (qtd. Parameswaran 356). Kingston, Tan and Chang too, look back to Chinese mythology, history and legend to re-vision and transculturate those stories in contemporary Asian American terms, thus combining American individualism and filial piety, the east and the west, tradition and modernity to create new hybrid 'third' identities. Kingston and Tan make use of the legend of Fa Mulan and transform them in the Asian American context.

Jasbir Jain in an article entitled "Geographical Dislocation and the Poetics of Exile," too, identifies two trajectories in diasporic writing—a process of self-discovery through history and memory or self-preservation through an act of transformation. Jain also points out how geographical and cultural dislocation also leads to the creation of what Homi Bhabha has referred to as "a third space." A diasporic author, while moving from one kind of affiliation (culture of his/her origin) to another (culture of adoption), may take recourse to fantasy in his/her narrative and this may perhaps be compared to Foucault's definition of heterotopia. Heterotopia, Foucault in his essay, "Of Other Spaces," (1967) explains, is to be contrasted with utopia. It is a countersite like a resting place, a boarding school, a museum, a library, a garden, a sanatorium, a prison, a brothel, a motel room, a theatre or a crematorium where "all other real sites that can be found within a culture are simultaneously represented, contested and inverted, " and where a juxtaposition of the otherwise incompatible can take place. The present epoch, in Foucault's opinion, is the epoch of space; "of simultaneity, of juxtaposition of the near and the far, of the side by side, of the dispersed" (1). And in this third space, identity is constructed through multiple specifics like language, myth, history, psychology, gender and race, and creation of the third space which reflects these complexities, which are directly connected with the subject's self-image and unconsciously inherited positioning. Thus space becomes an important determinant in the kind of relations which are produced as it provides a dynamics of history. And power structures indicating exclusion and inclusion are spatial in nature, as Edward Soja has pointed out, "The historical imagination is never completely spaceless and critical, social historians have written and continue to write some of the best geographies of the past" (Soja 14). It may be pointed out here that in Tan's narrative *The Joy Luck Club*, the club formed by the first generation mothers is also an instance of a heterotopic space which was formed in response to exclusion by the hegemonic culture. The club may be said to be a 'third' space where the elderly women played mahjong, danced and dined together, tasting each other's culinary delicacies; and this enjoyment transported them to an 'elsewhere,' where they could forget their painful past, their sorrows, and bond together to celebrate life.

A discussion of Divakaruni's first novel *The Mistress of Spices*, published after her short story collection *Arranged Marriage* will help to demonstrate how such a space is constructed wherein identity is interrogated and contested through the use of myth, fable and story-telling. The novel, also to a great extent, reveals Divakaruni's understanding of the human psyche, particularly female consciousness. Shashi Tharoor, in *The Los Angeles Book Review* has applauded Divakaruni's *The Mistress of Spices*, as he says: "Divakaruni has written an unusual, clever and often exquisite first novel that stirs magic realism into new conventions of culinary fiction and still simmering cauldron of Indian immigrant life in America." Tharoor too acknowledges that perhaps she is best at depicting the real America and has a "keen feel for immigrant life" (Rev).

The novelist also confesses to obliterating not only the boundaries between the real and the surreal, but also the "boundaries that separate communities and people," which leads to the main theme of the novel, as she points out in her Interview, "happiness comes from being involved in our human world" (Morton "The Spice of Life"). Divakaruni here dramatizes the conflict between the community and the individual, and empowers the feminine in connection with the community. Yet in the novel we find Tilo, the mistress of spices only being allowed by her mentor, the First Mother, who almost replicates patriarchy, to serve the needs of her own people, to "help her own kind," that is, the Indians, for the others "must go elsewhere for their need" (*The MOS* 70).

Debjani Bannerjee in her essay entitled, "'Home and Us': Re-defining Identity in the South Asian Diaspora through the Writings of Chitra Bannerjee Divakaruni and Meena Alexander," points out how in the novel national boundaries become "aggressive" and "all-important" in the diaspora as she says:

> But even within the structure of the fable Divakaruni has underscored the opaque nature of national borders. . . .National boundaries become aggressive, all important in the diaspora, as a way of defining identity, a liminality that marks the contours of one's experience, a platform for resisting co-optation by the dominantl hegemonic discourse. The store with its sacred, secret shelves functions as a geographical/textual space that is the repository of a monolithic national identity. The store represents a space for self-indulgence 'dangerous for a brown people who come from elsewhere to whom real Americans might say Why?' (23)

Tilo, the rebellious mistress however, transgresses the rules of the First mother, and serves an African American named Kwesi who frequented her shop for cure of ailments, and a Native

American whom Tilo calls Raven, and who with his idea of the 'earthly paradise' falls in love with Tilo. Divakaruni too confesses how apart from bridging the real and the mythic world she also took the literary risk of including three other ethnic groups in the novel—an African American, a native American and a Chicano man named Juan Cordero; perhaps suggesting that marginality itself can be a traumatic experience for all migrants who in some ways do not belong to discourses of the centre. At this point it is important to mention that when we examine the novels of Chang or Tan, we find that their narrative landscape consists only of Chinese American characters except for a few other white Americans or people belonging to other ethnic groups, for example, Rodale Taitai, the missionary in Chang's *Inheritance* and white characters like Ted (Rose Hsu's husband) and his parents in Tan's *The Joy Luck Club* who hover on the margin of the text. There could possibly be two reasons for this act of inclusion on Divakaruni's part. As a newly arrived first generation immigrant who came to America as a student, Divakaruni could easily empathize with other lonely immigrants like herself. Another reason could be Divakaruni's background of activism which made her sensitive to marginalized groups and individuals. In writing about "American" communities that are not perceived as "American" by the dominant group, the author redefines "America" as human and connected in contrast to capitalistic and isolated. Tilo's life in America thus, as has been suggested by Brunda Moka Dias, shifts from a solely South Asian context to an inter-ethnic, inter-racial context. With great human understanding, the author delineates the complexities in forging interethnic and interracial relationships. Divakaruni underscores the need to be wary of polarization of race and ethnicities; and understand the notion of power as that which includes the individual and community rather than one which conquers and divides (Dias 88-89). The novel could be easily read as a wake-up call (by the author) to all ethnic communities to form solidarity with other minority groups.

III

The narrative, with its plot of shipwreck and pirates is also reminiscent of Shakespeare's *The Tempest,* and Divakaruni also looks back to writers of her own native Bengali tradition like Bankim Chandra Chattopadhyay and old grandmother's tales of pirates and strange islands and magical transformations. Tilo, the Mistress of Spices, who survives a shipwreck, is reminiscent of Bankim Chandra's novel *Debi Chowdhrani* (1884) where he portrays the emergence of Prafulla, an ordinary housewife into a terrifying omnipotent bandit queen, embodying powerful feminine principle.

The novelist here destabilizes conventional notions of young and beautiful heroines, her protagonist instead, is a rebellious dark-skinned girl 'Nayantara' who by transmigration becomes an old woman and moves to Oakland, California, to open a spice store. Tilo, who survives the shipwreck, thus becomes a messiah for the Indian customers, and administers the oriental spices which almost 'sang back' (36) in her hands. Divakaruni here draws on Indian folk beliefs about the magical power of spices, but much of it is also her own creation. She warns her readers how one has to be careful while using the spices, and in the novel, makes the rules into laws from the divine realm; laws Tilo also could not transgress without serious consequences. It is interesting to note here that food or herbs as a therapy for healing is also inherent in the traditional Chinese cultural belief system. Mary Scott in an illuminating article entitled "Chinese Food" informs us that the traditional five tastes of Chinese cooking (sweet, sour, bitter, pungent and salty) should be balanced in seasoning a dish or planning a meal which, in turn, is derived from a traditional Chinese theory that the five elements—earth, fire, water, wood and metal—loosely correspond to a certain humor in the body. Any excess or shortage of any element in the body can be adjusted through a combination of diet and decoction that would act as a remedy for the imbalance (183-84).

Scott tells us how crabs should be eaten with ginger for the 'heat' or yang of ginger can be balanced with the 'cold' or 'yin' of crab (184). In *The Joy Luck Club* we find An-mei cooks crab with lots of ginger for a Chinese New Year celebration. Divakaruni too, in her novel, points out how oriental spices (which had turned western traders venture to the eastern world and in fact had been a prime mover and shaker of colonialism), if used in the correct combination, can result in curing physical and mental imbalances of individuals in the diasporic space.

Each chapter in the novel contains a little vignette about a spice—(turmeric, cinnamon, chilli, fennel, fenugreek, peppercorn, makardhwaj etc), which describes the role it plays in curing individuals of social, cultural and psychological maladies they may encounter while negotiating life in diasporic locations. Debjani Bannerjee reminds us that like the protagonists of her stories, the immigrant characters in her novel, *The Mistress of Spices* also "play out their conflicts in the theatre of the family, America is omnipresent but never at the centre of the stage. It is the internal logic of the characters that work through and reimagine identity in the new spatial parameters of the diasporic world" (12).

The *mistress* (emphasis added), the "deliberate gendering" (12) of the word to underplay the power associated with mastery, serves the overt and hidden needs of the Indian immigrants by recreating in her spice store a "little India" which boasts of all spices that ever were, including the lost ones and for whom the place is reminiscent of home where men and women come in search of peace and happiness. Saturday being a weekend, is especially a busy day as all Indians flock to Tilo's store for fresh home-grown methi leaves, pudina, and kum-kum powder (a red decorative liquid or power used by Indian women) to put on foreheads of married women, as well as CDs of Juhi Chawla-Aamir Khan blockbusters: A few customers are also happy to locate the Mysore sandal soap with its fragrance which reminds them of the 'fine' life in India:

> So many people on Saturday, it seems the walls must take a deep breath just to hold them in. All those voices, Hindi, Oriya, Assamese, Urdu, Tamil, English layered one on the other like notes from a tanpura, all those voices asking for more than their words, asking for happiness except no one seems to know where. (81)

At times however, Tilo, the ministering minstrel is quite distressed at the plight of the Indians in the diaspora and the intergenerational problems they face while negotiating life in the diasporic space. She emerges as a Prospero-like figure, who, with her magical concoction of spices, serves as a healer in communal regeneration, thus bringing back peace and harmony in the life of her community, as Trinh T. Minha says:

> In many parts of the world, the heaters are known as the living memories of the people. Not only do they hold esoteric knowledge, but they are also kept closely informed of the problems of their communities and are entrusted with all family affairs. In other words, they know everyone's story. . . .The very close relationship these healers maintain with their patients remains the determining factor of the cure. . . . The act of healing is therefore a sociocultural act, a collective, motherly undertaking. (Minha, *Woman* 40)

It is precisely for this act of motherly undertaking that the first mother transforms Nayantara, the young woman into an old woman, Tilo, who can serve as a healer of her community—a woman who will be free of male gaze and in whom every member can freely confide. It is indeed significant that Divakaruni makes use of 'metmorphoses,' one of the most important symbolic devices of magical realism as an important reference point in the novel. The paradigm of 'metamorphoses' can perhaps best explicate the postcolonial or diasporic condition where the subject is hybridized by history, belonging both to the East and the West, city and country, self and the other, home and abroad, nation and diaspora. Steven F. Walker while discussing Salman Rushdie's use of magical realist device of metamorphoses in an article entitled Magical Archetypes: Midlife Miracles in *The Satanic Verses*," explains that in magical realist terms, metamorphoses is as common an event as racist stereotyping in terms of social realism (351).

Indeed, peculiar to diasporic condition is the lack of stable identity, its propensity towards change and metamorphoses. It is interesting to note that Kafka who uses surrealist techniques in his novels, is one of Divakaruni's most-admired writers and his *Metamorphosis* has been listed by her as an all-time favorite book (Interview, *Barnes and Noble* 2004). For a migrant writer like Divakaruni, writing from an in-between space, transformation may symbolize a central metaphor for life. Her protagonist Tilottama also must transform into an old woman to serve as a healer of her community. Yet the process of metamorphoses can be strewn with trials, tribulations and personal sacrifices. Much different from the archetypal, docile mistresses, Tilottoma, by naming herself gives vent to the rebellious streak in her and justifies her naming: "I will be Tilottoma, the essence of til, life-giver, restorer of health and hope" (44).

The novel in a way, charts the difficulties and anxieties of assimilation for the first and second generation Indian Americans, and Tilo, the mistress has different concoction of spices to assuage the pain of both the generations, thus restoring peace and harmony in the family. She prescribes 'brahmi oil' for the grandfather to cool his nerves and a mixture of ginger, fenugreek and amchur so that Geeta finds courage and strength to take the right decision. Tilo, the mistress thus, has to perform a great balancing act and help the three generations of diasporic Indians discover their true selves and find out the right path.

In fact, far from liberating, diasporic experiences lead to practice of severe forms of gender oppression. Patriarchy severs a woman from her past and uproots her from her familiar surroundings. By physically taking a woman to her husband's home and forcing her to assimilate his world view, patriarchy can be equated with the process of migration wherein the subject in question is forced to adopt the host country's customs and social and cultural practices. Thus both patriarchy and migration entail a sense of discontinuity and sudden severance from the past. The diasporic male in such a situation formulates a belligerent male identity and goes back to an indigenous cultural past to counter various forms of marginalization in the host country. Repressing any deviant female behavior indicates that though the diasporic male may be marginalized in the public sphere, he has full control over his private sphere which includes his family. Mrs. Ahuja's story is a case in point. An immigrant woman, she had left behind the comfortable home of her father, a profitable tailoring business, a good life with women friends, and a substantial bank account to marry a violent alcoholic man, an NRI whom she had to consent to marry after seeing just his photographs. The real person who arrived three days before marriage turned out to be a much older version of the photograph—a balding, potbellied man, yet the young and beautiful Chowdhury girl had to reluctantly marry the man to save the family honor. Coming to America, Mrs. Ahuja had to bear the abuse of this violent man night after night, and confined within the space of the home, she was not allowed to work, as Ahuja said, "Ain't I man enough man enough" (16). One is here reminded of the abuse and violence Winnie in Tan's *The Kitchen God's Wife* is subjected to. As the Japanese soldiers continue to ravage the Chinese city of Nanjing, Winnie's body and mind suffer the trauma of rape and abuse. In fact, in situations of stress like war and dislocation, male members who suffer such unnatural conditions, become aggressive in their behavior towards their family (particularly towards the spouse and children). Wen Fu's extreme atrocity towards his wife and children led Winnie to wonder whether he was a human being or a monster. Just as Winnie suffered the abuse in silence, Mrs. Ahuja, the innocent and beautiful Chaudhury girl who had a comfortable life in India is hesitant to talk about her husband to the mistress as she cannot get rid of those voices of conditioning that have prescribed womanly duties for her, "but ah the voices, we carried them all the way inside our heads" (107). She also blames herself for her miseries, "Mataji, maybe some of it was my fault," (104) yet the mistress finds the refrain "my fault" to be one which women all over the world "have been taught to sing" (104).

Paula Caplan, in her book, *The Myth of Women's Masochism*, suggests how women can break the stereotypical image of women's masochism:

> This is a common pattern for women: blaming themselves rather than other people . . . because that is the 'feminine' thing to do. . . . Like the concept of original sin, the concept of women's innate masochism limits the definition of who we are and what we can become and makes us feel ashamed and self-blaming. Only by understanding how the myth grew and what perpetuates it now, only by learning to recognize the numerous forms it takes in our lives, can we demolish the myth and open wide the possibilities for women freely to be and do what they want. . . . To protect ourselves and others from destructive self-blame and unnecessary acceptance of a harmful status quo, we need to recognize the various guises the myth takes in our society. (6)

The Mistress of Spices, Tilo, performs an important social role by breaking women's stereotypical perception of themselves and helping them recognize their true strength. She prescribes fennel for Ahuja's wife to give her courage, but the lady too, has to help herself. Finally, by being able to speak out, Mrs. Ahuja, the immigrant woman, doubly subalternized by patriarchy and racism, is able to become Lalita, and escapes the tyranny of her husband who had ravaged her mind and body night after night. Similarly Weili in Tan's *The Kitchen God's Wife* becomes Winnie after escaping from the clutches of her brutal husband and runs away with a kind American man, Jimmie Louie, and is able to find true love. Mrs. Ahuja too, finally seeks shelter in a battered women's home and with the help of Tilo, the mistress, finds her true identity—her voice, mind and self.

In the novel, Divakaruni also gives us a glimpse into the lives of the rich Indian immigrant community, who in quest of acquisition of wealth in the materialistic Western society had to forego their cultural heritage and spiritual values: "The rich Indians descend from hills that twinkle brighter than stars. . . .their cars gleam like waxed apple, guide like swans over the potholes outside my store" (78).

Tilo in her store stocks up everything Oriental—extra long grain basmati rice, elephant-brand mustard oil, fresh lauki flown in from the Philippines and other authentic oriental spices which the rich Indians can afford to buy, for many of the first generation immigrants still eat delicacies like kheer pulao or achaar which reminds them of India in a foreign space.

Yet in spite of their affluence, Tilo finds a kind of vulnerability and emptiness as she looks into their inner lives, as she says: "beneath the shiniest armor, gold-plated or diamond, the beat of the vulnerable flesh" (80). The woman with oversize Bill Blass jeans and Gucci shoes and Dr. Lalchandani's wife who stares out of the bedroom window of her designer home while her husband is in bed with another woman are true evidences of the loneliness and isolation such women suffer in diasporic locations. Migration may have provided the women with material comfort but has deprived them of the support of friends and family members. As a result, they have no one to turn to, when faced with problems of raising children or coping with their marital discord. A similar crisis confronts the second generation daughters in Tan's narrative, *The Joy Luck Club*. They are too individualistic and too pre-occupied with themselves to provide support to each other. And just as the second generation Indian Americans turn to Tilo for advice and counselling, the second generation daughters in Tan's novel look up to their mothers for providing them with inner strength and support. The woman in Gucci shoes in Divakaruni's novel, *The Mistress of Spices,* too turns to the mistress for proper advice. Afraid that her son may be taking drugs as of late he had been hanging out with boys who "frighten her with their razor earrings and biker jackets and heavy boots as though for war, their cold, cold eyes and slits of mouths that are becoming his eyes, his mouth" (80), she feels quite helpless and rushes to Tilo for help. For the mother, Tilo prescribes hartuki, "shrivelled seed in the shape of a womb, which has no American name," yet it helps mothers "bear the pain that starts with the birthing and continues forever, the pain and joy both, tangled dark and blue as an umbilical cord around an infant's throat" (80).

Divakaruni, who had migrated to America at the age of twenty, realizes that with the change of locations, relationships change, and the ties that bind become unsteady, hence the reference to 'birthing,' 'womb' and 'umbilical' cord and other such symbols become significant for immigrants who lead lonely lives in diasporic locations. Yet it is not only the women and children but also the able bodied men who visit Tilo's spice store for remedies. Interestingly enough, Divakaruni chose the woman, Tilo, as a protagonist, a woman who could nurture, support and give emotional strength to men, women and children, as Iris H. Young has pointed out: "The gender socialization of women makes us tend to be more attentive to interactive dynamics than men and makes women good at providing empathy and support for people's feelings and at smoothing over interactive tensions. Both men and women look to women as nurturers of their personal lives" (Young 7).

In her second novel, *Sister of My Heart*, Divakaruni, as in Chang's narrative *Inheritance (*where she narrates the story of two sisters Junan and Yinan), tells the moving story of two cousins, Anju and Sudha, who born twelve hours apart in the upper middle class Chatterjee family of Calcutta, together experience the "joys, pains, mystical tales and tiresome tasks" that accompany growing up in a traditional Indian household in Calcutta. The story unfolds in the decadent Chatterjee mansion of Calcutta, Anju's house, in which both the girls live with their respective mothers and aunt Pishi, who had sought shelter with her brother's family since her widowhood at the age of eighteen. After the tragic demise of the fathers in a mysterious and reckless quest for a cave of rubies, Sudha and her mother with no other family and no means of financial sustenance, permanently reside in the Chatterjee household. Despite the socio-economic difference in the girls' background, a strong emotional bond develops between them, and though their lives are shaped by the three widows without any overt male domination, the spectre of imperialism and patriarchy seems to haunt their everyday existence. Divakaruni to a great extent feminizes the family space, yet there is a looming presence of colonial legacy and a male dominated past. The community in which the sisters live is a legacy of male ancestors, the upper middle class Brahmanical Chatterjee family whose women become upholders of culture and tradition. In the novel, as we have seen in our discussion of Chang or Tan's narratives, the private becomes the public, the personal becomes political/ social as intergenerational/ interpersonal conflicts, social contradictions, national/ transnational constructions of gender and issues of women's agency—all crystallize within the domestic space of the Chatterjee family.

The underlying tension between the desires of the mothers who embrace traditional Indian values and those of the cousins/ sisters who are more influenced by Western philosophy and culture is central to the evolution of the novel, as well as the growth of the female protagonists. Divakaruni very deftly captures the intricacies of middle and upper middle class social life and the position of women and their relationships in post-independent, postcolonial India. Social evils like discrimination against the girl child, exploitation and indignities of arranged marriage do exist, yet some amount of freedom like right to education and women meeting their husbands before marriage were permissible in society for women. Of course, difference in social and economic status was an important criterion for determining the degree of liberation a woman could enjoy. So, while Anju, who belonged to the upper class, could afford to concentrate on her studies and envision a career for herself, the restrictive demands of traditional Hindu female gender notions constrict Sudha's desires and she can only imagine herself in the stereotypical role of a good wife and mother. Her physical beauty is of course her advantage within the framework of the traditional Hindu-Indian family where 'beauty' is an important criterion to 'securing' a 'good husband.'

Things of course happened a little differently for Anju. While arranging marriage for her, her widowed mother, Gauri, made it clear that her daughter should be allowed to pursue higher education after her marriage when she moves to America. Sudha, who is socially and economically less privileged of the two is married to Ramesh, a well-settled boy from the orthodox Sanyal family of Bardhaman and falls a victim to the patriarchal structures of a colonized society. After marriage, she finds herself confined to the household space and instantaneously slips into the role of an obedient wife and meticulously performs her duties under the strict surveillance of a mother-in-law, the widowed, omnipotent matriarch who replicates patriarchy. When after their respective marriages, Anju visits Sudha at her marital home, the formidable massive brick gates and wall panels covered with fierce looking figures of 'yakshas' who guard the house, make her instantly 'dislike' the house, Anju is intrigued by little things she observes, which 'bite' at her like 'ants':

> The way Sudha serves the family at dinner time, even Ramesh's younger brothers, cleaning up their spills and removing their dirty dishes. The way her smile doesn't falter when one of the boys pushes away his plate, telling her—the cheeky brat—that the fish curry didn't turn outright. The way, whenever Mrs. Sanyal calls her, she drops whatever she's doing—even abandoning me in the middle of a conversation with an apologetic, 'Why don't you rest for a while, Anju'—to go to her." (194)

Divakaruni's women characters find a voice of resistance against this purpose of female education and it pains Anju to see the way Sudha toils at her marital home, cooking, cleaning, stitching the entire day and reflects to herself. "Is this what marriage is, this settling for the mediocre?" (195). In this context it would not be irrelevant to mention that during the late nineteenth century, particularly in Bengal, when women's education began, women themselves insisted that education should be made widespread for fostering feminine qualities like chastity, self-sacrifice, submissiveness, devotion, kindness and labour of love. Partha Chatterjee quotes Kundamala Devi, an advocate of women's education, and suggests how her observation points to the limited sphere of 'private space' which women envisioned for themselves; "see how an educated woman can do housework thoughtfully and systematically in a way unknown to an ignorant, uneducated woman. And see how if God had not appointed us to this place in the home how unhappy a place the world would be" (qtd. Chatterjee, 1993, 129).

Anju's own marriage is also not the ideal 'companionate' marriage she desired. Her fairytale romance with her liberal, Westernized husband, Sunil, receives a great jolt the day her orthodox father-in-law, in an altercation with his America-returned son, comments, "drinking and whoring . . . don't think the stories didn't get back to me." Later in bed, Anju reflects, Sunil hadn't even bothered to deny the accusations. Thus in Divakaruni's novel, selfhood and nationhood are problematized as in any encounter between the 'east' and the 'west.' Sudha is resigned to her lot and passively accepts the oppressive atmosphere of her marital home. As a young girl, she had fallen in love with Ashoke, but keeping in mind her age-old 'sanskar,' which she had inherited from her mother, she could not hurt her by defying her wishes, jeopardize Anju's marriage, or defame her family. Yet she shows exemplary courage and assumes the role of a 'virangana' when her husband's mother pressurizes her on aborting the female fetus she was carrying. She decides to have the baby alone and is able to escape from the repressive atmosphere of her marital home, which had become for her a place of exile, where through the ultra sound tests she had been subjected to (correctly amniocenteses which is legally banned in India; Divakaruni it seems, confuses between the two), her body becomes a site where politics of gender, sexuality, patriarchy and violence intersect. In Chang's *Inheritance* too, we find that after the birth of a daughter, Li Ang, Junan's soldier husband eagerly looks forward to the birth of a son. In feudal China, sons were considered to be assets in an agricultural society, as they would add to the labor force of the family. And Junan's mother, Chanyi, commits suicide after the astrologer predicts that she could only give birth to girl children. The bias against the female child was thus a common practice in both Chinese and Indian societies.

Coming back to Divakaruni's *Sister of My Heart*, in Anju, the bold and forthright sister, a student of English literature who interrogates the validity of the native culture, Divakaruni presents the cultural bias of the colonized hybrid. An ardent reader of Virginia Woolf's novel, *A Room of One's Own*, she still carries with her the colonial baggage. She easily falls in love with Sunil—the boy from America her mother had chosen as he too appears to be an admirer of Woolf. Later, realizing his deception, that he had used it as a ploy to impress her, she is disillusioned with Western sophistication. After migrating to America, she realizes that simply wearing jeans and sporting short hair are not true signs of emancipation.

A close reading of the events of the novel thus reveals that Divakaruni does not want the story to fall into a conventional binary between the orthodox East versus the liberating West. As already indicated, even Sunil and Anju's marriage belies the "ostensible equality" (Banerjee 19) of the 'companionate' modern marriage. While Anju wants Sudha to leave her marital home and have the girl baby alone, her husband Sunil, the liberated Western educated man, a resident of America, is quite reluctant to let his wife encourage her sister to walk out of her marital home as in India a lot of social stigma is attached to single mothers, as he says: "That's easy for you to say, Anju. You're safe here in America. Sudha's the one who'll have to face it every day. What kind of life will it be for her, alone with her daughter for the rest of her days, for who'll want to marry her after this? A social pariah. . . . May be abortion would have been the lesser of the two evils" (274). Even Anju is temporarily confused whether she had taken everything away from Sudha by her misplaced American notion of feminism and justice. The undertones in Sunil's arguments disturb her; she wonders whether she would also have had to abort her child had it turned out to be a girl.

An important theme which underlies Divakaruni's text is that oppression of women is carried out in diasporic locations too. Not only are women merely victims, they are also agents within the patriarchal project. Sudha's mother-in-law, as already mentioned, is a case in point, as she is the one who forces Sudha to abort the girl child and implores her son to go in for a second marriage.

Anju's accusation of her husband, Sunil, as an upholder of patriarchal values while pretending to be overtly westernized and liberated, raises important questions about whether gender subordination is reinforced or loosened through diaspora.

In an article entitled "Re-producing South Asian Wom(b)en: Female Foeticide and the Spectacle of Culture," Tej Purewal points out how a survey of maternity clinics and hospitals in Britain, US and Canada shows that a few hospitals refuse to disclose the sex of the child depending on the perceived ethnicity of parents. On the other hand there has been a mushrooming of private baby and gender clinics who have filled this gap providing scanning services irrespective of culture, ethnicity and race, on the basis of ability and willingness to pay the private fee. (147). Yet it is not actually known how many South Asians utilize this facility. Purewal appropriately points out how such a statistical analysis may have multiple ramifications as questions about who access these services and to what purpose remain unaddressed. Women's voice of dissent has been distinctly heard in recent times as she points out the fact that the patriarchal agents' opinion is opposed, ignored or even challenged is an important feature of how women have resisted and continue to resist the "modes of patriarchy" (149). Divakaruni's text too, charts a voice of resistance against discriminatory social practices.

The turn in the events of the narrative, however, show that Ashok whom Sudha had been passionately in love with, before her marriage to Ramesh, had still been waiting for her and he and his parents are only too eager to accept Sudha as his wife. In the end, Sudha, the timid Indian girl, who had known no other life than to serve her husband and in-laws, assumes the role of a virangana (woman warrior) and asserts her autonomous female identity. She moves to America to be with her sister Anju, though she realizes it will not be a fairy tale journey: "And suddenly I know this: I am going for Anju, yes and for Dayeeta, but most of all I am going for me" (316).

Sudha, in the end promises never to rely on a man again, and reflects on Anju's plans to start a clothes boutique together where she could be the creative head: "Why not? A future built by women out of their own wits, their own hands. A future where I lean on myself alone" (317). Like the character of Mulan in Walt Disney's animated film *Mulan* (where Mulan goes to battle in place of her father not simply out of filial piety, but in order to re-invent her selfhood,) Sudha asserts her identity and her individualism.

The novel thus, celebrates the triumph of selfhood and friendship between women, and Divakaruni here, like other post-colonial immigrant women writers of fiction, explores the genre of fictional autobiography to provide an alternative mode of narration in her attempt to break away from racial and patriarchal confinements. The cousins, Anju and Sudha tell their stories alternately and the novel unfolds through their first person binary narration. This mode of narration gives a certain degree of agency to the autobiographical subject. Ethnic writers like Hong Kingston, Amy Tan, Sandra Cisneros and Gloria Anzaldua have used this narrative technique, and Divakaruni, by her own confession, had been influenced by their writings as she had been by her own native tradition of autobiographical writing by women which emerged in the middle of the nineteenth century, influenced by the concept of the 'individual' among the English educated elite, as Partha Chatterjee tells us: "the immediacy, directness and the very artlessness of the form was seen to make it appropriate for an authentic "feminine" literary voice (Chatterjee 139).

The fictional autobiographical voice of Charulata in Tagore's *Nashtoneer* (*The Broken Nest*) where she writes about the Kali temple of the village which she traversed as a child is indeed a genuine voice of simplicity and charm much appreciated by Tagore himself (Chatterjee 139). Another instance of a genuine female voice which charts the life of a woman who emerges from the home to the world through the act of writing is Rassundari Debi's autobiography *Amar Jiban* which is, of course, a monologic representation, though a dialogue emerges from the narrative itself through juxtaposition with women of her family and community.

Rocio G. Davis, in an essay on Asian American autobiographical strategies, points out how the first person narrative form blends "selfhood and writing to stress evolving subjectivities, challenge contextual authority, or claim agency" (42). She also suggests that such texts often exhibit the writer's process of self-awareness and "struggle for self-representation through the narrative structure itself" (42). Divakaruni, in her novel *Sister of My Heart*, like her contemporary Chinese American writer Maxine Hong Kingston's *The Woman Warrior*, uses the fictional autobiographical form to show how the narrators juxtapose their lives with those women in her family and community (44). In such writing, Davis asserts, the 'writing subject,' views and writes his or her story from the "prism of intersecting lives" which is also dialogic in nature. Susanna Egan uses the term 'mirror talk,' to describe the process in which the (auto)biographer is the child or partner of the biographical subject and identity is shaped by the process of exploratory mirroring: "Such 'reflections' within a text where one person is formed in proximity to another, often but not always by genetic inheritance as well as by proximity in life" (qtd. Davis 45).

Thus relational life writing challenges the fundamental paradigm of the independent self of traditional autobiographies as well as the concept of monologic representation; it is basically dialogic in nature, and such representations underscore the relationship between individuals rather than individuals themselves, as Davis says: "To have one's opinions, perspectives and stories complemented or challenged by an (ostensibly) equally authoritative voice *within the text itself* stresses the dialogic element, making the relationship, rather than individuals, the centre of the text" (57).

It is clear that Divakaruni's primary focus in the novel, *Sister of My Heart* as in her other novel, *The Mistress of Spices* is human relationships, though in *Sister of My Heart*, relationship between sisters assumes greater importance apart from the mother-daughter bonding or women's relationship with each other and in the novel, the use of two narrators also helps Divakaruni achieve a balance of representation.

So friendship between women is an important aspect of Divakaruni's *oeuvre,* though we do get a glimpse of Divakaruni's sensitive understanding of the male psyche also through her portrayal of the tender aspects of father-daughter relationship in Singhji's concern and love for Sudha and also the selfless love of Ashoke for Sudha which cuts across all norms of patriarchy and male domination.

In Western fiction, the theme of bonding between sisters has been explored by Jane Austen in her novels *Pride and Prejudice* and *Sense and Sensibility* and by Louis M. Alcott in *Little Women*, though in *Jane Eyre*, the friendship between Jane, the protagonist and her childhood friend, Helen Burns is marginalized, and ultimately Helen dies and Mr. Rochester's other women Bertha Mason and Blanche Ingram are silenced so that Jane can emerge as the central woman is Mr. Rochester's life—his wife and the mother of his children (46-48).

It is important to mention here, that Divakaruni, who had known the terrible isolation of the newly arrived immigrant writer in the tradition of other ethnic women writers, particularly the African and Asian American women writers and other women of 'color' for whom ties with community and bonding with other women become an important feature of their writing, as a mode of survival in a racist patriarchal world.

Toni Morrison, the African American woman novelist, in an interview with Claudia Tate, writes about female friendship almost a century after Charlotte Bronte, and her comments on female friendship almost anticipates Divakaruni's by about two decades:

> Friendship between women is special, different, and has never been depicted as the major focus of a novel before *Sula*. Nobody ever talked about friendship between women unless it was homosexual, and there is no homosexuality in *Sula*. Relationships between women were always written about as though they were subordinate to some other roles they're playing. (Tate 118)

In *Sula* Morrison celebrates the friendship between the two women, Sula Peace and Nel Wright who, growing up in a black neighborhood in Ohio are almost two throats and one eye. Their mother's failure to meet their emotional needs brings these solitary girls together, although a rift occurs in their relationship after Sula's romantic involvement with Nel's husband. After Sula's death, Nel realizes in a rare moment of epiphany that friendship with Sula had been the most necessary part of her existence. So in *Sula*, Morrison goes out to show that the bond between women is deeper, more significant and permanent in nature than women's relationship with men. Yet Nel realizes the strength of this bond only after Sula's death when she is able to rise above female jealousy about her friend's relationship with her husband (53).

The female protagonists of Divakaruni's fiction too are able to overcome their petty rivalries and realize that loving their sisters/women friends can provide them with emotional anchorage as no relationship with men can. Women can truly love each other on equal terms; they can be true 'sisters' of the 'heart.' thereby emphasizing the emotional and not biological nature of their friendship. In her short story, "The Ultrasound," "Affair" and "Meeting Mrinal" anthologized in her collection of short fiction *Arranged Marriage*, Divakaruni celebrates female bonding and shows how women's love for each other surpasses all other bonds. While "The Ultrasound," an earlier short story version of *Sister of My Heart*, is about friendship between two cousins Runu (Sudha in *SOMH*) and Anju, living in two different continents, India and America, who love each other and provide the greatest support when Runu is forced to abort her female fetus and Anju suffers a miscarriage, in "Affair," the deep friendship between Abha and Meena is temporarily disrupted when Meena realizes that Abha is having a secret affair which she had not confided in Meena. However when Meena meets Abha to sort out matters with her, still jealous and angry, she sees in her own marriage the same emptiness in Abha's relationship with Srikant, her husband. She leaves her husband and meaningless existence for the uncertain pursuit of self-fulfillment and self-empowerment. Thus in Divakaruni's fiction, friendship between women overcomes all petty rivalry and jealousy and help women nurture themselves and realize their subjective self.

Asha too, in "Meeting Mrinal," realizes that she shares an inseparable bond with her childhood friend Mrinal, the apparently successful, free woman, who had been her greatest competitor in school. When she meets Mrinal, who had come to attend a conference in California, she is shocked at her tearful confessions of the emptiness of her life and can find courage to bear her individual sorrow of separation from her husband and the growing distance from her adolescent son. Though she maintains the façade of a happy and contented wife in her meeting with Mrinal, she comes back home and weeps for them both, for their lost dreams and their realization that "perfection was only a mirage" (*AM* 296). Anju too, in *Sister of My Heart* realizes that she loves Sudha unconditionally as she says: "I would love you . . . no matter who you were. I would love you because you love me. I would love you because no one else knows us like we know each other." (61). And in spite of marriage and the distance that separates them, Sudha is still the most important person in Anju's life, not Sunil, her husband.

So in the end, Sudha, realizing that Anju needs her and she also needs to make her journey to America for self-realization, sets forth to the 'terra incognita,' knowing fully well that her presence may cause problems and unhappiness in Anju's marriage. Earlier Sudha had also expressed her wish to share a man with Anju as the love between them is above all absolute: "If only Anju and I, like wives of the heroes in the old tales, could marry the same man, our Arjun, our Krishna, who would love and treasure us both, and keep us both together" (123).

Divakaruni, thus in her novel makes sisterhood or friendship between women her central theme, yet paradoxically enough, her theme also connects her with the pre-feminist Indian women novelists who celebrate the emergence of women's subjectivity and selfhood in a male-centred colonial world, where 'sisterhood' and women bonding with each other could be the only means of survival for women who silently and unquestioningly accepted male subordination as the women's lot. In what appears to be the first Indian novel, Hannah Catherine Muller's Bengali *Phulmoni O Karunar Bibaran* (1852) [a predecessor of Peary Chand Mitra's *Alaler Gharer Dulal*, published in Bengali in 1858 and *Yamuna Paryatan*, published in Malayalam in 1857], the Christian missionary novelist preaches how women can provide support to each other. The two protagonists, Phulmoni and Karuna give moral and emotional leadership to the women of the village in spite of its poverty, illiteracy and petty jealousies and are able to form a networking. Many other novelists of the period, especially the two women writers Anurupa Devi and Nirupama Devi wrote novels portraying women who move from strength to strength through bonding with each other, thereby resisting patriarchal domination (Barat 49-52).

Divakaruni retells and revisions the old Bengali women's novels in contemporary Asian American terms, stories through which the 'new' woman subject, the 'virangana' emerges whose tales seem to be 'déjà vu' as they have already been narrated by male novelists like Sarat Chandra Chattopadhyay, Bankim Chandra and Rabindranath Tagore. The constant reference to Rani Lakshmibai of Jhansi, or the Goddess Durga as the epitome of strength and courage invoked to empower Anju and Sudha throughout the novel reminds one of the literary representation of the 'virangana' celebrated in Michael Madhusudan Dutt's poems, of Shanti, the female revolutionary in Bankim Chandra's *Anandmath* or *Devi Chaudhurani*, the ordinary housewife who metamorphosed into the Bandit Queen in Bankim's novel by the same name. Divakaruni seems to suggest that the women of South Asian origin do not have to learn a new role to become activists, rather their collective memory, literature, ancient scriptures and tradition have to be retrieved.

Apart from Anju and Sudha, the three women characters in the novel—the two mothers and Pishi also move literally and figuratively from the 'home' to the 'world' like Bimala in Tagore's *Ghare Baire* (*The Home and the World*), the new woman who emerges in the liminal space between "colonial subjection and incipient nationalism." (Ray 6).

It is thus apt that the novel should end with Anju's reflection of the ties that bind the two sisters ready to usher in a new reality, a brave new world:

> We've formed a tableau, two women, their arms entwined like lotus stalks, smiling down at the baby between them. Two women who have travelled the vale of sorrow and the baby who will save them, who has saved them already. Madonnas with child . . . for now the three of us stand unhurried, feeling the way we fit, skin on skin, into each other's lives. (347)

The birth of Sudha's daughter, Dayita (beloved) thus signifies renewal, hope and healing. The novel, like Chang's *Inheritance,* Tan's *The Joy Luck Club* and *The Kitchen God's Wife* or Lahiri's *The Namesake* ends not with the celebration of assimilation, but with the creation of a new identity, a new life, a new home and a new meaningful present created from memories of "temps perdu" (lost/past times). Divakaruni's own observations pertaining to the responsibility of the ethnic author is noteworthy here as she notes in an edited collection of South Asian fiction and poetry entitled *Living in America:*

> The challenge lies in trying to bring alive, for readers from other ethnic backgrounds, the Indian and Indian American experience, not as something exotic and alien but as something human and shared. It lies in getting my own community to see the subject of my work (often the plight of women often origin struggling within a male-dominated culture,) even here in America. . . . But the opportunities are more important: to be able to straddle two distinct cultures . . . to destroy stereotypes and promote understanding between different sectors of the multicultural society in which we live; to paint the complex life of the immigrant with its unique joys and sorrows, so distinct from those of people who have never left their native land. (Divakaruni "Living" 28-30)

In a conversation with Rajini Srikanth, Divakaruni also confesses how a writer's responsibility should not concern itself with the reaction of majority culture but work with truth and honesty; and care for her characters as she says, "When we care for our characters, the readers will start to care for and about them" (99).

Divakaruni, like other immigrant writers (for example, Tan, Chang or Lahiri), writing from an in-between neo-colonial space, in her engagement with social issues relevant for migrants living in a new emerging space, shows her true commitment to her art, what Jean-Paul Sartre would term as 'art engage,' which gives the writer freedom to be an *'avant garde'* for truth; "creating, healing and always being herself" (Margaret Walker 106).

NOTES

1. As an Indian immigrant, hailing from an upper middle class family of Calcutta, Tagore had been a great influence on Divakaruni as she says in a conversation with Girija Sankar (*India Currents*, April 25, 2010): "I often go back to Tagore's works. . . . I find them amazing."

Arranged Nations: Rushdie, Divakaruni and Alexander

SAURABH BHATTACHARYYA
S.S. Mahavidyalaya, Chandraketugarh

One of the central facts about most of the identities we derive from the establishment is that they are involuntary for the individual. The same fact applies to the constructs of the nation and its ideologies in the postcolonial context and it has had serious consequences in a case like that of India where the classical form of nationalism based on the similarity of socio-ethnic origins is virtually impossible to hold up. The liberal nationalism espoused primarily by the Indian National Congress, ever since its inception in 1885, had however, proved inadequate even during the final years of the independence movement, let alone the time after it when it was thoroughly questioned. One of the most remarkable things about *Midnight's Children* (1981) is that it serves to bring into mainstream Indo-Anglian literature, the questions regarding the ideology of this nationhood in a narrative mode fitting with the questions it poses. This paper intends to read into these challenges into the ideology of the nation in *Midnight's Children* and the novels of two of the Asian American diaspora writers of the day, Chitra Banerjee Divakaruni and Meena Alexander, and try to locate the alternative modes of belonging that these narratives resort to in their quest for identity. In the way, the paper also will link up Saleem Sinai's homelessness with that of these later writers.

Midnight's Children presents multiple patterns of reading into the life of its central character, Saleem Sinai. Saleem represents on a personal scale a Muslim of Kashmiri parentage living through the years after independence to experience the trauma of the National Emergency. But he is also representative of the newly emerging nation, "a country which is itself a sort of dream" (159). There are seminal points in the text that define this myth of the nation. One of them is that when Nehru the first Prime Minister sends letters to all the midnight's children, and Saleem receives one of them. The idea of nationhood that Saleem represents and becomes linked to is in fact most clearly delineated in the letter Nehru wrote to congratulate the midnight's children. Thus his representation of the nation was not something that happened accidentally, like his development of the faculty of being a metaphorical All India Radio receiver by being able to hear others' thoughts, but is a kind of expected role that he is supposed to play; a role hurled upon him by the Prime Minister of this country: "Dear Baby Saleem, My belated congratulations on the happy accident of your moment of birth! You are the newest bearer of that ancient face of India which is also eternally young. We shall be watching over your life with the closest attention; it will be, in a sense, the mirror of our own" (167).

However it is not Saleem's life that alone reflects the history of the nation, the narrative does the same too. The lack of a linear development in the narrative is reflective of the resistance in the way of the development of the nation. It is the act of story telling that constantly digresses and disappoints the audience Padma with all possible means that subvert the sense of propriety of the narrative, nullifying the possibility of a narration that goes by the controls of the literary establishment of which the reliability of the narrator is a kind of foregone conclusion. The pickle-making is not only a metaphorical equivalent of the novel writing in which Saleem fails his audience Padma but it is also the technique adopted in the nation building which, like his narrative, is fated for disappointment. It is "the chutnification of history; the grand hope of the pickling of time" (642). The grand hope invariably alludes to that of the new nation, as also of Saleem who is supposed to represent it. The failure of the grand hope is the failure of the nation to build itself along the mythical lines, to live by the eloquent political rhetoric of its first Prime Minister which poor Saleem took too literally. At a later place in the novel he calls Nehru an "author of framed letters" (240). The reality of the situation of Saleem's family is brought about by another letter, also from the establishment itself that was not much late in coming, and perfectly counterpoised Nehru's letter. It was that which formally informed Ahmed Sinai that the state has frozen his assets. One of the minor characters sum up the matter in a more political tone: "Then let's see what kind of country we've ended up in!" (185)

There is in the historiography of *Midnight's Children*, a kind of photographical approach that even overcomes the "inevitable distortions of the pickling process" (644). Edward Barnaby has even gone to the extent of finding this photographic realism, which lurks through despite the unreliability of the narrator, posing a challenge to the general notion of the use of magic realism as the dominant narrative technique. And it is in these moments that the delineation of the nation comes out most explicitly. The letter that actually ruins the Sinai family for no apparent fault of theirs, standing in contrast to the framed letter bearing the promises of the mythical nation is one such moment. However, it also comes out in not so accurate moments of the narrative, particularly when Saleem deliberately mistakes the date of Gandhi's assassination. It does not qualify as a mistake in the narrative as Saleem at another point admits to making the mistake. If the reaction of Amina Sinai at the news of Gandhi's assassinator's name is a photographic moment already talked of, ""Thank God," Amina burst out, "It's not a Muslim name!"" (197), the mistake conveys the message that the fictional creation of the narrative is also a kind of creation of the nation and both are linked together though Saleem gets occasional chances of wish-fulfillment as a narrator. "In my India, Gandhi will continue to die at the wrong time," (230) he announces. Nevertheless, the next moment, we find him desperately trying to preserve the sanctity of the representative role of his narrative.

> Does one error invalidate the entire fabric? Am I so far gone, in my desperate need for meaning, that I'm prepared to distort everything—to re-write the whole history of my times purely in order to place myself in a central role? Today, in my confusion, I can't judge. I'll have to leave it to others. For me, there can be no going back; I must finish what I've started, even if, inevitably, what I finish turns out not to be what I began. (230)

And the solution to his crisis of being unable to form the unitary narrative that will reflect the possibility of the unity in the diversity that the nation and the framed letters ideally aim to attend to, comes in the very next line: "Ye Akashvani hai. This is All-India Radio" (230). It refers to the development of his magical ability to hear others' thoughts, be a kind of a radio receiver, where different voices coexist. And it is here that rests Rushdie's provisional substitute of a nation, as a kind of amorphous community. It is in the polyphony of the communities on the mental radio receiver that there is a proper representation of all the voices that constitute his substitute nation. The substitute to the nation is in the individual, the world of one's own and not ideologies of state polity, propagated by framed letters, concealing a coercive establishment that castrates in the name of development. It is the Midnight's Children Conference which he calls "my very own M.C.C." (287), that also offers a kind of substitute, albeit temporary. The form in which the narrator describes the transmissions received by his all Indian radio is in the Stream of Consciousness mode. While on the one hand the use of such a mode sets up a discourse countering the grand narrative of nationalistic ideologies exemplified by Nehru's framed letters or his 'tryst with destiny' speech, on the other hand it brings about the impression of homogeneity, rarely realized in the nationalistic set up imposed on Saleem from birth, in its refusal to follow the dictates of the linear narrative and grammar from without. It is Saleem's temporary substitute for a nation, a community that, as he himself says, places him at the centre rather than making him part of a system:

> Because the feeling had come upon me that I was somehow creating a world; that the thoughts I jumped inside were mine, that the bodies I occupied acted at my command; that, as current affairs, arts, sports, the whole rich variety of a first-class radio station poured into me, I was somehow making them happen . . . which is to say, I had entered into the illusion of the artist. (241)

The affiliation to the inward community compensates the failure to be a part of the fiction of the nation. It compensates for the doubts in the identity that the national selfhood cannot satisfy. To him there was "nothing but trouble outside my head, nothing but miracles inside it" (287).

It is this breakdown of the established concept of nationhood that is carried on in a different way by the other two writers under this study. The central issue of their novels is actually the negotiation of the two cultures, that of their ethnic origin and of their new home into which they "arrive." And, in this bipolarity, they develop a kind of transnationalism that becomes the answer to their quest for identity. If the earlier East-West relations have gone through the phases of the assimilation and limited abrogation, here is a renewed answer to the quest of identity that neither fully assimilates nor tries to abrogate, rather goes to find a kind of identity that fully suits the experience of fragmentation that marks modern diaspora consciousness. It is a kind of belonging rather than a negation, though this belonging is more internal than external. It is a belonging that does not seek the sanctions of the structures of power. And it is in here that it comes closer to the experience of Saleem Sinai in *Midnight's Children*. It is an important milestone in the changing modes of expression of the East-West conflict, and the representation of the identity that it evolves. The renewed identity represents itself as a kind of private, autonomous self, breaking the parameters set by the establishment, lending a kind of selfhood beyond nationalism. In the following parts of the paper, two novels by Chitra Banerjee Divakaruni, an immigrant writer who has been living in the United States since 1976, are taken up first to demonstrate the effects of *Midnight's Children*'s idea of the nation on the diaspora writers of the day.

When one comes to Divakaruni after Rushdie, the beginning of *The Vine of Desire* (2002) reflects the melancholy of isolation of Saleem and equally emphasizes on the self as a means of emancipation. "IN THE BEGINNING WAS PAIN. Or perhaps it was the end that was suffused with pain, its distinctive indigo tint. Color of old bruises, color of broken pottery, of crumpled maps in evening light." The "crumpled maps" represent a space limited by the boundaries of the nation that these writers defy both in physical and in emotional terms. In fact the desires of the lives of the diaspora protagonists are linked with this phenomenon of the "crumpled maps." In *The Vine of Desire*, the quest that animates the novel is that of finding the real identity of the diaspora Indian beyond the maps that has been crumpled by time and irreversible historical change. It is in this quest that all the characters move. Nation not only adopts the stance of the home with which to link up the migrant experience, it is also a kind of repository of patriarchy. Sudha's migration is a result of her rebarbative experiences with the systems of patriarchy. Going to America she adopts a new home and a new life of emancipation. It is her migrant experience that affords her a freedom that her homeland could not. However, if America provides a kind of realization of her femininity, it does not provide her a home in the complete sense of the term. Over there, she will not be subjected to the strict chores of patriarchy; she need not abort when she comes to know that she will bear a female child as she had to do in India. She does not have to go on playing the role of the perfect wife, irrespective of what she gets from her husband in return. She can enjoy her femininity with a married man of her liking without caring about social scandal. It is here that her role is not so much constructed by forces beyond her as is in her married life in India. Still America can only afford a fragmented self. Affiliation to its nationhood can hardly substitute her idea of a home. Both the women protagonists in the novel, Sudha and Anju, feel a kind of rootlessness in America. In spite of the fulfillment it affords over here, their life still remains fragmented. Their consciousness becomes a site of contested identities. "I want to bite into the apple of America. I want to swim to India, to the parrot-green smells of my childhood" (87), they feel.

Very closely related to Sudha's quest is that of Anju. She has the same origin as Sudha; but staying in America, she is in a position of relatively more personal freedom than Sudha. Like Sudha she also, at one point of her life, tried to be a perfect wife. Like Sudha she had failed. The depression following her miscarriage is deepened by her feeling of scattered identity, in her duality of belonging to two nations with widely different cultural traditions. While she has strong disgust towards certain aspects of her Indian heritage, she also feels protective towards it in the face of the Western tendency to stereotype it. But she does not leave her exile. She realizes that it is in the state of exile that she will have the distance necessary to understand both the cultures, of her home and of America. Rather than physically seeking refuge in either of the nations, she strives to encounter the fragments within herself through writing and joining a creative writing community. Here too, the disappointment of not being a part of the cultural tradition belonging to a nation turns her towards a community life. And it is here that she comes closer to Saleem and the diaspora sensibility of Meena Alexander's characters.

In Divakaruni, patriarchy seems to be one of the dominant aspects of nationhood. However, it is also the lack of belonging, the split identity of the diaspora situation that further complicates the effects of patriarchy. Her own recourse to literature was a kind of result of her homelessness in the US. Writing seemed to her a way of resisting the exile. Narrating the circumstances that led to her choice of the writing career, she says: "I couldn't go home. Lying on the bed I tried to visualize how it was back home, and couldn't. Writing made me remember. I wrote for myself, to keep linked, but never thought that I'd take up writing as a career one day," she recalls. "America made me a writer. Being in a whole different culture suddenly changed me. It made me question many things, especially about women's roles."

Divakaruni herself has found a convergence of her contested identities in interest groups of her community. She is a founder member of *Maitri*, a support group intended for the South Asian diaspora women. It deals with matters ranging from immigration to domestic violence and has established a helpline since 1991.

The same experience, drawn from her own cultural encounters in northern California, informs the protagonists of Divakaruni's other novels and short stories. Experiences of nationhood and patriarchy merge in the themes of her novels making them poignant narratives of the immigrant experience and the situation of women, particularly in arranged marriages. Like Rushdie in *Midnight's Children*, Divakaruni resorts to magic realism as a narrative mode in her first novel *The Mistress of Spices* (1997). Commenting on the novel Divakaruni writes: "I wrote in a spirit of play, collapsing the divisions between the realistic world of twentieth century America and the timeless one of myth and magic in my attempt to create a modern fable" ("Dissolving Boundaries"). The diaspora sensibility and the feelings of not belonging to the nation of immigration seem inseparably linked. "The spices of true power are from birthland" (3), the mistress of the spices in the novel, Tilo, declares. Tilo's life strangely bears close resemblances with Saleem being gifted like him of special abilities, in her case it is an ability to see into the future. Her childhood is similarly chequered though much more insecure than Saleem's. The trauma of homelessness accompanies her right from birth when she was named Nayan Tara. Almost deserted by her family for being a female child, she is taken off by pirates into the sea. With her magical abilities she comes to know of a magic island ruled by the "Old One" and manages to gain a new identity there, with a new name and new powers. She comes to know of the healing powers of spices and got the new name Tilottama.

The idea of the breakdown of the purposes of the nation on the individual thus features from the very beginning. If her exile is prompted by the ineffectuality of the nation of her birth in protecting her, the magic island may stand for a kind of substitute nation that empowers her with a new identity. Remarkable is the fact that her new name, with its mythological import, to which Divakaruni even alludes in the novel, is a kind of constant reminder to the situation of exile. Her stay in Oakland is an exile too. Despite her empowerment, she has to encounter the effects of patriarchy specific of her nation of birth when Indian women like Ahuja's wife, who has a real name Lalita but is known by her marital identity, or the rich women of Indian origin who are economically empowered by their NRI status, but still live with their "vulnerable flesh" (80), tell her their stories. The nation or the political establishment projects itself through one of its most potent components—patriarchy. In the secure home in America the "vertigo of homelessness" (137) continues to exist. It continues till the rebirth of Tilo with a new face and a new identity, as the partner of Raven, the reformed face of western emancipation, not so much at the institutional level as at the personal.

Coming back to *Midnight's Children*, it is not a novel which provides the experiences of the diaspora in the way the other novels under our study do. Saleem never moves out of the subcontinent. Yet, in a way it does actually provide an insight to the experience. He faces the immigrant crisis in his own home as the nation that he banks his identity on never actually materializes. It remains the fictional creation of the framed letters. Meena Alexander, our next author under study writes novels that question the concept of the nation, from both the locations. Beside challenging the constructs of nationhood of India in the way Saleem does in *Midnight's Children*, they also question the status of émigré nationality in the West, which they cannot be comfortable with as they stand in the way of ascertaining their own identity. Consequently, they form an identity out of myth and history, memory and nostalgia, in the way Saleem builds it.

When this memory works it tends to break the barrier of the nation in a way that is autonomous with the self. It is then that nostalgia comes to serve as the primary definitive force that could bring about a kind of belonging. And it is over here that the experiences of life in India and America come together in a process of denationalization to form component parts of the same consciousness. In fact, the realization comes close to the situation of Saleem in *Midnight's Children.* In *Fault Lines* (1993) she professes in having "possessed many souls, many voices in one dark body" (2). It reminds one of Saleem's multiple impersonations, feeling the voices of the entire varying multitude in him:

> At one time I was a landlord in Uttar Pradesh, my belly rolling over my pajama-cord as I ordered serfs to set my surplus grain on fire . . . at another moment I was starving to death in Orissa, where there was a food shortage as usual: I was two months old and my mother had run out of breast-milk. I occupied, briefly, the mind of a Congress Party worker, bribing a village schoolteacher to throw his weight behind the party of Gandhi and Nehru in the coming election campaign; also the thoughts of a Keralan peasant who had decided to vote Communist. My daring grew: one afternoon I deliberately invaded the head of our own State Chief Minister. . . . And finally I hit my highest point: I became Jawaharlal Nehru, Prime Minister and author of framed letters. (240-41)

It is the understanding of what Benedict Anderson calls "large cultural systems" (19) that preceded the construction of the nation that the multiple voices reflect.

In our study on Meena Alexander we would concentrate on two of her novels, *Nampally Road* (1991) and *Manhattan Music* (1997). In both these novels the prime protagonists are women and among the questions that come up, the idea of the nation in the accepted sense of the term or rather the lack of that is one of the key issues. In *Nampally Road*, the protagonist Mira reaches a critical point of her life when she returns after completing her studies in England to a newly independent India with an idealism to serve the country with her literary endeavour. At the beginning, her idea of her home had been perfectly in accordance of the dictates of national history and the ideals of nationalism that the independence movement had modelled itself on. However, soon upon reaching her home, she found herself drawn towards the prevalent socio-political turmoil of the 1970s that question the bases of the nation-building process. Her involvement lays bare before her the failure of the national enterprise in the traditional sense. Nehru, the "author of framed letters" (241) for Saleem, seemed like "an aristocrat lacking a phone line with the future" (57). The failure of the nation state and the power structures that foster its establishment come out most succinctly in a seminal episode in the novel. A poor Muslim woman Rameeja is raped by the policemen. The episode, followed by what it unleashes, expose the myth of the unity in diversity to Mira, she starts questioning the ideals on which this welfare state has been based. Nationhood and the identity it hurls upon an individual unawares, all seems to be exploitative constructs of the same patriarchy that defines the norms of the race and gender. She can no longer remain content with writing as a meaningful vocation since the postcolonial world around her "was too visible, too turbulent already to permit the kinds of writing I had once learned to write" (32). But like Saleem she needs substitutes. It is she who ultimately finds her companionship not so much in the identity dictated by the establishments of power than in something that she discovers inwardly, just as Saleem does through the strange faculty he develops. It is the realization that involved the individuals around her much more concretely than the anachronistic idea of the nation. It is a feeling of an understanding that has always been with her. "The life that made sense was all around me in little Mother and Ramu and the young students, the orange sellers and the violent and wretched, ourselves included. It was already there" (28).

Once the socio-political sense of nationalism is thwarted, Mina strives to find another substitute. In her quest for a group to identify with, she realizes like Saleem that "the self is always . . . broken" (92). But she also feels the necessity to "leapfrog . . . over the black fissures" (92). Having lost her national identity she seeks a collective identity in a community, realizing in her a sense of multiple lives, a kind of emancipating quest "from one woman's body into another" (91). It is in the attachments of the community bound together by experiences based on gender and class that finally provides her with a real identity. It is acknowledged neither by the mechanism of the establishment, nor by the structures of power or political authority built upon the unrealized ideals of nationhood. It is a kind of communion based on similarity of socio-cultural experiences. She declares her multilayered identity in the community of women in a language that evinces fullness rather than fragmentation in this multiplicity.

> As for the Indian past, what was it to me? Sometimes I felt it was a motley collection of events that rose in my mind, rather like those bleached stones in the abandoned graveyard the boy picked his way through. I had no clear picture of what unified it all, what our history might mean. We were in it, all together, that's all I knew. And there was no way out. (28)

The Indian past thrust upon by the discourses of nationhood appears obscure. It is replaced by the community that is more palpable and real. These lines obviously remind one of Saleem's contesting the hierarchical nationalistic discourse with a more polyphonic one founded on similarity of experiences.

It is the same kind of identity that Sandhya, one of the central characters in *Manhattan Music* seeks, though she is placed in a diametrically opposite position to Mina. If Mina's predicament is consequent upon her homecoming, for Sandhya her realization comes from her experiences in the West. She had followed her husband into the US. Her exile is thus not voluntary, neither does it emancipate her. It is a following of the dictates of patriarchy. Draupadi, another female character in the novel is almost her foil. She has been born of an émigré family; her only attachment to India is in her name and in her constant reminder of not belonging fully to the American society in which she works as a free lance journalist. Nevertheless she cannot find her identity in the present context. While like Gogol in Jhumpa Lahiri's *Namesake* she cannot find any reason why she was named Draupadi instead of Dorothy, she also cannot remain at ease with the racist American society. She finds that her situation of belonging to two cultures actually contest her affiliation to either of them. She tries to find her home in the tradition of her ancestors. Yet the homelessness that Sandhya experiences, in being too bound to her original homeland is counterpoised with that of Draupadi, who cannot relate herself with a tradition constructed by memory and nostalgia derived from ancestry, constructed in countering numerous dislodgments, not an actually realized feeling.

Memory ties Sandhya to the past. Almost in a literal sense, she shuttles between the deathbed of her father in India, where her identity of an Indian daughter manages to take hold of her, and the alien New York with her husband Stephen. It is memory that prevents her from adapting totally to her immigrant status. And it is this kind of identity that Draupadi desires in her. But the experiences that lend this identity are so distant in her case that she fails to achieve it. There is a desire in her to adopt a kind of hybridity as her performance piece, in which she evinces a kind of fusion of Indian and US history, shows. Still she rejects her hybridity in favour of a more secure mooring, which, however, evades her. She realizes, "All she had were whispers, shards of songs, torn phrases, and could they add up to a heritage? Still, as a human being, she felt she had a right to anything out there. And what came from India was closer" (520). This is again a rejection of nation in the institutional sense and a kind of adherence to the psycho-ethnic constructs of the home, as opposed to the geopolitical identity of physical location.

For Sandhya the US cannot be her home. It is too institutionalized to be so. She however, finds for herself a kind of altered home. It is, again, a community rather than a geographical location. It is that of women like her who voice their sufferings. And it is here that her quest for identity completes itself. She neither relates to the hegemony of power, nor towards a reality that is physically absent around her. Her renewed identity is much more concrete than tagging oneself with the memory of the culture. The community is of Indians no doubt, but it is a kind of belonging that requires neither governmental nor patriarchal sanction. "Sandhya felt she had entered a country where she needed neither passport nor green card, nor any other signs of belonging. She sat back in the plastic chair to listen to the testimonies of the women on the platform" (211). While the passport and the green card are all emblems of institutional authority and sanction defining identities hurled on by the establishment, which she no longer requires, the plastic chair also serves as an image that deinstitutionalizes her identity, making it personal and beyond the powers of the establishment to mould.

Saleem is an émigré on the inside, while Sudha, Anju, Tilo, Mina, Sandhya and Draupadi are émigrés on the outside as well. Their experiences are similar and the solutions they seek to their crises are similar. The way Saleem responds to this crisis is different. Yet a similarity of pattern can be traced in all their responses. The diaspora sensibility, whether inward or outward, does not seek a kind of self-identifying affiliation to the changed co-ordinates of the nation that the émigré migrates to. Rather, they cannot but create the reflections of their own nationhood in their own self, despite all its oppressive insensitivity. Some reject it; others try to renew its understanding. However, in the long run, it is neither patriarchy or sectarianism nor the cultural imperialism implicit in development that satisfies the need of the individual lost to his nation. It is human relationship, sometimes individual, sometimes communal, based on the sameness of experience that creates the collective identity nationality is supposed to invest the individual with. If the mechanism of the nation becomes irrelevant for them in its implication of giving a particular identity, its symbolic role gets played by communities and conferences, that empowers from within rather than from without.

Works Cited

Alexander, Meena, *Nampally Road*. San Francisco: Mercury, 1991.

_____, *Manhattan Music*. San Francisco: Mercury, 1997.

_____, *Fault Lines: A Memoir*. New York: The Feminist P at the City U of New York, 1993.

Barnaby, Edward. "Airbrushed history: photography, realism, and Rushdie's *Midnight's Children*." *Mosaic: a journal for the interdisciplinary study of literature*, 38:1, March 2005, pp. 1-16.

Benedict Anderson, *Imagined Communities: Reflections on the Origin and Spread of Nationalism*, rev. ed. London: Verso, 1992.

Biswas, Ranjita. "Queen of Dreams." *Span* January/February 2007: 7.

Divakaruni, Chitra Banerjee. "Author Essay: Dissolving Boundaries." *Boldtype*; an Online Literary Magazine. Issue 3 May 1997. http: www.randomhouse.com/boldtype/0597/divakaruni/essay.html

_____, *The Mistress of Spices*. New York: Anchor, 1997.

_____, *The Vine of Desire*. 2002. London: Abacus, 2003.

Rushdie, Salman. *Midnight's Children*. 1981; London: Vintage, 2006.

A Comparative Study of Chitra Divakaruni and Jhumpa Lahiri's Diasporic Experiences

VIDYA P. VERMA
Viva College, Mumbai
&
YOGITA VERMA
R.J.I.T., Tekanpur, Gwalior

Indian Americans (or Asian Indians) are Americans of Indian ancestry and comprise about 2.81 million people, alone or 3.18 million, combined with one or more races, about 1% of the U.S. population, the country's third largest self-reported Asian ancestry after Chinese Americans and Filipino Americans, according to American Community Survey of 2010 data. The U.S. Census Bureau uses the term Asian Indian to avoid confusion with the indigenous peoples of the Americas commonly referred to as American Indians. Indian English literature has produced a range of writers who are being recognized as the powerful writers of the Indian immigrant writings and have earned name and fame worldwide. V.S. Naipaul, Vikram Seth, Shashi Tharoor, Amitav Ghosh, Agha Shahid Ali, Kiran Desai, Arundhati Roy, Chitra Banerjee and Jhumpa Lahiri are the few India based writers. This paper attempts to examine the basic themes of Chitra's *Oleander Girl* (2013) and Jhumpa's *The Lowland* (2013). Chitra Banerjee's works primarily deal with various shades of the experiences of the immigrant women. Her novels *Sister of My Heart* (1995), *The Mistress of Spices*

(1997), *The Vine of Desire* (2002), *One Amazing Thing* (2011) and her recent novel *Oleander Girl* (2013) are the fine exposure of different shades of identity crisis and quest of freedom and dependence of Indian immigrant women. Lahiri's work shows her obsession with the Diasporic world of Bengali families migrated from India to the United States of America. Lahiri's stories deal with individuality, communication gap between the first and second generation, addiction, secret love, parenthood, family relationship, emotional and physical disconnectivity, Indian American identity and diasporic experiences of immigrant families in USA.

Chitra Banerjee Divakaruni (born Chitralekha Banerjee, 1956) is an Indian-American author, poet, and the Betty and Gene McDavid Professor of Writing at the University of Houston Creative Writing Program. Her short story collection *Arranged Marriage* won American Book Award in 1995, and two of her novels (*The Mistress of Spices* and *Sister of My Heart*) were adapted into films. *Mistress of Spices* was shortlisted for the Orange Prize. Divakaruni's works are largely set in India and the United States, and often focus on the experiences of South Asian immigrants. She writes for children as well as adults and has published novels in multiple genres, including realistic fiction. Chitralekha Banerjee was born in Kolkata, India. She has two brothers. She received her B.A. from the University of Calcutta in 1976. That same year, she went to the United States to attend Wright State University where she received a master's degree. She received a Ph.D. from the University of California, Berkeley in 1985 (Christopher Marlowe was the subject of her doctoral dissertation). Divakaruni put herself through graduate school by taking on odd jobs, working as a babysitter, a store clerk, a bread slicer in a bakery, a laboratory assistant at Wright State University, and a dining hall attendant at International House, Berkeley. She taught at Foothill College in Los Altos, California and Diablo Valley College. She now lives in Texas, where she teaches at the University of Houston Creative Writing Program.

Divakaruni is a co-founder and former president of *Maitri*, a helpline founded in 1991 for South Asian women dealing with domestic abuse. Divakaruni serves on its advisory board and on the advisory board of a similar organization in Houston, Daya. She also serves on the Houston board of Pratham, a non-profit organization working to bring literacy to disadvantaged Indian children

Chitra Banerjee is a mesmerizing storyteller. Her latest book, *Oleander Girl*, keeps you engrossed from start to finish. It is an exciting exploration of modern India with characters who are easy to understand and care about. Orphaned at birth, seventeen-year-old Korobi Roy has enjoyed a sheltered childhood with her adoring grandparents. But she is troubled by the silence that surrounds her parents' death and clings fiercely to her only inheritance from them: the love note she found in her mother's book of poetry. Korobi dreams of one day finding a love as powerful as her parents' and it seems her wish has come true when she meets the charming Rajat, the only son of a high-profile family.

But shortly after their engagement, a heart attack kills Korobi's grandfather, revealing serious financial problems and a devastating secret about Korobi's past. Shattered by this discovery and by her grandparents' betrayal, Korobi undertakes a courageous search across post-9/11 America to find her true identity. Her dramatic, often startling journey will, ultimately, thrust her into the most difficult decision of her life. Korobi Roy has been strictly but lovingly brought up by her grandparents following the tragic loss of her parents after her birth. She is engaged to be married to a handsome and rich young man and seems fated to a charmed if tradition-bound life. But then Korobi's grandfather dies, and everything changes. A dark secret is revealed, and it sets Korobi on a mission to America to discover a part of her past she never knew existed. The journey not only leads Korobi to new discoveries about herself but also triggers new challenges and discoveries for her prospective in-laws, The Bosses, and her fiancé Rajat, who are already facing business challenges in the changing and unsettling Indian political and social climate. Even her grandmother, already struggling with the loss of the man who dominated her life for many years and now also separated from the granddaughter she has raised, has to learn and grow as she finds new roles for herself. Korobi and Rajat are forced to grow up by these circumstances. One of the great things about this story is that it is not only the lovers who have to learn and grow and face challenges and failures as well as successes. The book explores what happens when everyone's seemingly stable life is shaken in many ways. Even the minor characters are fully realized and involved in facing their own evolution as they react to their problems and position in life. The insights into such issues as racism and the class system in India, the volatile and sometimes violent confrontations between Hindu and Muslim, bosses and workers, tradition and change, are fascinating and are integrated fully into the plot in a seamless manner so that one is enlightened without any extraneous explanation necessary.

Jhumpa Lahiri, born on July 11, 1967, is an Indian American author. Lahiri's debut short story collection, *Interpreter of Maladies* (1999), won the 2000 Pulitzer Prize for Fiction, and her first novel, *The Namesake* (2003), was adapted into the popular film of the same name. She was born Nilanjana Sudeshna but goes by her nickname (or in Bengali, her "Daak naam"). Jhumpa Lahiri is a member of the President's Committee on the Arts and Humanities, appointed by U.S. President Barack Obama. Her book *The Lowland*, published in 2013, was a nominee for the Man Booker Prize and the Fiction. Lahiri was born in London, the daughter of Indian immigrants from the state of West Bengal. Her family moved to the United States when she was two; Lahiri considers herself an American, stating, "I wasn't born here, but I might as well have been." Lahiri grew up in Kingston, Rhode Island, where her father Amar Lahiri works as a librarian at the University of Rhode Island. Lahiri graduated from South Kingstown High School and received her B.A. in English literature from Barnard College in 1989. Lahiri then received multiple degrees from Boston University: an M.A. in English, M.F.A. in Creative Writing, M.A. in Comparative Literature, and a Ph.D. in Renaissance Studies. She took a fellowship at Provincetown's Fine Arts Work Center, which lasted for the next two years (1997-1998). Lahiri has taught creative writing at Boston University and the Rhode Island School of Design. In 2001, Lahiri married Alberto Vourvoulias-Bush, a journalist who was then Deputy Editor of *Time* Latin America, and who is now Senior Editor of *Time* Latin America. Lahiri lives in Rome, Italy with her husband and their two children, Octavio (b. 2002) and Noor (b. 2005). Lahiri's early short stories faced rejection from publishers "for years." Her debut short story collection, *Interpreter of Maladies*, was finally released in 1999. The stories address sensitive dilemmas in the lives of Indians or Indian immigrants, with themes such as marital difficulties, miscarriages, and the disconnection between first and second generation United States immigrants. Lahiri later wrote, "When I first started writing I was not conscious that my subject was the Indian-American experience. What drew me to my craft was the desire to force the two worlds I occupied to mingle on the page as I was not brave enough, or mature enough, to allow in life." The collection was praised by American critics, but received mixed reviews in India, where reviewers were alternately enthusiastic and upset Lahiri had "not paint[ed] Indians in a more positive light. However, according to Md. Zia-ul Haque, a poet, columnist, scholar, researcher and a faculty member of the English department at Sylhet International University, Bangladesh, "But, it is really painful for any writer living far away in a new state, leaving his/her own homeland behind; the motherland, the environment, people, culture etc." *Interpreter of Maladies* sold 600,000 copies and received the 2000 Pulitzer Prize for Fiction (only the seventh time a story collection had won the award). In 2003, Lahiri published *The Namesake*, her first novel. The story spans over thirty years in the life of the Ganguli family. The Calcutta-born parents emigrated as young adults to the United States, where their children, Gogol and Sonia, grow up experiencing the constant generational and cultural gap with their parents. A film adaptation of *The Namesake* was released in March 2007, directed by Mira Nair and starring Kal Penn as Gogol and Bollywood stars Tabu and Irrfan Khan as his parents. Lahiri herself made a cameo as "Aunt Jhumpa."

In *The Lowland* (2013), two brothers bound by tragedy; a fiercely brilliant woman haunted by her past; a country torn by revolution: the Pulitzer Prize winner and # 1 *New York Times* best-selling author gives us a powerful new novel—set in both India and America—that explores the price of idealism and a love that can last long past death. Growing up in Calcutta, born just fifteen months apart, Subhash and Udayan Mitra are inseparable brothers, one often mistaken for the other. But they are also opposites, with gravely different futures ahead of them. It is the 1960s, and Udayan—charismatic and impulsive—finds himself drawn to the Naxalite movement, a rebellion waged to eradicate inequity and poverty: he will give everything, risk all, for what he believes.

Subhash, the dutiful son, does not share his brother's political passion; he leaves home to pursue a life of scientific research in a quiet, coastal corner of America. But when Subhash learns what happened to his brother in the lowland outside their family's home, he comes back to India, hoping to pick up the pieces of a shattered family, and to heal the wounds Udayan left behind—including those seared in the heart of his brother's wife. Suspenseful, sweeping, piercingly intimate, *The Lowland* expands the range of one of our most dazzling storytellers, seamlessly interweaving the historical and the personal across generations and geographies. This masterly novel of fate and will, exile and return, is a tour de force and an instant classic.

The Lowland is her fourth book—all of them woven around the theme of dislocation of immigrants, cultivating the angst of those pining for the ones who left; the late knowledge in life for the ones who left that there are no places to hide in this world, especially from one's own guilty self. Culture for Lahiri is both hyper-local and disingenuous, a fickle companion to build a foundation upon when it comes to matters of the sub-conscious and the soul, helplessly drawn to shores far away when assimilated life beckons from close by. She effortlessly creates conflict in comfort, comfort in conflict. In *The Lowland*, Lahiri also seems to have unfinished business left from the Bengal of the 60s, the period from which her previous, debut novel *The Namesake* also emanated. Both are family sagas, both feature a couple catapulted to America from Kolkata, to live a life which at least one of them—the wife—did not plan emotionally or psychologically, then delivers a baby. Elements of discord and alienation, hope and rejection, love and loss between spouses in *The Lowland* are themes that were nurtured in *The Namesake,* as well as her past two short story collections, *Interpreter of Maladies* and *Unaccustomed Earth. The Lowland*, steeped in the violent and outlawed Naxalite movement of the 60s, revolves around the lives of brothers Subhash and Udayan, in Kolkata, and the enigmatic Gauri, the woman destined to become the wife of both of them. First, to the charismatic revolutionary younger brother Udayan, whom she loves, and then when pregnant with his child, marries the sedate and moderate scholar Subhash, who studies and lives in Rhode Island, after Udayan is shot by the police. His death, though, remains a mystery that hovers like a jack-in-the-box that threatens to startle the reader at any turn of the page throughout the book. Subhash convinces Gauri to marry him for the sake of the unborn child, even though his parents oppose it. Gauri sees it as an escape from the place where everybody, except her brother, has rejected her, for her alliance with Udayan and his incendiary politics. In America, Gauri caves in to her first love—the study of philosophy. She starts to focus her attention and more time on taking classes at the local university, even as Subhash becomes the role model of a pristine father to Udayan and Gauri's daughter Bela. His greatest fear is the child coming to know that he is not her real father, even as his marriage to Gauri starts to crumble. Bringing matters to a head are Subhash's ageing parents in Kolkata, whom he finds increasingly hard to ignore, and yearns to take care of. Lahiri superbly juxtaposes the tug-of-war between Subhash's comfortable life on the East Coast in America versus the debilitating life of his parents on the East Coast in India, where his intrinsic memories also live on, and he cannot tear away from. Like a patch of land at the back of his house in Kolkata, which becomes submerged during the monsoons—a lowland—and emerges again when the rains abate, showing also two distinct ponds side by side separated by an embankment, the two cultures he wears and breathes, often become inseparable, distinct at the same time. After the death of Subhash's father, his mother, who is going senile, starts to clean the detritus of the two ponds with her bare hands—the rotten waste she surfaces symbolic of her and her husband's dashed ambitions and hopes of living in a joint family with their sons and families, the modern indestructible plastic refuse uncovered, of the negligence by her sons. The research-heavy early chapters, on the Naxalbari movement, and then the ultimate realization that here is a novel which defied conventional wisdom—to let it gain life in itself as it rolled on, but instead was scripted to perfection—is an aberration too. The plot is simple, boxed in, conclusive; the course of the lives of most of the characters chalked with studied finality seems to have halos of ghosts of other characters from Lahiri's past books. The act of rebellion by Gauri for self-identity and the way she charts her independent life in America stands out. Her unjustifiable character and the shades she's given, is perhaps a way out for Lahiri to turn the tide of a routine in a story that had otherwise the makings of a repetitive throw of a yo-yo, yet again.

Both Chitra Banerjee Divakaruni and Jhumpa Lahiri are writers of diaspora and show the diasporic sensibility in almost all their works. They show deep concern for the Indian Americans and bring forward in their works the issues of diasporic families living in the United States of America. Chitra Divakaruni admits that it is the familial tie that binds her with other Indian-origin writers including Jhumpa Lahiri. She says while she and Jhumpa Lahiri live and work in different cities and hence can't meet each other as often as they would have liked, they know each other quite well, interacting closely on the panels of literary festivals around the world.

Bibliography

W.W.W.dnaindia.com
W.W.W.Khaleejtimes.com
En.wikipedia.org/wiki/Indian—America
en.wikioedia.org/wiki/Jhumpa Lahiri
en.wikipedia.org/wiki/Chitra-Banerjee-Divakaruni.

'Draupadi' speaks through Pratibha Ray and Chitra Divakaruni

ANJU JAGPAL
Govt. P.G. College, Ambala Cantt.

Draupadi of the *Mahabharata* has been one of the most tragic and contentious characters of archetypal women in the Indian imagination since the inception of the great epic itself. Considered to be the cause of tremendous destruction of human race and the harbinger of one of the greatest wars, she has also been assigned the proud place among the *panchsatis* and *panchkanyas.* Though she has been "counted among the five supremely virtuous women, honoured as 'Panch Sati,'" yet "in mythology, the name Draupadi still bears stigma and is often contemptuously uttered by people in society." She has neither been accorded the due respect and reverence, nor has she been considered the epitome of virtues to be emulated by other women. She is rather ridiculed and rejected for her polyandrous marriage to five Pandava brothers. The stories of her birth, beauty, learning, pride and haughtiness suffice to intimidate the wilful and the ambitious woman in a patriarchal society even today as she has been alleged of transgressing the normative socio-cultural boundaries many a time and duly punished for those audacious acts.

According to Chaturvedi Badrinath, "The *Mahabharata* never stifled Draupadi's voice." One cannot challenge or refute this assertion entirely, yet the question arises whose voice has it actually been? Is it really Draupadi who speaks or is she just a mouthpiece of the author/s of the epic? If she herself had the liberty to put forth her mind, why could she not defend herself and why did she choose the epithet of a cursed woman for all times to come? Where was the need to retrieve her sobbing silences and her agonized self from the archives of cultural history and coax her to speak up now?

C.R. Deshpande very rightly says, "Over the years of its existence the *Mahabharata* has been playing a very important role not only in the lives of the people of India but also in the lives of the people of South East Asia. . . . The *Mahabharata* has not only influenced the literature, art, sculpture, and painting of India but it has also moulded the very character of the Indian people." He agrees with Oldenberg: "in the *Mahabharata* breathe the united soul of India and the individual souls of her people." Dr. V.S. Sukhantar claims, "Whether we realize it or not, it remains a fact that we in India still stand under the spell of the *Mahabharata*. . . . Venerable for its very antiquity, it is one of the most inspiring monuments of the world and an inexhaustible mine for the investigation of the religion, mythology, legend, philosophy, law, custom and political and social institutions of ancient India." Thus, the *Mahabharata* is not just an epic of the ancients; it is a living tradition and the very life source of Indian socio-political and cultural moorings. We derive sustenance and recheck our facts going back to our ancient sources to justify our present and take pride in being their inheritors. Since we are the inheritors and the past belongs to us all, we can also take the liberty to move toward the hind side and inspect and project what has somehow been left out or overlooked for a long time and also to re-examine and reinterpret the established facts through different canons.

It is hardly disputable that ours has been a largely patriarchal society and in such a society woman is merely an appendage to man, sans identity and voice of her own. Like other soulless things, she is also a 'thing' for the consumption of man. Uma Chakravarti digs out the episode of Gargi challenging Yagnavalkya in the debate. Moreover, how she is intimidated into silence. The daughter of a famous philosopher, Gargi shoots sharp questions regarding soul which is considered a prohibited subject for the lesser beings and "instead of answering them, he [Yajnavalkya] abruptly ended the debate with a typical assertion of brahmanical male power: 'Do not, O Gargi, push your inquiry too far lest your head should fall off.' Thereupon Gargi fell silent." Chakravarti observes that it is noteworthy that "while recourse to violence is actually necessary to tame or break the resistance of men who need to be subordinated the mere threat of violence is enough to silence women."

Draupadi, however, breaks her silence only after the worst imaginable happens to her in the court of the Kauravas in the presence of all her male elders and her five mighty husbands. None but the divine comes to her rescue, whereas, bound by their duty, their *dharma,* all present in the court, including Dharamraj, Yudhishthir and Bheeshma Pitamah become the mute spectators of the most horrible insult meted out to a helpless menstruating woman. No one has any answer to her appeals and questions. For her defeated eldest husband, the codes of his *dharma* are far more important than the respect and dignity of his wife. It is only her vengeful vow and curse of total annihilation of the Kauravas and the powerful yet emasculated onlookers, that prompts Dhritarashtra to seek forgiveness from Draupadi for the wrongs done to her and he begs her to ignore the regrettable incident. It has been a blot on our cultural heritage as there is hardly any parallel anywhere of such a heinous crime and physical punishment as public disrobing of a royal woman. This event also reinforced the patriarchal conviction that a wife is man's property and he has the right to put her on stake like his other belongings.

After such a rejection and abuse of her person, Draupadi was left only with two choices—either to end her life and put to shame, utter subjugation and constant threat of similar penalty the whole womankind forever, or to avenge the wrong keeping herself inflamed. A woman of mettle, she took to the latter recourse, which accelerated the Great War of Mahabharata. Even today, she is held responsible for that enormous devastation and is considered the cause of patricide and fratricide. Had she chosen death, instead of revenge to reclaim her self-respect, who would have set the moral order right in favour of the poor woman? Had our history been any better supporting the transgression and bruised egos of Duryodhan and Karna, rejected in the *swayamvara*? Could it have been as great a monument as the *Mahabharata* is considered today, had Draupadi not taken the responsibility of salvaging her own honour? Isn't it ironical that the wife of five supreme men of her times, in essence Draupadi was all alone in her life and death except the steady support of Krishna who was her *sakha*? Since she was born of sacrificial altar, the cruel fate even denied her the comforts of a mother's lap where she could bare her heart and soul without qualms. Her uttered words were heard and recorded but what about those that remained buried deep like smoldering cinders under the ashes of her apparent being concealed with her tangled tresses? Both Pratibha Ray and Chitra Banerjee Divakaruni have tried to give a breather to Draupadi persuading her to narrate her own story revealing the secret sore-spots of her dejected being to the prejudiced world in their fictional works *Yajnaseni, the Story of Draupadi* and *The Palace of Illusions* respectively. This paper is an attempt to study and understand Draupadi from the perspective of these two women writers and assess to what extent they have succeeded in redeeming the respect and reputation of this victimized woman.

Pratibha Ray was the first Indian woman to be presented the Bharatiya Jnanpith's prestigious ninth Moortidevi Award in 1993 for her novel *Yajnaseni.* As very significantly noted by Jaiwanti Dimri, "According to Ved Vyasa, this epic examines, by and large, the basic dharmas of religion (Dharma), money (Artha) and salvation (Moksha):

What is in this epic
On Dharma, Artha, Moksha,
May be elsewhere
What is not in this epic
Is nowhere else. (*Mahabharata* 62:53)

(Interestingly, one of the Dharmas, Kama is missing here.)," yet one finds this epic replete with the incidents of Kama that hurl forth the narrative, except the birth of Draupadi and her twin brother Dhrishtadyumna, who are born of the sacrificial fire. Born of the fire of *Yajna,* Pratibha Ray's Yajnaseni is full of youth and exquisite beauty that had the potential of making "mighty Time . . . [stand] still" at the moment of her birth. (7) She earned her father's instant approval and affection as her birth was accompanied by a prophecy: "This woman has taken birth to avenge your insult. She has appeared to fulfil a vow. By her, dharma will be preserved on this earth, kshatriyas will be destroyed. She will be the destroyer of the Kauravas." (8) She is fondly named Krishnaa, the dark complexioned one and her father gleams with pride and satisfaction as he pledges softly, "O Krishna! It is to you that I shall offer my Krishnaa. . . . The finest of Aryavart's heroes! The greatest warrior and dharma-establisher!" (9)

On the other hand, Chitra Banerjee Divakaruni's Draupadi was "the Girl Who Wasn't Invited." (1) Insisted by the girl to tell her stories to counter suffocation and claustrophobic atmosphere of her father's palace, her Dhai Ma tells her "When your brother stepped out of the sacrificial fire onto the cold stone slabs of the palace halls, all the assembly cried out in amazement . . . when you emerged from the fire, our jaws dropped. It was so quiet, you could have heard a housefly fart." (1-2) In stark contrast to her brother who was fair, noble and calm, she was dark, clumsy and hasty. When the boy emerged, some voices emerged too and declared to the king: "Here is the son you asked for. He'll bring you the vengeance you desire, but it'll break your life in two"; still the father welcomed the son with open arms. Then appeared the girl, uninvited and the voices spoke again "Behold, we give you this girl, a gift beyond what you asked for. Take good care of her, for she will change the course of history" (4-5). Hesitatingly, King Drupad picked them up and named the son Dhrishtadyumna, destroyer of enemies and the daughter was called Draupadi, daughter of Drupad. The girl remembers how her father wanted to pick up his son "to show to his people. Only my brother that he wanted." (6) Yet he was forced to pick the girl up as well, as both the children held each-other's hand stubbornly.

This initial denial of a girl child is typical of Indian mind-set and so deep-rooted in our psyche that it seems a naturalized response. Draupadi remembers this rejection even though her father tries to indulge her as she grows up, yet she could never trust him completely ever in her life. Her inequitable status in comparison to her brother singes her soul and makes her confidence dwindle many a time even in the prophecy made at the time of her birth. She is denied that education which is considered essential for her brother and she resents this fact as much as "the thick gray slabs of the walls—more suited to a fortress than a king's residence." (6) She dreams indulgently and waits for the prophecy to come true to justify her birth and existence, yet is sceptic about her being chosen by the fate to change the future course of history. Desperately she wants to prove her worth as she knows and accepts it candidly, "what my father did not find useful, he removed from his life." (6) She is restless and impulsive and her queries never end. Time and again she is reminded by her Dhai Ma to contain herself and not to have very high hopes about her future lest they should incite her to transgress the boundaries fixed for women. She is forcibly initiated into the course of femininity as becoming of a princess whereas her heart lies somewhere else. She wants to learn the art of statecraft and be proficient in the wielding of arms if she is the chosen medium for such a critical mission in her life. She surreptitiously joins her brother and his tutor during his lessons and is dissuaded repeatedly from such an impish act. She resents most the tutor's declaration that "women were the root of all the world's problems." (24) She questions every injunction laid down in the *shastras* that limit women's existence and invite the wrath of her father and Dhai Ma along with her brother's and his tutor's.

The seeds of dismissal sown in her childhood never let her accept her father's home as her own. She is unable to grow her roots and bond of affection except with her brother and the Dhai Ma. She yearns for her own home and often imagines "When I had my own palace . . . it would be totally different . . . a riot of colour and sound . . . elegant as crystal . . . precious, like a jewel-studded goblet . . . it would mirror my deepest being. There I would finally be at home." (*POI,* 7) She imagines her future palace to be in complete contrast to that of her father which lacks life, colour and mirth. In fact, it represents her father's sole motive of life that is to take revenge, which saps him of all his vitality and overpowers his existence completely. Draupadi's mere desire and imagining a palace of her own, which would reflect her true self reveals her love for life and yearning for her own space and freedom.

Another cause of Draupadi's rejection was her dark complexion, which was and is still considered to be a major drawback and most unfortunate for a girl. It gave her many a sleepless nights to her as well to her attendants who tried assiduously to lighten her complexion till Krishna assured her that a girl as dark as Draupadi was also capable of changing history. To relieve her of her distress he says, "A problem becomes a problem only if you believe it to be so. And often others see you as you see yourself." (9) As an acquaintance and a trusted person Krishna aids her at the moments of confusion and difficulties, and gradually becomes an integral part of her life. Divakaruni's Draupadi is fascinated by Krishna, as she could not decipher his 'chameleon' like character and capabilities to fit into the role, as was the need of the time and situation. It was he, who groomed Draupadi's confident self, cultivated and sharpened her mental faculties, challenged and rectified her obsolete beliefs, asked about her future hopes and aspirations and provided her the information of the outside world denied to her inside the walls of her father's dungeon-like palace. She later on realizes that she herself was the cause of Krishna's frequent visits to her father's kingdom, though there was no element of desire in this relationship whereas, Ray's Yajnaseni is thrilled with "some unknown sensation . . . every pore in [her] skin throbbed with joy . . . a heavenly, pure, sweet stream of love drenched [her] heart . . . eyes brimmed over" the moment she hears Krishna's name for the first time. (9) Even without having seen him, she accepts him as her future husband as her father's desire is the same. Her friends and maids further fuel her desire for Krishna and tease her in his name.

Divakaruni's Draupadi spends her childhood craving for the love and attention of her father. Her life is strictly regimented and secluded. She feels deprived and discriminated against in the male-dominated world as she is an unwanted and uninvited girl child. Devoid of a milky complexion and feared as the carrier of the seeds of an unknown cataclysmic event of future, she is considered a peril that emerged out of sacrificial altar. She leads an uneventful life and is shunned like an ill omen by the family of her father until she assertively takes up the challenge and joins the royal procession to a Shiva temple confident of her beauty and grace. There she mesmerizes everyone with her bluish hue and elegance and "Overnight . . . became a celebrated beauty!" (10) She makes use of her physical charms to punish the tutor of her brother who declares women to be "the path to ruin." (24) A smile from her lips makes him lose his balance and "manuscripts fell, helter-skelter, from his hands." (25) She is thrilled to find this source of power which earlier she was unaware of. This awareness of the potential of her beauty instills confidence as well as pride in her.

Draupadi is also aware of the perils of her beauty yet she realizes that only her physical beauty has provided her the visibility she had always craved for. Yajnaseni, too, is aware of her heavenly beauty and its effect upon others, yet she is cautious and prays to the Almighty for giving her strength to bear the insults and calumny that would be the corollaries of her fate. She, too, starts interrogating the whole scheme of things and indulges in self-dialogue the moment she emerges out of the altar. Her questions underline the pain and fear that she is born with and they are the questions of all women of all ages: "Should only women be forced to be the medium for preserving dharma throughout the ages? Is it woman who is the cause of creation and destruction? Sita had to become the medium of destruction of Lanka and the establishment of Ram's rule. . . . The intention behind Lord Ram's birth was fulfilled. But ultimately, what did Sita get? The sentence of exile from Rama! Public test of chastity! . . . To hide her sorrow, shame and insults Sita sank into Earth's lap." (8)

Her questions also highlight her assertive and inquiring self who would not succumb to circumstances without resistance even though she has been born with a decided destiny. She scans the severely patriarchal moves of destiny and wonders why her brother alone has not been assigned the task of restoring the moral order of the world. She scrutinizes everything minutely and has the desire to reach the very core of things. To quench her thirst of knowledge, her father would organize many discussions and would invite learned scholars, poets and wise men. She was not denied the knowledge of *shastras* and her father tried his best to equip her for her future destiny. Even sage Ved Vyas approved of her craving for learning and affectionately guided her in the lessons of life, whereas Draupadi had an entirely different experience with him. It is he, a fortune-teller, who unveils what future has in store for her and, thus, prepares her for the destined destiny. He tells her categorically: "Destiny is strong and swift. You can't trick it so easily . . . your own nature is going to speed its process. . . . Your pride. Your temper. Your vengefulness." (40) He suggests her to hold back her question, her laughter and her curse at three specific occasions of her life as it might diminish the catastrophe to come yet he is convinced that "Only a fool meddles in the Great Design," as destiny is born out of lifetimes of karmas and is too powerful to be changed. (40) In a way, Draupadi is being foretold about the future events and unconsciously she gets mentally prepared for them even though her conscious mind resents and questions the validity of such predictions. Her Dhai Ma assures her of the improbability of having five husbands and makes reference to *shastra* and her austere father who would never allow such a scandalous thing ever happen to his daughter.

Draupadi feels empowered with her new name Princess Panchaali that the sage gives her, impressed by her fortitude and savours the strength attached to it, yet she feels disheartened to imagine other unfortunate incidents foretold in the same breath. She quite often ruminates if she has any control over her destiny and life! If everything has already been decided and fixed, and she is merely a puppet, then why did the sage warn her to control herself on specific occasions? Why did he not own the whole responsibility of writing her fate in the book of destiny? Why is he trying to shift the onus to her feeble shoulders referring to her past karmas, which she is not even aware of? Thus, her mind is pestered with many unsolved mysteries while she has only hints about the incidents of her future. As if concerned about her unfortunate life, destiny designs to equip the disgruntled Draupadi for her future; a sorcerer arrives from nowhere and rigorously trains her in the art of surviving under all conditions. She drills into her romantic soul, the venomous and harsh truth of worldly wisdom and shatters her myths of true love. At every severe turn in her future, Draupadi is reminded of her teachings that prove useful.

However, the news of her *swaymvara* tickles her out of her fear and pain and again she is lost in the dreams of her fulfilling married life. She is jolted out of her expectations with immediate understanding that she is "nothing but a worm dangled at the end of a fishing rod." (57) The conditions of her *swaymvara* are laid down by Drupad keeping in view Arjun's valour. She mocks at the very farce of this notion where a girl is projected to be exercising her free will in the choice of her life partner while the conditions for the same are laid down by the males of the family. She resents the fact that she is merely a pawn to be sacrificed at the altar of marriage to make Drupad realize his dream. She is warned by her brother not to make a wrong choice at her *swayamvara*, thereby openly limiting her choice to Arjun, whereas the mere portrait of Karna has set her heartbeat faster and she starts identifying his pain and rejection with that of her own. She has to thwart her heart's desire to save her brother's life and she openly raises the issue of Karna's low birth refusing him any right to contest in her *swayamvara.* Though her heart bleeds for him, yet the trap of destiny is too mighty to be evaded. She has already been forced to commit the first blunder, which Ved Vyas had warned her against.

Yajnaseni, on the other hand, is pining for Krishna as her future husband oblivious of her destiny that has five husbands for her. None can fathom her dejection and hurt when Krishna politely declines the offer and instead proposes his *sakha* Arjun for her. After some initial hesitation, her father happily accepts the idea of this alliance as it would assuage his bruised ego and materialize his plans of taking revenge. She accepts Krishna's verdict and surrenders her will for the sake of her father's honour, but the news of Pandavas' death in the *Lakshagrah* creates gloom in the palace and she herself becomes sceptical about her impending *swayamvara.* Her suggestion to cancel the event is rebuffed by her brother, as it would bring dishonour to the whole Drupad clan. Again, she has to surrender her will in the name of honour and prepare herself for the collective gaze and ridicule of the contestants, as she is sure that no one of the contestants would be able to face the challenge successfully. Everywhere there are murmurs of resentment regarding the stringent conditions to win her as one after the other contestant fails and she herself confesses, "I hated myself for having sat so long before such lust-driven eyes. I felt soiled." (41) She also becomes ambivalent about the conditions but could do nothing except wondering if her father wanted her to lead a life of celibacy.

The whole narrative of *swayamvara* underlines how a woman is reduced just to a body devoid of any self-esteem and voice. The Yajnaseni on display to be won by the best warrior and hero is nothing more than a medium to quench the thirst of revenge for her father, and for the contestants she is an exotic and mesmerizing female body, which would enhance their prestige and prove their superiority over others. Some of them are also planning to abduct her when Karna appears as a contestant and her saviour. Impressed by his valour she becomes hopeful and secretly starts desiring for the success of this young man when her brother interferes and Karan is rejected on account of his low birth. At this instance also, she is helpless and feels muted even though secret desire and respect for Karna has erupted in her heart and she sympathizes with him in her heart of hearts. She also feels guilty for his insult in the open court, yet in the court of men, she is simply an adjunct who is not allowed to voice her mind. Even though there is no role of Yajnaseni anywhere and her fate is decided by the males, she is held responsible almost by all the contestants for their failure and collective shame, which is writ large on their faces.

Won as trophy by Arjun in the guise of a mendicant, both Draupadi and Yajnaseni had to leave Drupad's home and were divided among the five brothers as an object. Kunti in Ray's novel feels repentant having pronounced the verdict unknowingly and sincerely seeks the way out for Yajnaseni. She sympathizes with her daughter-in-law and understands the plight of women kind. When Krishna and sage Narada convince her that only a united marriage could keep the Pandava brothers united for the cause of greater benefit of humanity, she gives her consent.

On the other hand, Divakaruni's Kunti is a prototype of possessive mother who is jealous of her daughter-in-law lest she should surpass her authority over her sons. She deliberately wants Draupadi to be divided among five brothers like an object as she is aware that such an arrangement would never allow Draupadi to exercise her sexual charms on the mightiest Pandava Arjun, who would also resent his wife being shared among the rest of his brothers. Like a seasoned player and crafty mother-in-law, she contrives the situation and asserts her unparallelled authority to seal Draupadi's fate forever. Draupadi could never forgive Kunti for this act and their relationship turned out to be a constant tug of war and none would forgo an opportunity to slight and overthrow the other whenever the chance occurred.

This division among the five brothers like an object not only brings her ridicule from society and Kauravas, Arjun, too, penalizes her for the rest of her life for consenting to the collective marriage. On the other hand, Karna leaves no opportunity to slight her for his rejection, whereas at some instances, he comes to her rescue and his wife confesses Yajnaseni being his inspiration and the greatest object of love and reverence. Again, she is considered responsible for the demeaning behaviour and ultimate fall of this great warrior. Is it justified to consider Draupadi's silence as the root cause of Karna's grief? In fact, she becomes just an immediate objective correlative for his seething anger, ignominy and frustrated dreams of his life. Why is it that the history of revenge is always written on woman's body?

Again, like an object she is pledged and lost by Yudhisthir in the game of dice and molested publicly in the court. Her body becomes the bone of contention among the cousins. Hitherto silent Draupadi decides to articulate the wrongs done not only to her body and honour but also to her soul, and salvage her female pride and entity. The politics of space and security advocated by society in the institution of marriage and family gets exposed here in its most deteriorated way. One finds her donning the role of a radical feminist where she deconstructs many of the traditional myths related to *dharma* and patriarchy. The elderly people present in the court including Bhishma and many of the learned *gurus* had no straight answer to her questions. It is the divine intervention of Krishna, her *sakha* that saves her and none of her five husbands. Even then, she did not leave her husbands and readily accompanied them to the forest for a long exile. However, she is alleged by society of having an extra-marital affair with Krishna who is her only solace. Her opponents describe her as nothing more than a whore and openly ache for her. Her whole life is reduced to a tale of unending strife and miseries which none of her five husbands understands. Every one of them has a grudge against her as all of them want her all for themselves. Was it her desire to be divided among the five husbands? Has it been very easy and convenient for her to take care of all the five husbands all her life yet have none to rescue her when she needed them the most? Why could Arjun not assert his exclusive right over her when it was being suggested that she should be divided among the five brothers like an object? Was he not concerned more about his own *dharma* as a son and a younger brother than about Draupadi's welfare? Why did the *Dharmaraj* Yudhisthir consent to his mother's will immediately and could not come out with any other option? Did they all not surreptitiously desire to own her the moment they saw her? Did the rest four not envy Arjun secretly? Was it not suggested to her that she was the only means to keep the Pandavas united for the larger good? Did Vasudev not express his suspicions that she might become a cause of enmity among the five brothers if she refused to marry them all? Did she not consent for the sake of Arjun's *dharma* and his safety? Then why was it that none of them considered himself responsible for her welfare and she was taken as the chief cause of their troubles and disputes with the world? All her husbands had other wives as well and she had no exclusive claim on any of them, and yet she is ridiculed and taunted by the world for marrying five men and leading an unchaste life like that of a prostitute. Arjun, whom she loves primarily and unconditionally, locates non-existent motives behind her consent and scoffs at her for hankering after power and position, as only the eldest brother could accord her the status of the Chief Queen. So, he finds one or the other pretext to stay away from her to penalize her.

Ray's Yajnaseni and Divakaruni's Draupadi in one voice coax and challenge the reader to determine her share in the massive destruction that followed the war of *Mahabharata.* How far was she responsible? Did she desire the kingdom refusing to follow the footsteps of her mendicant husband without knowing his real identity? Did she have no right to avenge the wrongs done to her pride and honour? The strife existed there between the Kauravas and the Pandavas for kingdom and power and the ruse became Draupadi. She is remembered even in our history as the chief cause of the war amongst brothers and a large-scale destruction of the *Kshatriyas* but how many of us know about her role and contribution in uniting the non-*Kshatriya* and tribal races and ensuring their unflinching support for the Pandavas? The history of our memory has skipped her role as the *Annapurna* when she takes food only at night after satisfying the hunger of all, including the beasts, birds and insects of the forest during the period of their exile.

Divakaruni raises a very pertinent issue regarding a woman's desire to have a home of her own, a place where she belongs and which reflects her own persona. Like any other girl who feels unwanted at her father's home, Draupadi also aspires to have a palace of her own. But the palace of her dreams turns out to be the palace of illusions as she dreams of being the mistress of this palace, forever enjoying a perfectly blissful life in the company of her husbands. Very soon, this very palace turns out to be the reason of her distress, incredible insult and grief. For the rest of her life, she keeps longing for her own rightful space and home and the memories of her palace of unparallelled beauty haunt her till the end. Through Draupadi, Divakaruni seems to ask if it is so great a demand of a woman to have her own home and space where she could grow and nurture her roots. The diasporic woman writer, twice displaced from her home and homeland is acutely aware of Draupadi's dilemma. Once her assigned role is completed and she is released from her body, she finds her palace waiting for her in the other world. It is here and now that she recognizes the futility of desires that chase humans during their lifetime propelling them into the pit of untold suffering and misery, whereas the real 'home' promises liberty from worldly illusions and cares.

Finally, there is no disjunction between Ray's Yajnaseni and Divakaruni's Draupadi, as they proceed on the final journey. Their fate is identical. On the way to heaven, Yajnaseni is left behind when she slips and gets injured. None of her husbands even slows down and the very *Dharmaraj* Yudhisthir forbids Bhima from looking back. She is astounded to find this stark streak of self-centredness in her eldest husband and realizes how all his life has been a steady performance to attain *moksha.* That is why he could never behave as a human being; he had no compassion for the suffering wife and was only passionate for achieving the ultimate goal of salvation. This realization and retrospection make her transcend her womanly existence and she rejects the very idea of *moksha* which disconnects a person from his humaneness. Invoking Krishna, her only *sakha* and saviour, she prays to him to make her indivisible and destroy all her agonies and sorrows. Merging her soul in the super soul of her God, she decides to take birth repeatedly as a human being in the universe of Krishna to contribute in its spiritual growth. She wants to come back to bring peace and happiness to everybody as Krishna resides in every soul and is the only truth and sustenance in the world of suffering. How could she not surrender to Krishna who even after parting from his mortal form comes to his dying *sakhi* and assures her of his perennial presence? Her egoless transcendental state also poses a question if there is at all any solution to a woman's problem in the world of men. She has come to the realization that "a world enveloped in the darkness of danger and difficulty and error can only be uplifted through spiritual consciousness." (398) She attains the Krishna consciousness and prays for four boons before her death—"no woman will ever have several husbands at a time, . . . Do not let even the enemy grieve for his sons," "let no woman be put to public shame ever again," "make women beautiful, but do not make men so lustful" and "because of race, religion, language and colour let no country split into parts like Hastina and Indraprastha." (396)

The contemporary woman in our society is still seeking the solution to all these problems and challenges. Whenever there is a war, women suffer the most. None of Draupadi's wishes seems to have been granted by the almighty, again raising the question if God resides only in the woman's soul and there is only one man, Krishna. If it is so and every soul is a female soul, then from where comes so much of brutality and suppression that gets reflected in the unequal world of men and women? Perhaps, the questions would never end and the only solution would emerge through spiritual consciousness. This seems to be the united message of both Ray and Divakaruni through the persona of Draupadi/ Panchaali/ Krishnaa/ Yajnaseni, who has attained the ultimate realization that it is only the Divine, who could assure human beings of unflinching support and unconditional love.

This consciousness of the all-benevolent Divine sets her tormented soul free and she completely surrenders and dissolves her sceptical self to be awakened to the final reality.

Representing the Ethnic Body in Bharati Mukherjee, Rohinton Mistry and Chitra Banerjee Divakaruni

ALESSANDRO MONTI
University of Turin, Italy

Gleaming steel sinks hopelessly stained with yellow turmeric; shelves groaning under the load of housemade chutney; the stale pungency of curries haunting American flats; makeshift bedrolls (Indian style) spread on the floors of sitting-rooms to accommodate guests or, worse, querulous mothers-in-law. These or other unsavoury and untidy displays of ethnicity mark the writing of the diaspora, from Bharati Mukherjee to Chitra Banerjee Divakaruni. We should construe them as re-imagined tokens of ethnic belonging, as sad proofs of permanent disavowing difference and failed integration, of which *Wife* (1975, by Bharati Mukherjee) represents a valuable case in point.

The unsanitised condition of the flat in Calcutta (with particular emphasis on the damp toilet) or the repetitive chores requested by the traditional preparation of food constitute the rough backdrop that motivate Dimple's refusal in conforming to the usual tasks and roles claimed by the traditional Hindu marriage. Such disavowal of duties stands behind the rebellious untidiness that in *Wife* makes a battleground of the otherwise modern and comfortable American flat in which Dimple lives after migrating to the West with her husband.

The *adharmic* quality displayed by her uneasiness in fulfilling the auspicious identity of a bountiful Lakshmi complicates as it were the image of this regressive return to domestic life. Her dis-accommodation does not imply the nostalgia for a *deshi* way of life. It rather suggests a post-feminist rehearsal of the ethnic juxtaposition between the opposite personae of *Lakshmi* and *Alakshmi*. The issue concerns here the continuity or discontinuity of *stridharma*, viz. the question if a migrating woman may still conform to established type and rules of imposed behaviour.

To understand the roots of this conflict, we should compare the feminine resistance in *Wife* to the male sense of sexual possession (the ideology of the *pati* as I would claim it) enhanced by Bharati Mukherjee in her short story "Nostalgia" (*Darkness*, 1985). Here behind the hysterical return of the male migrant to embarrassing autochthonous practices of toilet behaviour lurks the bitter sting of refused feminine availability.

As a matter of fact, an analogous atmosphere of crisis loads both *Wife* and "Nostalgia," these two narratives sharing an intimate sense of loss and betrayal of integration. In particular, the short story forelights the residual sting of ethnicity that we should be able to detect in the behaviour of the male protagonist, this feature suggesting a sad failure of relocation, given the crucial regret that the successful migrant nurtures for a pristine *deshi* attitude of patronising and domineering privilege.

This undialogic feature of ethnicity (a notion that we should discuss in terms of ambivalence) is constituted as a bitter pun in the short story "Squatters" by Rohinton Mistry (*Tales from Firozsha Baag*, 1987). The momentous clash of accumulated meanings with its ensuing intimations of difference either in Standard English (to squat, primarily "to live in an empty building or an area of land without the permission of the owner") or in *swadeshi* idiom (in which it means almost exclusively "to sit on one's haunches, usually while defecating")[1] indicates the interstitial position of the shifting migrant. His physiology and corporeal regulations cannot be accommodated within the sanitary practices of Western usage.

The same miscegenating qualities of permanent mis-education, conveyed by the truncated movement that rejects achieved measures of cultural fitness, come again to the surface in a further short story, "A Father" (*Darkness*). Here the figure of the "refurbished" migrant is *de facto* deconstructed by the violent and uncompromising reaction against the daughter, one that yields too easily to free ways of life. The disjunction of purposes within the family is handled by the writer with an excessive overloading of tension, whose key motif is given by the revengeful and oppressive icon of Kali. In this short story, ethnicity is astutely construed in terms of devotional folklore and frightened taboos, so as to sidestep cleverly whatever realistic analysis concerning the anguish of relocation.

To me, the ethnic lesson conveyed in "A Father" seems to coincide quite disturbingly with the traditional portrayal of the sulky half-tamed native in the colonial script. Let's consider, for instance, "Little Henry and His Bearer" by F.A. Steel (*In the Guardianship of God*, 1903). This early representation of how a Hindu clings to his own rites when he gets in touch with an alien culture foregrounds measures of compulsory devotion to Kali, so as to anticipate the tremendous effects of behavioural regression exposed by Bharati Mukherjee in "A Father."

However, it would be possible to equate the scared and violent reaction of the displaced migrant father to the murderous attack against the husband in the final page of *Wife*. Here the conflict between Hindu traditions and the American ways of life involves a double process of psychic disintegration. The migrating wife views the American world exclusively through the agency of television, the prison-house of marriage forbidding the woman a direct knowledge of reality.

Such a repeated and vicarious act of gazing on the part of the protagonist posits a mediated vision of the world outside the flat. The TV screen becomes the window open onto a blank wall, as to suggest an implied mimicry of *purdah*. Paradoxically, the confined woman grounds her own perception of the American society on an act of gazing that surrogates the direct and free perception of reality. In other words, she imagines the world beyond her rooms. As a consequence, she considers the external events as if they were an illusory pageant, devoid of any substantial quality of truth: a *lila*, to adopt Hindu lexicon.

The serialization of the American reality in terms of distanced flashes and fragmented visions transfers the visualized images of violence from the TV screen to a crucial representation of ethnic character. The strategy of self-defence enacted by the woman because of her indirect gazing seems to be the agency that determines compulsory reactions of murderous behaviour. The wife rescues herself from her imagined terrors by assuming the avenging and killing role of the Devi. Thus she ultimately transfers the serialized events of violence watched on TV into the redeeming sequences of Hindu myth. She becomes the triumphant and warlike image of the Goddess killing her demon foes.

Such reshaping of the feelings of fear and loneliness in the lives of the migrants substitutes the glamour of the ethnic mytheme for the estranging nakedness of solitude and failure. This rendering of the ethnic heritage in the fiction of the expatriate writer is often "nautcherized" through sentimentalizing procedures of saddened remembrance, so as to evoke a nostalgic frame of mind, devoid however of the stigma that the notion of a return to the ethnic type seems to entail for Bharati Mukherjee.

The point may be argued apropos of C.B. Divakaruni, whose short stories dealing with lines of missed opportunities and grievous relationships defuse whatever resistant stance of unyielding ethnicity. Whereas Bharati Mukherjee and Rohinton Mistry introduce Western everyday gadgets or manners of life as agencies of discomfort, C.B. Divakaruni incorporates these fashionable shibboleths into an upgrading Western canon that indicates social prestige and happy prosperity.

As a consequence the lives of her migrant women are measured against the permanence of such cherished possessions indicating achieved financial success. This condition of relative affluence seems to authorize whatever step to growth and fresh beginnings in life. Throughout these Westernizing short stories, the Indian pre-migration background stands sharply outlined as a memento against the obsessive tyranny of the past. However, these intimations of ripeness are made impossible in the event of economic insufficiency.

Thus, the short story "Silver Pavements, Golden Roofs," in *Arranged Marriage* (1995), impresses a mawkish turn to the failed and stunted lives of an elderly and saddened couple of migrants, giving way to melancholic terms of romantic and unrealistic remembrance of India, as a counterpoint to the feeling of implied revulsion and withdrawal into the past caused by the bleak life and the violent surroundings that mark the dreary suburban milieu in which they are socially relegated.

The seclusion that in *Wife* circumscribes the migratory act of the woman must be understood as a sign of patriarchal imposition (a domineering attitude that survives, as it were, the passage from India) becomes in "Silver Pavements, Golden Roofs" the product of raw racial hostility, or rather the sad consequence of a faulty upward dynamism. The inadequate saris and the clumsy overcoats worn by the two women in this short story, as a shabby and pathetic defence against the snow and the icy weather of North America, stand in paradigmatic and complementary relationship with the costly designer dresses (Gucci, Armani and the like) that are shamelessly exhibited throughout the pages of *Arranged Marriage*.

We should compare this re-accommodation of values to the updated consideration granted to ethnicity by the socialite fiction of the non-expatriate writer. In Shobha Dé, the regional lexicon of traditional Indian clothing spotlights measures of select sophistication and highly elaborated practice in mundane wisdom. This refurbished rehearsal of a *deshi* heritage does not consider ethnicity to be in stark opposition with the Westernization of manners and cultural mimicry. The case is quite different with Bharati Mukherjee and Rohinton Mistry: both writers introduce Bakhtinian sequences of folkloric time, so as to deconstruct the superficial Westernization of the migrant, given their emphasis on the "clownish" and the "cynical" and finally the "grotesque allegorization" of the encounter between cultures.[2] Now emerge straight physiological themes that concern issues of corporeal organization which replace the too easy pathos of *Arranged Marriage*.

This crucial shift in the fictionalized biographies of the migrant is paradoxically grounded on the parodic interruption of physiological regularity. In "Nostalgia," the protagonist reverts revengefully to unwestern practices of corporeal behaviour, unsanitizing as it were his assimilation into America, whereas in "Squatters" Rohinton Mistry adopts a grotesque allegory of failed assimilation, one that concerns again practices of physiological expulsion. We should contrast the use in Mistry of the Bakhtinian interrupted defecation series with the circumstances of Gargantua's delivery, an event in which the series of birth and defecation intersect each other.[3]

According to Bakhtin, the construction of "crude and unmediated connections" between phenomena that are otherwise kept separate (such as the case of birth and defecation) involves both procedures of disunification (in the abstract series that isolate the body and its functioning from that which Bakhtin terms the "idealistic" or "idealized" strata) and simultaneously concerns "the bringing together of that which had traditionally been kept distant and dis-unified" (170). In "Squatters," the idiosyncratic interpretation of corporeality thwarts the should-be regular movements of the migrant, so as to impede his rebirth into the new Canadian world. Of course, such folkloric rendering of a dis-accommodated "concrete human corporeality" negates a positive ending (in the sense conveyed by Rabelais) to the serial sequence defecation-birth, or metaphorical change of identity.

Both in "Nostalgia" and in "Squatters," the human body constitutes the concrete and unique measuring rod for the passage from the "sealed off sequences of an individual life" to folkloric lines of representation that embrace a shared experience. Instead of resorting exclusively to a world of interiority, both authors deal with physiological acts of the body which cannot be made public but whose full significance should not be restricted to mere questions of individualized growth. Rohinton Mistry laughs his un-defecating migrant out of Canada and by doing so he introduces a clash of cultures that "exceeds the boundaries of any individual personality" (239).

It is worth noticing that in *Family Matters* (2002) also, Rohinton Mistry associates powerful images of regressive behaviour with a sad manifestation of physiological decay. In this novel, the surging decay of Nariman's body provokes the very signs, implying "destruction and strife," of which Bakhtin speaks (171). We must extend the meaning of this counter-epiphany, so as to embrace the notion of a self-destructive society that rejects what everyone values, linked with measures of organic growth and development.

In *Family Matters*, Rohinton Mistry transfers the discourse of power and hegemony from the selective organization of postcolonial nationhood, such as exposed in *A Fine Balance*, to the circumscribed and private world of the family group. As a consequence, he depicts the dark side of the nostalgic return to tradition and cultural (or religious) heritage. His latest novel suggests an atmosphere of ethnic intimacy turning sour, the magnified isolation of the would-be growing self from the roots that have shaped it.

NOTES

1. Of course, the pun here is about "squatter" meaning "illegal occupant, intruder" (also "to squat," synonymous with "to be external") and the definition given by S. Mutiah in *Words in Indian English*, 1991, and reproduced in my text.
2. M. Bakhtin, *The Dialogic Imagination*, Austin, University of Texas Press, 1988, p. 170.
3. *Ibidem,* pp. 171-72. "Thus, Gargantua's birth: it is portrayed with a clownish cynicism, with precise anatomical and physiological details—Gargantua's mother, who had eaten too much tripe, suffers a prolapsus of the rectum resulting in severe diarrhoea (the defecation series) and then the birth itself: 'Thanks to this unfortunate accident there took place a weakening of the uterus; the child leapt up through the Fallopian tubes to a hollow vein and, scrambling across the diaphragm to the upper arm where this vein divides in two, he took the left fork and crawled out through the left ear.' Here, grotesque fantasy is combined with the precision of anatomical and physiological analysis."

Bibliography

Divakaruni, Chitra Banerjee, *Arranged Marriage*, London, Black Swan, 1997.

Mistry, Rohinton, *Tales from Firozsha Baag*, Markham (Ontario), Penguin Canada, 1987.

_____, *A Fine Balance*, London, Faber & Faber, 1996.

_____, *Family Matters,* London, Faber & Faber, 2003.

Mukherjee Bharati, *Wife,* Markham (Ontario), Penguin Canada, 1990 (1975).

_____, *Darkness,* New Delhi, Penguin Canada, 1990 (1975).

NOTES

1. Of course, the pun here is about squirrel meaning "tree-climbing" [illegible] ... as synonymous with the [illegible] and the definition [illegible] in [illegible] [illegible] a typical [illegible].
2. M. R. [illegible], *The [illegible]*, Austin: University of Texas Press, 1958, p. 170.
3. *[illegible]*, p. 172. Thus [illegible] is [illegible] with a [illegible] [illegible] and physical [illegible] [illegible] [illegible] [illegible] [illegible] suffer [illegible] of the [illegible] [illegible] [illegible] [illegible] [illegible] the [illegible] [illegible] [illegible] Thanks to this [illegible] [illegible] [illegible] a [illegible] of the [illegible] [illegible] through the [illegible] [illegible] a hollow [illegible] across the [illegible] to the appearance where this [illegible] [illegible] [illegible] of the [illegible] and [illegible] out through the [illegible]. Hence [illegible] with the precision of [illegible] physiological [illegible].

BIBLIOGRAPHY

Divakaruni, Chitra Banerjee. *Arranged Marriage*. London: Black Swan, 1997.

Mistry, Rohinton. *Tales from Firozsha Baag*. [illegible] (first published [illegible]).

——. *A Fine Balance*. London: Faber & Faber, 1996.

——. *Family Matters*. London: Faber & Faber, 2002.

Mukherjee, Bharati. *Wife*. [illegible]: Penguin (India), [illegible] (1975).

——. *[illegible]*. New Delhi: [illegible] (1989).